Transnational Cosmopolitanism

Based on the theoretical reconstruction of neglected post–World War I writings and political action of W. E. B. Du Bois, this volume offers a normative account of transnational cosmopolitanism. Pointing out the limitations of Kant's cosmopolitanism through a novel contextual account of *Toward Perpetual Peace*, *Transnational Cosmopolitanism* shows how these limits remain in neo-Kantian scholarship. Inés Valdez's framework overcomes these limitations in a methodologically unique way, taking both Du Bois's writings and his coalitional political action as texts that should inform our theorization and normative insights. The cosmopolitanism proposed in this work is an original contribution that questions the contemporary currency of Kant's canonical approach and enlists overlooked resources to radicalize, democratize, and transnationalize cosmopolitanism.

INÉS VALDEZ is an assistant professor of political science at Ohio State University. Her work has appeared in the *American Political Science Review*, *Political Research Quarterly*, and *Political Studies*, among other outlets. She is the recipient of the Laurance S. Rockefeller Visiting Faculty Fellowship at the Princeton University Center for Human Values (2017–2018) and a Humboldt Research Fellowship for Experienced Researchers (2018–2021).

Transnational Cosmopolitanism

Kant, Du Bois, and Justice as a Political Craft

INÉS VALDEZ
Ohio State University

CAMBRIDGE
UNIVERSITY PRESS

CAMBRIDGE
UNIVERSITY PRESS

University Printing House, Cambridge CB2 8BS, United Kingdom

One Liberty Plaza, 20th Floor, New York, NY 10006, USA

477 Williamstown Road, Port Melbourne, VIC 3207, Australia

314-321, 3rd Floor, Plot 3, Splendor Forum, Jasola District Centre, New Delhi - 110025, India

79 Anson Road, #06-04/06, Singapore 079906

Cambridge University Press is part of the University of Cambridge.

It furthers the University's mission by disseminating knowledge in the pursuit of education, learning and research at the highest international levels of excellence.

www.cambridge.org
Information on this title: www.cambridge.org/9781108704809
DOI: 10.1017/9781108630047

First published 2019
First paperback edition 2020

A catalogue record for this publication is available from the British Library

Library of Congress Cataloging in Publication data
NAMES: Valdez, Inés, 1975- author.
TITLE: Transnational cosmopolitanism : Kant, Du Bois, and justice as a political craft / Inés Valdez.
DESCRIPTION: Cambridge, United Kingdom ; New York, NY : Cambridge University Press, 2019. | Includes bibliographical references and index.
IDENTIFIERS: LCCN 2018048993 | ISBN 9781108483322 (hardback) | ISBN 9781108704809 (paperback)
SUBJECTS: LCSH: Cosmopolitanism. | Kant, Immanuel, 1724-1804–Political and social views. | Du Bois, W. E. B. (William Edward Burghardt), 1868-1963–Political and social views. | BISAC: POLITICAL SCIENCE / History & Theory.
CLASSIFICATION: LCC JZ1308 .V35 2019 | DDC 303.48/201–dc23
LC record available at https://lccn.loc.gov/2018048993

ISBN 978-1-108-48332-2 Hardback
ISBN 978-1-108-70480-9 Paperback

For Philipp and Lea

[A] prominent man who was trustee from Haverford College wrote [to *The Crisis*] to cancel his subscription . . . He said that, to his horror, while he was in London in 1924, he found that we were picketing The Strand with placards concerning lynching in the United States and he thought that it was a very bad way of washing the dirty linen of our own country in a foreign land. I read it with a degree of amusement and then replied that I was going to wash the linen anywhere I got soap and water.

W. E. B. Du Bois, interview with Moses Asch, 1961

Contents

Figures

Acknowledgments

Writing this book would not have been possible in the absence of the rich interlocking communities of colleagues, friends, and family that, at different stages and in different ways, supported me in this endeavor.

I am thankful to Michael Lienesch, who was the first interlocutor in my efforts at reading Du Bois transnationally. I am grateful to Jeff Spinner-Halev and Susan Bickford, who worked patiently with me on my first critical engagement with cosmopolitanism and – along with Desmond King and Rainer Bauböck – supported me every step of the way thereafter. Lawrie Balfour sat with me in a stairwell of the Palmer House Hilton in Chicago when I could only describe the project with keywords, remaining in conversation about the project ever since, which has been invaluable.

Throughout the writing of the book, I was fortunate to engage in conversations about the various chapters with audiences at Columbia University, Cornell University, Goethe University Frankfurt, Humboldt University of Berlin, Indiana University Bloomington, McGill University, Ohio State University, Princeton University, Saint Louis University, Torcuato Di Tella University, University of British Columbia, University of Chicago, University of Illinois at Urbana–Champaign, University of Minnesota, University of Pennsylvania and University of Virginia. I also presented previous versions of the chapters at the meetings of the American Political Science Association, Midwest Political Science Association, International Studies Association, and the Association for Political Theory. In these fora or elsewhere, one or more of the chapters benefited from the engagement of Arash Abizadeh, Begüm Adalet, Ishan Ashutosh, Wendy Belcher, Duncan Bell, Craig Borowiak, Yvonne Chiu, Julian Culp,

Marina Duque, Lisa Ellis, Rainer Forst, Jason Frank, Jill Frank, Loren Goldman, Reena Goldthree, Arbel Grinner, Brian Herrera, Jakob Huber, Desmond Jagmohan, Anna Jurkevics, Steven Kelts, Nazli Konya, Alexander Livingston, Catherine Lu, Katherine Marino, Lavender McKittrick-Sweitzer, Jeanne Morefield, Dirk Moses, Benjamin Mueser, Naomi Murakawa, Sankar Muthu, Emily Nacol, Daniel Nemser, Anne Norton, Paulina Ochoa Espejo, Tejas Parasher, Jennifer Pitts, Camille Preel-Dumas, Adolph Reed, Carly Regina, Olimpia Rosenthal, Diane Rubenstein, Hope Sample, Tessy Schlosser, Andrew Schroeder, Ryan Shah, Amy Shuster, Rogers Smith, Anna Stilz, Kirstine Taylor, Chris Tenove, Alexander Thompson, Robert Vitalis, Srdjan Vucetic, Joel Wainwright, Timothy Waligore, Alexander Wendt, Melissa Williams, Elizabeth Wingrove, Yves Winter, Automn Womack, Lea Ypi, and Peng Yu.

Lawrie Balfour, Adom Getachew, Juliet Hooker, Eric MacGilvray, Inder Marwah, Ben McKean, and Michael Neblo read the whole manuscript and sometimes several versions of particular chapters and provided wise advice, as did the anonymous reviewers for Cambridge University Press. One of them, Michael Goodhart, was as generous as to provide more of his incisive, yet generous, feedback on a subsequent version. My editor, Sara Doskow, and the remarkable production team at Cambridge University Press, did the rest.

I also owe deep thanks to the many research assistants at Ohio State who – at different stages of this project – performed timely research on the history of late eighteenth-century warfare, twentieth-century black newspaper coverage of Du Bois, and everything in between. These are Rahel Admasu, Rachel Beery, Alisha Bhagwat, Jada Earl, Anthony Fasano, Hyeji Kim, Alexandra Konicki, Nate Leeson, Madeline Marshall, Lauren McDermott, Kasey Powers, Maria Vargo, Elvis Saldias Villarroel, Robin Smith, Kaitlyn Willette, Erik Wisniewski, and Cecilia Wolf. I am also thankful for the support of the staff members at Ohio State, Princeton and the Hanse Institute for Advanced Study in Delmenhorst, who made the journey much smoother logistically than it might have been: Alicia Anzivine, Steven Blalock, Diana Camella, Dawn Dissette, Susanne Fuchs, Robb Hagen, Maureen Killeen, Jill Klimpel, Melodie McGrothers, Andrew Perhac, Courtney Sanders, Laurie Skoroda, Charles Smith, Christina Thiel, Jessica Valsi, and Susan Winters. I also thank the *American Political Science Review* and Cambridge University Press for permission to reproduce portions of Chapter 1 that appeared in that journal under the title "It's Not About Race: Good Wars, Bad Wars, and the Origins of Kant's Anti-Colonialism" (111 (4): 819–34).

There is probably no topic beyond that of my research that has occupied my thinking as much during the preparation of this manuscript as that of writing. To Michelle Rivera-Clonch and Maurice Stevens I owe thanks for teaching me that academic writing is a practice and helping me get better at it. I am thankful for Alyson Price's shrewd engagement with my writing in uncountable versions of each of the chapters. To my accountability partners – Amna Akbar, Ishan Ashutosh, Katherine Borland, Murad Idris, Katherine Marino, Miranda Martinez, Jennifer Mitzen, Nada Moumtaz, Miriam Thaggert, and Sara Watson – I owe thanks for listening to my writing plans and sharing theirs with me. Writing would not have happened if it was not for the many writing partners writing alongside me at Ohio State University and Princeton University: Ruha Benjamin, Katra Byram, Adriana Dawes, Marina Duque, Arbel Grinner, Andrew Leber, Tasleem Padamsee, Sara Rodriguez-Argüelles Riva, Johanna Sellman, and Leslie Weingard.

Friends and family sustained me through the writing of this book, and through the more disjointed explorations that preceded it. In Buenos Aires, Carlos Acuña, Roberto Gargarella, Elizabeth Jelin, and Catalina Smulovitz were generous enough to orient me as I considered and while I pursued doctoral studies abroad. Kevin Morrison – who I miss dearly – and Marcela Gonzalez Rivas welcomed me to Durham in 2002. In Chapel Hill, the friendship and scholarship of Chris Gaffney, Amber Knight, Hollie Mann, and Allison Rovny kept me intellectually engaged and sane throughout my PhD. The company and conversation of friends new and old in Buenos Aires, Columbus, Florence, Toronto, and beyond meant I never had to think alone, so more thanks go to Amna Akbar, Dóra Beszterczey, Mat Coleman, Theresa Delgadillo, Lilia Fernández, Lori Gruen, Lynn Itagaki, Paloma Martinez-Cruz, Nada Moumtaz, Paulina Ochoa Espejo, Laura Pszemiarower, Anita Saha, Ted Sammons, Johanna Sellman, Michael Shifter, Jennifer Smither, Alex Street, Srdjan Vucetic, and Shannon Winnubst.

I spent the 2017–2018 academic year as a Laurance S. Rockefeller Visiting Faculty Fellow at the Princeton University Center for Human Values, where I found the time and space that allowed me to complete the last two full drafts of the manuscript. I could not have asked for more, but, in addition to that, I had the collegiality and intellectual support of Charles Beitz, Desmond Jagmohan, Melissa Lane, Steve Macedo, Philip Pettit, and Anna Stilz, as well as the extended community at the center. I completed the copy edits and proofs of this book while a Humboldt Stiftung Fellow at the Hanse Institute for Advanced Study, where

I benefited from a rich and interdisciplinary community and a fabulous writing space. Before that, leaves supported by the Department of Political Science and the Mershon Center for International Security Studies allowed me to write the bulk of the manuscript, for which I am very thankful.

Only late in the project did I fully realize its autobiographical connotations. My parents, Gilberto Valdez Herrera and Patricia Tappatá, met when they both participated in networks of political solidarity established among young Latin American activists associated with liberation theology. Growing up in Lima and Buenos Aires I was never removed from the contentious democratic politics of the region. My mother's commitment and work on questions of displacement, memory, and historical injustice are, in retrospect, a central influence on my thinking. My sisters Patricia, Paula, and Jimena – spread out throughout the world as they are – were always present, in sisterhood.

My partner Philipp Rehm was steadfast in his support and encouragement throughout this project, and was always at hand to read, listen, and discuss its progress, and also when I was taking a break from it. My daughter Lea brightens my days with her enthusiasm for life, unending creativity, and budding commitment to justice. I dedicate this book to them.

Abbreviations of Works by Immanuel Kant and W. E. B. Du Bois

In alphabetical order, see Figures 1.1 and 3.1 for chronological order.

KANT

APPV [1798]:	"Anthropology from a Pragmatic Point of View," in (2007) *Anthropology, History, and Education*, eds. G. Zöller and R. B. Louden (Cambridge: Cambridge University Press).
CoB [1786]:	"Conjectures on the Beginning of Human History," in (1991) *Kant: Political Writings*, ed. H. S. Reiss (Cambridge: Cambridge University Press).
CoF [1798]:	"The Conflict of the Faculties," in (1996) *Religion and Rational Theology*, eds. A. Wood and G. di Giovanni (New York: Cambridge University Press).
CoJ [1790]:	*Critique of Judgment* (1987) (Indianapolis, IN: Hackett Publishing Company).
DHR [1777]:	"Of the Different Human Races," in (2013) *Kant and the Concept of Race*, ed. J. M. Mikkelsen (Albany: State University of New York Press).
DPP [1794]:	"Drafts of *Perpetual Peace*," in (2016) *Lectures and Drafts on Political Philosophy*, ed. F. Rauscher (Cambridge: Cambridge University Press).
IUH [1784]:	"Idea for a Universal History with a Cosmopolitan Purpose," in *Kant: Political Writings*.

LCFS [1794]:	"Letter to Carl Friedrich Stäudlin. December 4, 1794;" in (1999) *Correspondence*, ed. A. Zweig (Cambridge: Cambridge University Press).
LCS [1793]:	"Letter to Carl Spener. March 22, 1793," in *Correspondence*.
LFTG [1794]:	"Letter to François Théodore de la Garde. November 24, 1794," in *Correspondence*.
MoM [1797]:	"The Metaphysics of Morals," in (1996) *Practical Philosophy*, ed. M. J. Gregor (Cambridge: Cambridge University Press).
MoMV [1793/1794]:	"Kant on the Metaphysics of Morals: Vigilantius's Lecture Notes," in (1997) *Lectures on Ethics*, ed. P. Heath and J. B. Schneewind (Cambridge: Cambridge University Press), 249–452.
MPC [1774/1777]:	"Moral Philosophy: Collins's Leacture Notes," in (1997) *Lectures on Ethics*, 37–222.
NaF:	*Notes and Fragments*, ed. P. Guyer (2005) (Cambridge: Cambridge University Press).
OCS [1793]:	"On the Common Saying: This Might Be True in Theory but It Is of No Use in Practice," in *Practical Philosophy*.
RA [1780s]:	"Reflexionen Zur Anthropologie" ["*Reflections on Anthropology*"] in *Anthropologie (Band XV)*. Kant's gesammelte Schriften. Akademie Ausgabe – Electronic Edition.
RJGH [1785]:	"Review of J. G. Herder's Ideas for the Philosophy of History of Humanity," in *Anthropology, History, and Education*.
TPP [1795]:	"Toward Perpetual Peace," in *Practical Philosophy*.
UTP [1788]:	"On the Use of Teleological Principles in Philosophy," in (2001) *Race*, ed. R. Bernasconi (Malden, MA: Blackwell Publishers).

DU BOIS (ONLY WORKS CITED TWO OR MORE TIMES, OTHER CITATIONS FOLLOW STANDARD FORMAT)

AMER [1922]:	"Americanization," in (1996) *The Oxford W. E. B. Du Bois Reader*, ed. E. J. Sundquist (New York: Oxford University Press), 383–4.

APMH [1930]:   "Africa, Its Place in Modern History," in (1977)
                 Africa, Its Geography, People, and Products and,
                 Africa, Its Place in Modern History (Milkwood,
                 NY: KTO Press).

APT [1943]:   "Africa at the Peace Table," *Negro Digest* 1:75–9.

ARW [1915]:   "The African Roots of War," *The Atlantic Monthly*
                 115 (5):707–14.

AW [1947]:   *An Appeal to the World*, ed. W. E. B. Du Bois
                 (New York: National Association for the
                 Advancement of Colored People).

BAO [1933].   "On Being Ashamed of Oneself," in (1986) *The*
                 Oxford W. E. B. Du Bois Reader, 324–8.

BRA [1934].   *Black Reconstruction in America: 1860–1880* (1998)
                 (New York: The Free Press).

CD [1934]:   "Counsels of Despair," *The Crisis* 43 (6):1258–9.

CDCP [1945]:   *Color and Democracy: Colonies and Peace* (New
                 York: Harcourt, Brace and Company).

CNA [1926]:   "Criteria of Negro Art," in (1996) *The Oxford*
                 W. E. B. Du Bois Reader, 324–8.

CR [1897]:   "The Conservation of Races," in (1986) *W. E. B. Du*
                 Bois Writings, ed. N. Huggins (New York: The
                 Library of America), 815–26.

DD [1940]:   *Dusk of Dawn. An Essay toward an Autobiography*
                 of a Race Concept (1997) (New Brunswick, NJ:
                 Transaction).

DP [1928]:   *Dark Princess: A Romance* (2007) ed. H. L. Gates
                 (New York: Oxford University Press).

DW [1920]:   *Darkwater: Voices from within the Veil* (1999)
                 (New York: Dover).

EPC [1919]:   "Editorial [On the Pan-African Congress]," *The Crisis*
                 17 (3):111–12.

ETHBM [1919]:   "An Essay toward a History of the Black Man in the
                 Great War," in (1986) *Du Bois*, ed. N. Huggins
                 (New York: Literary Classics of the United States),
                 879–922.

FA [1919]:   "The Future of Africa," *The Crisis* 17 (3):119–21.

IMA [1961]:   Du Bois, recorded autobiography. Interview with
                 Moses Asch.

LN [1923]:   "The League of Nations," *The Crisis* 27 (1):7.

NMRO [1925]:   "The Negro Mind Reaches Out," in (1997) *The New Negro: Voices of the Harlem Renaissance*, ed. A. Locke (New York: Touchstone), 385–414.

NNWN [1935]:   "A Negro Nation within the Nation," *Current History* 42 (3): 265–70.

NSS [1935]:   "Does the Negro need Separate Schools?," *The Journal of Negro Education* 4 (3):328–35.

NW [1900]:   "To the Nations of the World" (with Alexander Walters, Henry B. Brown, and H. Sylvester Williams). Speech given at the Pan-African Association Meeting.

PAM [1945]:   "The Pan-African Movement," in *History of the Pan-African Congress*, ed. G. Padmore (London: The Hammersmith Bookshop).

PE [1926]:   "Peace on Earth," *The Crisis* 31 (5):215–6.

PFR [1923]:   "Peace and Foreign Relations," *The Crisis* 27 (1):9–10.

PODR [1900]:   "The Present Outlook for the Dark Races of Mankind," *The A.M.E. Church Review* 17 (2):95–110.

RA [1942]:   "The Realities in Africa. European Profit or Negro Development?," *Foreign Affairs* 21: 721–32.

SAST [[1896].   *The Suppression of the African Slave-Trade to the United States of America, 1638–1870* (1969) (New York: Schocken Books).

SBF [1903]:   *The Souls of Black Folk* (1997) eds. D. W. Blight and R. Gooding-Williams (Boston: Bedford/St. Martins).

TA [1952]:   "The Acquittal," in *W.E.B. Du Bois Writings*.

TN [1915]:   *The Negro*, (2005) (Baltimore: Black Classic Press).

W [1927]:   "War," *The Crisis* 33 (4): 179.

WC [1925]:   "Worlds of Color," *Foreign Affairs* 3 (3):423–44.

Introduction

Taking the Cosmos in Cosmopolitanism Seriously

A meeting in Paris in 1919 challenged in word and deed the Western claim that Africans could not self-govern. To this day, neo-Kantian cosmopolitan political theory cannot properly grasp what made this meeting so radical. This is because of the grounding of cosmopolitan theory in Kant's political writings, whose seemingly global orientation is – when closely examined – narrowly concerned with the dangers of colonial conflict for Europe and cannot on its own provide a normative vision of world justice. In this book, I propose a theoretical framework of *transnational cosmopolitanism* – built upon the neglected work of W. E. B. Du Bois – to make sense of this event and other forms of transnational solidarity that contest the exclusionary structure of domestic and international realms of politics. Transnational cosmopolitanism is not tautological, it directs our attention to the *political craft* through which global injustice is contested and alternative organizations of the world are imagined. The concern with global forms of injustice makes this framework cosmopolitan. But the conviction that global injustice is best reconstructed by attending to interconnected yet local forms of domination and the forms of transnational solidarity that emerge therein makes it transnational. These forms of solidarity inaugurate counter-publics that mark themselves off from the dominant public and belong neither to the domestic nor to the international realm, but straddle them.

But back to 1919, just as Western powers were meeting in Versailles, W. E. B. Du Bois hosted the second Pan-African Congress in Paris. In this meeting, Africans and African Americans congregated in order to pressure the delegates at the peace table to consider the interests of people of color in the United States and the world (*FA*, 111). The United States and England denied visas to potential attendees not already in Paris, but the meeting took place nonetheless with attendees from over fifteen countries. Du Bois's plan for the German African colonies, which he had already sent to Woodrow Wilson, structured the agenda. This plan proposed that decisions on the fate of these colonies be made by a "public opinion" composed of chiefs and educated subjects from these colonies, along with the educated members of the African diaspora and the French and British colonies (*FA*, 119). These claims, and the actual gathering organized in Paris, undermined Western claims about subject peoples; their inability to self-govern was falsified by the very presence of these subjects, who – regardless of their different affiliations – came together to enact a new anti-colonial counter-public, i.e., a public that marks itself off from the dominant public, where it would have been received with hostility (Warner 2002, 81).

This new public converged around an understanding of the struggle against racial injustice in the United States being entwined with the fight against colonial rule in Africa. This public was neither domestic nor international, but relied on horizontal coalitions of subjects at the receiving end of imperial powers and spoke against Western powers' postwar consensus and the racially unjust United States polity. In so doing, this intervention highlighted the exclusionary nature of "international society" as well as the duplicity of an internally racialized United States performing as a liberal world power. At the same time, this event established ties of solidarity among differently located racialized subjects, which aimed to envision a world that need not predicate the freedom of some on the colonial or neocolonial oppression of others.

The gathering in Paris can be categorized neither as domestic nor as an international forum, thus falling into what I call "transnational politics." What is notable about this event, however, is how difficult it is to categorize it within the dominant coordinates of the contemporary neo-Kantian literature on cosmopolitanism (Benhabib 2004, 2006; Bohman 2007; Habermas 1997, 2001; Kleingeld 2012; Ypi 2012), itself an important strand of the contemporary debate on cosmopolitanism and global justice. Within political theory, cosmopolitanism is typically associated with an account of what justice is and requires a series of institutional prescriptions that contribute to realizing those requirements.[1]

---

[1] A second variant of cosmopolitanism is more directly indebted to Rawls's *Theory of Justice* and *The Law of Peoples*, and occasionally borrows from Kant's cosmopolitan

More broadly understood, however, cosmopolitanism is the area of inquiry that seeks to conceptualize questions of injustice and political responsibility at the level of the cosmos, based on the axiom of equal concern for all subjects regardless of membership or affiliation. If we are interested in theorizing injustice and political responsibility, we must grapple with the fact that, just as in colonial times, two features characterize our world: (1) injustice operates transnationally (i.e., affecting groups within and outside the West in ways that have affinities) and (2) vulnerable groups are excluded from representation in domestic spheres in the West and the non-West, and, as a consequence, in the international sphere. Focusing on the transnational character of injustice means acknowledging that multiple sets of dynamically overlapping and interacting social fields exceeding the national "create and shape seemingly bordered and bounded structures, actors, and processes" (Khagram and Levitt 2008, 26). This does not mean abandoning the domestic realm as an important sphere of politics, because the nation state is an inescapable social phenomenon that must be considered, even if not necessarily frame the inquiry (Seigel 2005, 63). It does mean that cosmopolitan approaches must theorize the distinctiveness of transnationalism to connect localized forms of domination and struggles with global economic and political structures (Mohanty 2002, 501).

The inability of neo-Kantian cosmopolitanism to grasp and theorize an event like the Pan-African Congress in 1919 speaks to deeper problems in this theoretical framework that prevent it from properly grasping contemporary questions of *transnational* injustice and the *political craft* through which subaltern actors contest these structures. These problems arise from the limitations of Kant's cosmopolitanism itself, but reappear in the accounts of neo-Kantian scholars in ways that curtail their ability to consider transnational injustice and transnational politics.

Kant's cosmopolitanism, developed in *Toward Perpetual Peace* (from now *Perpetual Peace*) and his *Doctrine of Right*, and the discussion of colonialism contained therein, are considered one of the bedrocks of the contemporary reconstruction of the Kantian cosmopolitan project. Yet, despite the apparently global motivation of his intervention, I show that both Kant's anti-colonialism and its role in his cosmopolitanism have actually narrower motivations. I argue that Kant's *Perpetual Peace* was

notions (Rawls 1999a, 1999b). I address this literature in the conclusion and elsewhere (Valdez 2019).

written out of concern for European stability and the progress of this continent toward peace. Each of the three "Definitive Articles" in this essay aims to come to terms with sources of instability and conflict that imperil the road toward European peace, including the third article, which contains the discussion of colonialism. While there is a moral condemnation of colonialism in the third article and one of settlement in the *Metaphysics of Morals*, these are not well-elaborated critiques and are compatible with hierarchical beliefs about race and civilization, which Kant explicitly espoused in earlier work. This is the *problem of hierarchy*. Rather than coming to grips with the nature of colonial injustice or exploring the political agency of the colonized (visibly at play in the Haitian Revolution as Kant was writing), the bulk of Kant's discussion in the third article focuses on *intra*-European colonial *conflict in* the colonies. In other words, rather than the relation of colonizer–colonized, Kant's focuses on intra-European conflict in faraway lands, which he judges too unbridled to contribute to the virtuous process of asocial sociability, which he believed would channel European conflict toward peace. This was his main concern, a concern that has little correspondence with the questions of global injustice that we face today. This is the problem of *correspondence*.

The evidently problematic commitment to racial and civilizational hierarchy in Kant has been shed by neo-Kantians, whose theories are genuinely egalitarian and concerned with the whole world, rather than just Europe. However, by maintaining other features of the Kantian framework, they inherit a framework that has little correspondence with our problems today. Thus, even if their goal is genuinely to advance a theory of *world* justice by embedding their theorization on Kant's framework, their vision of today's cosmopolitanism remains unwittingly centered in Europe (i.e., Eurocentric). This appears in three features of their theorizing:

1) Federative Eurocentrism: neo-Kantian scholars tend to remain (to different degrees and in different forms) within the Kantian framework that sanctions the domestic and international realms as the only spaces where politics takes place. In this they abide by the federative structure of Kant's cosmopolitanism.

2) Unworldly Eurocentrism: scholars do not consider intellectual resources and political practices from outside the West. This is despite the fact that this region has historically been at the receiving end of global wrongs (which cosmopolitanism aims to right) and

that it has, as a consequence, a well-developed tradition of thought and political practice with insights about global injustice.

3) Ahistorical Eurocentrism: neo-Kantian scholars tend to focus – sometimes critically – on a Western genealogy of international institutions (including the League of Nations, the United Nations, and the European Union [EU]) and overlook other instances of transnational cooperation taking place at the margins, like the Versailles example mentioned earlier.

In practice, these three forms of Eurocentrism result in neo-Kantians' tendency to engage in four interrelated practices of theorizing. First, because of their indebtedness to Kant's federative framework of cosmo-politanism, neo-Kantian scholars think of progress toward cosmopolitan-ism vertically, as a problem that requires democratization domestically and the gradual integration of these democracies into regional institutions in the style of the EU (Habermas 2000, 2006; Ypi 2012; sometimes Bohman 2007; Forst 2012). Second, because of their lack of attention to anti-colonial critiques of Western domination, some neo-Kantians think of Western democracies as the most developed ones and those that – once enlightened – will lead the project of cosmopolitanism. These two practices of theorizing overlook the problem that Western democracies actively sustain unjust power relations in the international sphere, of which they are the main beneficiaries. This puts in question the dictum that enlightened democracies will develop cosmopolitan orientations, and is akin to deferring to the privileged for a view of justice. Moreover, the fact that some states sustain unjust power relations also truncates the process of vertical integration of gradually democratizing polities, because imperfect democratic regimes in the Global South are signifi-cantly indebted to external constraints (Forst 2015). Third, a related practice of theorizing posits the model of the EU as a script for other regions to follow or as a model to extend to the rest of the world. This again reflects the Kantian federative model, and involves an assessment of the EU as an imperfect but improving script of federative peace that simply needs to be further extended for peace and justice to expand as well. Yet, the idea that the form of organization of a dominant region of the world can be extended is inconsistent; because the well-being and prosperity of Europe depends on a historically and presently unjust world, its model is simply not reproducible in the world sphere. Fourth, building upon a Kantian framework that considers the domestic realm paramount, some neo-Kantian scholars treat the cosmopolitan realm as one of morality, with politics restricted to the domestic and international realms (Benhabib 2006; Habermas 2006). This strategy obscures the political activity undertaken beyond the domestic and international spheres by a variety of actors that operate transnationally to put forward alternative models of organization at the world level.

As a consequence of these three forms of Eurocentrism and the related practices of theorizing, neo-Kantian frameworks offer narrow accounts of cosmopolitan normativity and politics. First, by not engaging non-European intellectual and political resources, neo-Kantian scholars miss the centrality of racial regimes of imperial and postimperial domination operating within Western regimes and transnationally theorized by this tradition. This is a central *political* feature of the way in which authority and domination were organized, one that was still prevalent when the League of Nations and United Nations were founded. Second, by not deviating too much from the federative model, neo-Kantians overlook transnational forms of solidarity and cooperation that result in important political actions in line with the cosmopolitan project of justice. These forms of organization offer *normative* scripts of justice that require exiting exclusionary domestic and international realms of politics. Third, by overlooking transnational thinking and political action spearheaded by subaltern groups, they also miss normative and political dimensions of the struggle for justice that makes advances toward cosmopolitanism possible. Among these dimensions are the centrality of mutual identification and solidarity in the political craft of cosmopolitanism, and their role strengthening political agency and transnational coalitions that are the condition of possibility of cosmopolitanism.

To address these problems, I propose a theoretical framework of transnational cosmopolitanism that draws on the neglected post–World War I work of W. E. B. Du Bois.[2] This approach centers questions of identity, transnational solidarity, and anti-colonial counter-publics, and thus transfigures accepted divisions between domestic and international politics. A transfiguration amounts to a radical and qualitative break that does not claim to culminate or perfect existing structures but instead departs from them (Benhabib 1986, 41–2). In the case of the transnational cosmopolitanism I reconstruct, the transfiguration is threefold.

---

[2] My claim is not that W. E. B. Du Bois is the only scholar missing from this conversation, but that Du Bois's long and prolific career as a scholar and activist makes him a privileged source for a critique of neo-Kantian cosmopolitanism and a coherent and comprehensive approach to cosmopolitanism in its own right.

First, a transformation in consciousness allows domestically marginalized subjects to reenvision themselves as part of a transnational collective. Second, this transformation is enabled and advances the formation of a counter-public that relies on ties of solidarity and a common sense of imperial temporality as bloody and radical regress, rather than progress. Third, these twin realizations in turn feed into new disruptive forms of politics that intervene in spaces of domestic and international politics and demand justice and reparation. The goal of this engagement is to present Du Bois as a global political thinker who deserves pride of place in the literature on cosmopolitanism.[3]

Transnational cosmopolitanism transfigures cosmopolitanism and, in so doing, reconceives its normative impetus. The proposed approach does take equal concern as a motivation but it refuses to design all-encompassing institutions and universal principles of inclusion, and to adjust existing political action to fit existing domestic and international realms. Moreover, transnational cosmopolitanism does not theorize the present based on models of politics indebted to a European ideal of convergent republicanism and international federation. Instead, transnational cosmopolitanism focuses on three under-theorized dimensions of cosmopolitanism. First, transnational cosmopolitanism starts from the acknowledgment of the common transnational origins of injustice (i.e., the ontological point). This acknowledgment implies, second, that political arenas and systems of accountability that exceed the domestic and the international spheres must exist to track and contest these origins (i.e., the political point). Third, to track arenas where transnational injustice is politicized, cosmopolitan theorists must relocate the cosmopolitan subject away from the charitable Westerner and toward subaltern colonized and

---

[3] I have a profound debt to the dynamic literature in African and African American Studies on Pan-Africanism, "vernacular" and "colored" cosmopolitanism, and historical accounts of transnational coalition making (Briggs 2005; Hooker 2017; Horne 1986, 2009; M'bayo 2004; Makalani 2011; Mullen 2003; Nantambu 1998; Shilliam 2015; Slate 2012a; Stephens 2005; Von Eschen 1997). My aim here is to position Du Bois as a global thinker and an interlocutor in the political theory of cosmopolitanism. By doing so, I go beyond Pan-Africanism by focusing on Du Bois's interest in establishing affinities and extending solidarity beyond Africa and toward Asia and the Americas. Vis-à-vis the historical reconstruction of realms of solidarity among Africans and Afro-diaspora, and Asians as forms of "colored cosmopolitanism," I show the purchase of the writings of one participant in this movement and the instances of coalition making for theorizing cosmopolitanism. As a consequence, my focus is on a more textured analysis of the normative and political dimensions of Du Bois's writings and political practice, and how they should inform theorizing of cosmopolitanism in contemporary political theory.

neocolonized subjects who take seriously the questions of identity, political subjectivity, and solidarity, tying together marginalized subjects located inside and outside the West (i.e., the ethical point).

By relying on Du Bois's multi-genre writing, his autobiographical reflections, and his political action, the conceptualization of transnational cosmopolitanism I put forward highlights the *political craft* that underpins projects of cosmopolitanism. Attention to political craft allows us to uncover events that are unintelligible to existing frameworks of cosmopolitanism, like the one that took place in Versailles in 1919, and focus on their political and normative import vis-à-vis a project of world justice. In this sense, attending to political craft is not simply to "illustrate" abstract cosmopolitan theories, but to vastly alter their theoretical presumptions and normative priorities (Ackerly 2018, 9, 14, 26; Goodhart 2018, 12–17; Lu 2018a).[4] In this book, I highlight forms of hospitable communication between marginalized subjects that put the exclusions of sanctioned realms in sharp relief. This engagement questions basic theoretical notions of sovereignty, the people, and political subjectivity by transnationalizing them. I further show that these exchanges were built upon networks of solidarity that exceeded borders, and that they successfully constituted a dynamic counter-public with a shared temporality and public will distinct and opposed to those of mainstream European publics. The normative insights of the grounded character of cosmopolitanism and its attention to non-Western spaces of colonial or postcolonial oppression, however, do not simply follow from the marginal locations of the groups engaged.[5] The marginal character of the writings and political action of Du Bois is *not*, in and of itself, a reason for engaging with his thought. As Luciana Cadahia and her coauthors argue, the

---

[4] This project also has affinities with Michael Neblo's defense of a "cooperative mode" between normative political theory and empirical social sciences. While in this project I set out to "cooperate" with the historical context and political action of W. E. B. Du Bois, it is no less true that one of the things I expect from this engagement is guidance for the workability of the normative theorization of cosmopolitanism (Neblo 2015, 10).

[5] While Du Bois is, technically, a Westerner, his was a critical voice that explicitly contested central tenets of American democratic exceptionalism and Western civilizational discourse. Moreover, throughout his life, Du Bois aligned himself with and contributed to consolidating a host of non-Western currents of thought, including Ethiopianism, Pan-Africanism, and Afro-Asianism. He could, perhaps, be usefully understood as part of what is currently known as "the Global South in the West" (Grewal 2013, 6). This caveat allows me to otherwise maintain the distinction between the West and non-West, assuming "West" still usefully tracks the site of imperial and postcolonial capitalist power without denying the internal heterogeneity of the West and/or the fuzzier divisions between these spaces upon which transnationalism approaches rightly remark.

periphery does not necessarily, i.e., just because of its site of enunciation, hold a truth forgotten by the center (Cadahia et al. 2018, 9).[6] Instead, what counts is the ability of marginal thinkers and their proposals – often resisted at the time and ignored in contemporary scholarship – to make us reconsider ways of seeing the world, normative priorities, and under-theorized questions. In this book, I show that transnational cosmopolitan-ism offers powerful insights with which to theorize injustice, trans-national politics, and solidarity in ways that will revitalize and democratize the project of cosmopolitanism. These insights include both tools for better conceptualizing contemporary global challenges, in the sense of acknowledging their political character, *and* a reorientation of the normative priorities of cosmopolitan projects.

In particular, the transnational cosmopolitanism I propose is a norma-tive account, which is not committed to abstract derivations of ideal forms of institutions that will secure justice globally. Instead, trans-national cosmopolitanism is *grounded* in concrete experiences of oppres-sion and the political practices of the struggle against it, including the conceptions of justice and practices of freedom developed in the struggle. Moreover, the cosmopolitanism proposed is *relational*, to the extent that it emerges from forms of political action dependent on intersubjective identification and the establishment of ties of solidarity among subjects engaged in common struggles locally and transnationally. This cosmo-politanism is also *dialectical*, to the extent that it takes struggles for emancipation to be always incomplete, because they are either non–all-encompassing or because power structures reorganize and new oppos-itional claims emerge. Because it is grounded yet concerned with global (in)justice, the cosmopolitanism of this project is decidedly *transnational*.

---

[6] This is made clear by Clifford Bob's work on transnational movements whose goals are decidedly non-emancipatory (2001). Moreover, a reliance on the thought and political action of a thinker like Du Bois must also acknowledge the normatively problematic way in which power circulated within transnational coalitions themselves. Du Bois's supportive stance toward non-Western empires, his exclusionary attitude toward black women, and his patronizing stance toward Africans all fall within this category. These features of coalition making, even the more horizontal kind that took place among marginalized subjects of empire, speak of the inevitable deviation of hospitable relations toward attempts to establish mastery theorized by Jacques Derrida (2000). This feature of hospi-tality need not prevent us from considering Du Bois – or anti-colonial thinkers more broadly – as productive normative resources to rethink cosmopolitanism. Rather, it should further affirm the importance of scrutinizing the democratic character of transnational encounters and the publics and institutions that are built upon them in the theorization of cosmopolitanism.

By this I mean that it finds the meaning of *global* justice and emancipation in the *particular* way in which actors throughout the world experience injustice and converge in recognizing that the oppression they face is connected to racialized and imperial forms of global power. In other words, what justice requires is attention to what located subjects conceive of as properly emancipatory transformations, which may not coincide across spaces. This is not because their subjection is not a matter of "global justice," but because the common set of global forces affecting them and other located subjects are refracted through local conditions, historical constellations, and particular forms of colonial rule and/or state power. This form of inquiry augments, challenges, and redirects the contemporary discussion on cosmopolitanism. The fact that Du Bois is the core source of my inquiry and the perspective of black Americans and colonial peoples is central in his work does not mean this is a "vernacular" project. This is because these perspectives are required resources for rethinking global justice so as to better track oppression and the normative priorities of those whose needs it wishes to serve. By conceptualizing the problem of race-based, colonial, and semi-colonial domination, and attending to transnational identity, solidarity, and political subjectivity, transnational cosmopolitanism contributes to the project of universality understood as the process of contestation of existing universals (Balfour 2011, 132–3; Butler 1996; Ingram 2013, 156–7; McKean 2017). Attending to those subjects and instances of domination that are not intelligible in the standard notion of universality assumed in frameworks of political theorizing is necessary, because the emancipation of those subjects constitutes the very possibility of universality.

The notion of transnational cosmopolitanism proposed is normative as well as political. It is normative because it contains an account of (in)justice that is rooted in the political experiences, practices, and thinking of actors struggling against conditions indebted to global social, political, and economic forces. Yet, the normativity of my account does not depend on a vision of justice as an ultimate ideal, but, first, on the construction of a composite picture of injustice based on the experience and political action of oppressed actors and, second, on the recovery of the aspirations toward justice contained in the struggle. This vision of justice, moreover, changes as actors reconceive of themselves as political subjects and as conditions of injustice gradually subside or mutate. In other words, just as bourgeois freedom, which emerged in opposition to absolutism, contained patriarchal and racialized exclusions and was ill-equipped by design to assist women and colonial subjects in their struggles (see Pateman (1988), Mills (1997), and Getachew (2016), among others). Kant's exploration of what was required to attain peace among relatively equal European states engaged in imperial conquest helps little in figuring out what global justice requires in a colonial and postcolonial world. The notion of transnational cosmopolitanism I propose is also political, in the sense that it conceives of justice as dependent on what Brooke Ackerly – following Arendt – terms "the political life (not just the political rules) of human association and disassociation" with a "focus on how we act together" (2018, 19). This does not mean conflating the normative and the political. Instead, it is to say that, just as power inequalities and oppressive social norms are constructed by humans collectively (Ackerly 2018, 9–10) (the political), normative principles emerge from political processes in which these institutions are contested through the enunciation of principles that are enacted, contested, and revisited (the normative).

PAST AND PRESENT, CENTER AND MARGINS, AND THE QUESTION OF INTERPRETATION

The reading I propose in *Transnational Cosmopolitanism* carries with it important interpretive implications regarding how we approach historical political thought when our goal is to theorize for the present. In conceptualizing transnational cosmopolitanism, I engage with Kant, neo-Kantians, and Du Bois while placing interpretive authority in the present. Such a reading involves keeping in mind that the primary goal is not exegetical loyalty, but to uncover the ability of past thinkers to contribute to our projects today. This involves identifying the racial and civilizational hierarchies in their writings and exploring how such hierarchies affect the frameworks we may extract from them. At the same time, placing interpretive authority in the present allows us to propose creative, anachronistic, and exegetically disloyal readings that can reorient normative principles for contemporary use (Leslie 1970, and Chapter 2). In this book, those creative readings rely on the productive juxtaposition of Kant, neo-Kantians, and Du Bois. This is not to say Kant's principles can be "recovered" once they are reread through Du Bois, or to say Du Bois's work alone can ground a novel cosmopolitanism. Instead, juxtaposed, or, in Jane Gordon's terms, "creolized," readings make us aware that moments of closure in one author can lead to openness when read alongside a different author or historical time. This practice, moreover, shows that cases of sedimentation in Enlightenment thinking about the

Other can find fluidity when juxtaposed with those addressing the project from below (Gordon 2014, 11). Unlike comparison, juxtaposition does not presume "stable and discrete traditions of thought," but considers the possibility that the very boundaries between traditions may be "contingent products of political power" (Gordon 2014; Hooker 2017, 14). The result is a study in contrasts, which vastly exceeds the realm of Kant's imagination to transfigure hospitality and complementarity to serve the radical politics of opposing colonialism and neocolonialism. This is not to say that Kant contains a kernel of these struggles, but rather that the juxtaposition illustrates at once the limits of the Enlightenment tradition and the need for political theorists to incorporate new voices, texts, and actions as richer normative scripts with which to tackle racism and imperialism as central forms of injustice cosmopolitanism must consider. In this book I highlight in particular questions of identity, solidarity, and transnational counter-publics, which have been given little weight in contemporary neo-Kantian accounts of cosmopolitanism, but have played a central role in the thinking and action of anti-colonial political actors, and can productively reorient the normative priorities of cosmopolitanism. I make these claims in four steps, corresponding to four modalities of interpretation.

First, I propose a novel historical reading of Kant's *Perpetual Peace*, which rereads his anti-colonialism alongside the historical background of the colonial locales Kant mentions in his cosmopolitan article (Chapter 1). This reading highlights important limitations of the original Kantian framework in terms of both the hierarchies of race and civilization it contains (*the problem of hierarchy*), and the lack of correspondence between the problems he was facing and the ones we face today (*the problem of correspondence*). For my analysis of the problem of correspondence I rely on David Scott's notion of the problem space, i.e., "an ensemble of questions and answers around which a horizon of identifiable stakes (conceptual as well as ideological-political . . .) hangs" (2004, 4–5). My original reading considers the problem space to which Kant's cosmopolitanism responded and concludes it was, in essence, Eurocentric, i.e., concerned primarily with the stability and maturity of nascent republics, the stability of Europe, and its progress toward peace. Kant's anti-colonialism, in this reading, is motivated more by an effort to shelter Europe from the unconventional and barbaric conflict *among* Europeans taking place *in* the colonies and less by a concern with the standing of colonial subjects and the injustice of colonialism. This is ill-fitted to consider the deep inequalities between the West and the non-West and the continued racial divides at the domestic and international level – including political phenomena that exceed the domain of the nation state – that occupy us today. Therefore, unmodified, Kant's thinking has limited correspondence with our problems today. Moreover, it is likely that Kant's anti-colonialism does not undo his well-known hierarchical under-standings of civilization and race, which remain an important building block of his understanding of progress, and raises the problem of hierarchy.

Interpretively, this is the "step of contextualization," which requires analyzing Kant's context of writing carefully in order to understand the historically specific challenges he faced, the questions he was answering, and – ultimately – what he was doing by conceptualizing the realm of cosmopolitanism.

In a second step, I consider how the problems of hierarchy and corres-pondence continue to condition neo-Kantians in their theorization of contemporary cosmopolitanism and – in particular – its transnational dimensions (Chapter 2). In particular, I identify three forms of Eurocen-trism that appear in some form in the neo-Kantian literature on cosmo-politanism, discussed earlier (i.e., federative Eurocentrism, unworldly Eurocentrism, and ahistorical Eurocentrism). As I note in Chapter 2, the three forms of Eurocentrism I identify do not necessarily appear in each and every one of the scholars I engage with, nor do they appear in the same form, but are nonetheless telling of the indebtedness of this literature to Kant's preoccupations in the late eighteenth century, which limit cosmopolitan theorizing today. Interpretively, this is the "step of decon-struction," in which we single out the hierarchies that structured Kant's thought and interrogate current neo-Kantian thinking to see if they still permeate these frameworks. This is in order to amend these frameworks, discard parts of them, and/or focus on developing theoretical approaches that directly address – rather than assume away – hierarchy.

In a third step, I juxtapose Kantian hospitality with Du Bois's anti-colonial transnational action and suggest the latter transfigures the notion of hospitality by bringing to the fore forms of collective identification that exceed the domestic sphere and inaugurating spaces of politics that are neither domestic nor international (Chapter 3). Here, I introduce the notion of transnational cosmopolitanism by centering the question of horizontal ties of solidarity built upon common experiences of racial and imperial domination that result in coalitional political practices. This framework requires the transfiguration of hospitality, i.e., its re-cognition as a horizontal practice among those who are subject to colonial power, in a way that centers hierarchy as a theoretical problem that cosmopolitanism must face. Moreover, by addressing the problem of hierarchy (by making it a normative priority to theorize injustice and those movements that challenged it, in this case, via non-Western perspectives and actors) also furthers the correspondence of transnational cosmopolitanism with the postcolonial world we face today.[7]

This is the "political interpretive step," in which I evaluate whether theoretical insights are usable to address the challenges we are facing today and answer the questions that are most pressing. While a thorough reconstruction of such present challenges would entail a book-length project of its own, my transnational cosmopolitanism keeps in mind the postcolonial era in which we live and centers questions of unequal sovereignty, racialized labor exploitation, and neoliberal capitalism. Addressing the way in which these forces result in localized forms of oppression, which, while diverse, are arguably rooted in a transnational matrix of power we need to reconstruct in order to counter, surely calls for tools Kant could not have provided. These phenomena require a theoretical framework that can grapple critically with questions of power, race, and oppression, rather than consider the problem of peace as one of gradual domestic democratization and convergence into federations of a group of relatively equal states. This is not to say that the world Du Bois inhabited was the neoliberal world we live in. Yet, the construction of a transnational cosmopolitanism that attends to the transnational character of imperial power and racial injustice, as well as instances of transnational political action disruptive of white diplomacy contains resources better aligned with today's challenges.

A fourth stage of interpretation requires reaching outside the Western canon for interpretive authority, attending to the subaltern experience and the theorization of the global condition. In particular, it involves finding interlocutors who can help scholars of cosmopolitanism conceptualize the way in which racialized forms of domination took shape and were transformed during the two centuries separating us from Kant; how these forces were resisted and overcome; and how they underlie our current condition. I identify this step as the "cosmopolitan interpretive

---

[7] As noted earlier, and as it will become clear throughout the manuscript, the incorporation required is both intellectual (i.e., of non-Western or marginalized Western theorists) and political (i.e., of those instances of political action that emerged to challenge colonial and postcolonial systems of domination).

step" (borrowing from Farah Godrej's reflections on cosmopolitan modes of inquiry [2011]), where I engage with Du Bois to conceptualize transnational cosmopolitanism. This engagement, however, requires cosmopolitanism to attempt a different tempo in its approach to the past. It requires interpretive techniques that engage patiently and with perseverance with the character of colonialism in our recent past and which, in Theodor Adorno's terms, linger with the particular (1978, 77; see also Saward 2011). This implies, first, acknowledging that the international public sphere was, for a century and a half after Kant, an imperial sphere of European cooperation devoted to – among other things – organizing colonial domination. This acknowledgment should be followed by the incorporation of intellectuals of color as interlocutors, because they conceptualized with precision these forms of domination and hierarchy in the international sphere and put forward powerful conceptions of transnational solidarity and emancipatory politics devoted to counter them. The attention required to recover these voices contrasts with the rapid genealogy of the twentieth century implicit in the neo-Kantian cosmopolitan literature; a gradual but certain extension of the public sphere through the League of Nations, the United Nations, and the EU, and a narrative that privileges human rights. The alternative orientation I propose still requires the careful reconstruction of the meaning of texts but goes beyond it by interrogating – rather than assuming – both the legacies of hierarchical dimensions in the normative substance of frameworks and the correspondence between these insights and our current challenges.

This is the exercise occupying the second half of this book and constitutes its core, constructive contribution, i.e., the conceptualization of transnational cosmopolitanism. Substantively, the joint reading proposed allows us to switch from a Kantian focus on the tension between nominally equal sovereign states and an overarching cosmopolitan authority (Flikschuh 2010) to the different problem of the drastically unequal conditions of sovereignty peoples experience around the world. It allows us to think of progress toward cosmopolitanism not in terms of the gradual democratization of states aided by a global human rights regime (Benhabib 2004) or as a project led by benevolent Western citizens and/or states, but as a process requiring scrutiny of how Western democracies are involved in forms of domination domestically and abroad. Moreover, instead of looking at questions of local and transnational loyalty as potentially contradictory (Nussbaum 2008; Scheffler 2002), the reading I propose allows us to find transnational affinities that may be stronger between differently located subjects of domination than between marginalized groups and their co-nationals, and may underlie transnational coalitional politics of emancipation in the present.

In particular, W. E. B. Du Bois's thought and political craft, including his experience spearheading fora of alternative internationalisms, provide the ideal resource for enriching the normative content of cosmopolitanism (Chapter 3). Because of the obstacles he found within the American polity and his understanding of the transnational character of racial domination and imperialism, Du Bois's thought and action made creative use of diverse spheres of politics, often in coalition with other subjects of imperial power. The notion of transnational cosmopolitanism I propose normatively centers questions of transnational identity-based solidarity and multiple loyalties (Chapter 4), and the forms of political action and counter-publics that opposed domination (Chapter 5). This theorization goes beyond simply assuming equal concern and instead performs it by exploring the meaning of identity, solidarity, and political subjectivity for subaltern groups that sought to overcome injustice in the post–World War I era. This exploration shows transnational solidarity can underpin emancipatory forms of subjectivity conducive to political action, which contrasts with the way in which identity figures in neo-Kantian scholarship. Moreover, I reconstruct how transnational consciousness and solidarity emerge in tandem with the inauguration and development of anticolonial counter-publics where the claims of those excluded from Western polities or the Western international sphere can air and politicize their grievances and engage in coalitions to overcome them. By building upon Du Bois to conceptualize transnational cosmopolitanism, I benefit from certain features unique to his work: its extension and duration, as well as its coincidence with historical moments of great transformation; its tendency to oscillate between the theoretical and the autobiographical; and the public character of his reflections on the experiential, the political, and the historical. Rather than aiming to reconstruct a coherent Du Bois, I read the transformation of his thinking, along with the political and the experiential, in order to recover the meaning of his thought. In other words, I consider the evolution of the text itself as a source of meaning (Bryant 2007, 19). The revisions in Du Bois's thinking convey important insights about the way in which he navigated the affinities and contradictions between the knowledge he acquired; the life he experienced; the political situations he faced and those he initiated; and the particular subjectivities that were imposed on him and that he shaped in turn throughout his life.

The four interpretive steps outlined are often entangled in the task of theorizing, but distinguishing them clarifies the normative stakes associated with each stage. For example, even if – as Pauline Kleingeld argues (2007, 2014a) – Kant had overcome his racist beliefs and upheld a nascent egalitarianism by the time he put forward his critique of colonialism, this does not mean Kant is an apt guide for our thinking on cosmopolitanism today. Moreover, even if we are able to confidently reconstruct a coherent picture of the Kantian system of Right that is faithful to Kant's intentions, this does not mean this framework carries particular authority over the questions we are supposed to answer today. In other words, we should let go of two forms of interpretation that maintain the authority of the past, i.e., those that consider exegetical accuracy of primary importance and those on which Kant's problem space still has a hold. Both of these forms lead us astray on the question of correspondence, preventing the accurate and critical reading of contemporary challenges. Prioritizing exegetical authority implies that our primary aim is not to theorize cosmopolitanism for our times, but to reconstruct Kant's cosmopolitanism with the greatest possible accuracy, a goal which may in fact detract from disloyal readings of his thought that would have emerged with an interpretive authority securely rooted in the present. Moreover, when the focus on exegetical accuracy is tied to a defense of Kant as an egalitarian thinker – despite the availability of only speculative evidence – the problem is that the project of theorizing cosmopolitanism to undo the legacies of racial and colonial hierarchy, cedes space and attention to the goal of defending Kant as an ultimately egalitarian and anti-imperialist thinker (Dhawan 2016). But deferring to Kant's diagnosis of the problem space is problematic because it encases cosmopolitan challenges in the Kantian problem space. In so doing, it proceeds under the assumption of sameness rather than attention to difference that would be dictated by equal concern. Sameness implies that simply expanding Kantian-inspired institutions to the world will result in inclusion, as opposed to considering how those institutions themselves established difference and ordered it hierarchically as the starting point of our theorization. Moreover, this interpretive strategy prevents us from attending to practices of contestation of colonial power and listening to subjects that read cosmopolitanism in contrasting ways, and thus significantly impoverishes our theorization of the politics and normativity of cosmopolitanism.

Furthermore, the four steps of interpretation make clear that the explicit or implicit repudiation of hierarchy in Kant by neo-Kantian scholars, when followed by the simple extrication of his cosmopolitan thought from his system, as if it could stand alone, avoids the consideration of the ways in which hierarchy remains associated with the framework and reproduces hierarchy in the ways outlined earlier. Without an explicit engagement with the legacies of hierarchy, neo-Kantians may fall into what Jeanne Morefield calls the "politics of deflection" (Morefield 2014, 16) For my purposes, deflection means that, while Kantian hierarchy is acknowledged, the next step is either to assume it disappears in later writings or to consider it inconsequential for the broader Kantian system. Thus hierarchy "fall[s] just outside our peripheral vision" (Morefield 2014, 16–17) and is never made the principal focus of *cosmopolitan* theorization. This means the remains of hierarchy that permeate the framework are neither explicitly theorized as such nor countered through a substantial amendment of the framework. It is in this sense that Kant continues to be our problem, because the dominance of his framework in contemporary accounts still filters out certain features of the world and prevents cosmopolitans from effectively engaging with transnational forms of injustice and politics.

CONTRIBUTIONS AND PLAN OF THE BOOK

The proposed mode of interpretation brings about an innovative approach to theorize cosmopolitanism transnationally. Adding the adjective "transnational" to "cosmopolitanism" is far from redundant. Instead, it substantively changes cosmopolitanism by bringing into view overlooked structures of domination and the political craft through which cosmopolitan projects come about. In the process, it radically transforms the normative orientation of cosmopolitanism and the way in which it is theorized in at least four ways.

First, transnational cosmopolitanism reconstructs the heterogeneous way in which racial structures of power became grounded in diverse moments and spaces through the slave trade, slavery, settler colonialism, apartheid, and racial disenfranchisement. In so doing, it recognizes that world injustice is better understood as sustained *at once* by unjust domestic, international, and transnational forms of power and must be tackled accordingly.

Second, and as a consequence of the previous point, transnational cosmopolitanism argues that to tackle world injustice normatively, it is necessary to look beyond state and interstate politics and toward the political craft of cosmopolitanism that takes place outside these fora. These practices contest the separation of realms that underlies democratization and vertical integration in the neo-Kantian literature. By tracking transnational political action by subalterns, transnational cosmopolitanism normatively indicts the project of simply extending multilateral institutions and spaces of Western solidarity toward the rest of the world, for it shows that they operated and operate to exclude them and sustain injustice.

Third, transnational cosmopolitanism highlights the importance of identity-based forms of transnational solidarity that nurture emancipatory political subjectivity and support transnational counter-publics operating at the margins – although in conversation with – colonial and neocolonial fora. The myriad forms of identity making that ground transnational cosmopolitanism emerge locally but are politically expansive and conducive to identification with differently located subjects similarly affected by forms of oppression that exceed the national.

Finally, a framework of transnational cosmopolitanism transfigures extant understandings of cosmopolitanism, communication, and hospitality. Cosmopolitan politics are transfigured through the transnational and solidaristic political craft of subaltern actors who do not currently have a voice domestically and internationally. These political exchanges give rise to processes of will-formation inaugurating counter-publics that aim not to reform sanctioned realms of politics, but instead overcome them, given their role in sustaining domination.

In the rest of this book I support these arguments. Chapters move through the four stages of interpretation to critically scrutinize the Kantian and neo-Kantian literatures and – via the writings and political craft of W. E. B. Du Bois – transfigure this approach to bring about a transnational cosmopolitanism. Chapter 1, "The Limits of Kant's Anti-Colonialism and His Philosophy of History," is devoted to contextualization. This chapter delves into the context of politics, economics, and war that motivated Kant to write *Perpetual Peace* in 1795, the essay that introduced his cosmopolitanism. I examine, for the first time alongside this essay, the historical events taking place in the six colonial locales Kant mentions in the section on cosmopolitanism and find they were all sites characterized by strong *intra*-European conflict. Based on this examination, I argue that the goal of Kant's cosmopolitanism was to prevent the multiplicative effect of these entanglements in the development of republics in Europe and the progress of this continent toward peace (Valdez 2017). The theorization of a cosmopolitan realm was Kant's amendment of his philosophy of history to prevent the nonconventional warfare, which characterized colonial explorations in the late eighteenth century, from upsetting Europe's path toward progress. This interpretation suggests, first, that Kant's anti-colonialism formed part of his teleological reflections on the likelihood of European peace rather than a full-fledged emancipatory cosmopolitanism, which raises the problem of correspondence. The embeddedness of Kant's system in his philosophy of history also limits the use of his framework for normatively considering questions of political agency and emancipation among those at the receiving end of colonial domination, which were unaccounted for by him. Second, the proposed interpretation shows that the civilizational and racial hierarchies in his framework are compatible with his cosmopolitanism, raising the problem of hierarchy. Readers less interested in the exegetical scrutiny of Kant's cosmopolitanism, anti-colonialism, and teleology, may be content with the discussion in the introduction and conclusion of Chapter 1. These sections summarize the argument and briefly anticipate the implications for the critique of neo-Kantian approaches and the motivations for the development a transnational cosmopolitan approach based on Du Bois's global thought and transnational political practice.

Chapter 2, "Vertical and Horizontal Readings of Kant's Principles," is devoted to deconstruction and political interpretation. This chapter scrutinizes the principles of Kant's cosmopolitanism with the greatest currency in contemporary readings, including hospitality; the interconnected and complementary character of the domestic, international, and cosmopolitan realms; and cosmopolitan patriotism. I consider the work of scholars like Seyla Benhabib, James Bohman, Rainer Forst, Jürgen Habermas, Pauline Kleingeld, Brian Milstein, and Lea Ypi and show that the problems of correspondence and hierarchy curtail the efforts of this scholarship to grapple with the transnational. I trace, in particular, the effects of privileging federative forms of cosmopolitan institutionalization, the lack of engagement with anti-colonialism as an intellectual tradition and political practice, and the little attention given to alternative transnational formations in the twentieth century. I show that it is not uncommon for this scholarship to privilege the West as the initiator of cosmopolitan relations, give priority to domestic politics when in tension with cosmopolitanism, and propose to solve the legitimacy gap through vertical/regional integration. I contrast these readings with a disloyal reading of Kant that open the concepts of complementary and hospitality to more horizontal readings.

Chapter 3, "Du Bois and a Radical, Transnational Cosmopolitanism," inaugurates the step of cosmopolitan interpretation. In this chapter, I contrast Kant's and neo-Kantian accounts of cosmopolitanism with a

Duboisian theorization of the common character of injustice found in colonialism, neocolonialism, and post-slavery societies. In so doing, I transfer interpretive authority to those at the margins of empire who offer a transfigured notion of hospitality, i.e., a form of communication that leads to radical departures from existing separations between the domestic and the international at the level of identity, solidarity, and public will. This transfiguration is evident in Du Bois's aesthetic turn, i.e., how he relocates African Americans and other subjects of color away from the places assigned to them by racist scripts and reconfigures the shape of community of fate away from the domestic and toward the transnational. I illustrate these claims with Du Bois's writings and the analysis of three events he spearheaded in the interwar and post–World War II periods; the 1919 Pan-African Congress, his participation in the San Francisco Conference as an advocate for the colonies in 1945, and the submission of a petition to the United Nations denouncing the violations of African Americans' human rights by the US government. Based on this, I conceptualize a framework of transnational cosmopolitanism, which I contrast with notions of cosmopolitan patriotism.

Chapter 4, "Race, Identity, and the Question of Transnational Solidarity in Cosmopolitanism," continues the task of cosmopolitan interpretation by tracing Du Bois's gradual detachment from Western teleologies of progress and his conceptualization of notions of transnational political subjectivity and solidarity grounded on forms of mutual identification that respond to racialization. I argue that, in a world in which injustice is transnational, processes of group self-definition may be more conducive to developing a cosmopolitan orientation than national, regional, or international fora. This cosmopolitan orientation becomes transnational when it moves to identify common threads of injustice between the conditions that affect local groups and those affecting groups outside the nation-state (i.e., the ontological point), allows for the establishment of ties of solidarity with subjects so affected (i.e., the ethical point), and for the engagement in joint political action to ameliorate their condition (i.e., the political point). The transnational subjectivity that emerges is historically grounded and identity based but also politically malleable, rather than sovereign. Moreover, it is anti-statist because its transnationalism makes it bound to open spaces of claim making beyond the state.

Chapter 5, "A Transnationally Cosmopolitan Counter-Public," complements Chapter 4 by showing how a sphere of public opinion based on an anti-colonial "imagined community" was built alongside and in conversation with the process of formation of a transnational political subjectivity. This chapter conceptualizes the transnational counter-public through an engagement with Du Bois's writing and editorial practices in *The Crisis* in the 1920s. While not formal, this sphere of transnational public opinion contested the hegemony of empire and addressed several loci of authority. In particular, this sphere served the functions of diagnosis, connection, counter-sovereignty, and political activation. These functions stand in contrast with the imperial imaginaries of the era, and are a needed complement to the critical literature on empire, which downplays the political character of imperial discourse.

The Conclusion returns to the main insights of the book, reviews the proposed notion of transnational cosmopolitanism, and reflects on the critical insights that it offers another contemporary cosmopolitan tradition, that of the global justice literature. In so doing, it encourages the contemporary political theory of cosmopolitanism to attend to the many "parallel Versailles" that may be taking place today, and take seriously their insights as resources for theorizing. In closing, I reflect on the way in which such transnational formations may be normatively central for offering alternative scripts of global politics when they are needed to counter the current populist backlash against globalization.

The Limits of Kant's Anti-Colonialism and His Philosophy of History

It is only fitting to start an examination of cosmopolitanism by revisiting Immanuel Kant's *Toward Perpetual Peace* (from now on, *Perpetual Peace*). Written in 1795, *Perpetual Peace* is one of the most read and debated texts in Kant's corpus. Moreover, the stark critique of colonialism contained in its third article is at the core of contemporary thinking on cosmopolitanism. This is the case in spite of remaining disagreement about many of the central claims in this text, including the grounds of his anti-colonialism, its compatibility with racial and civilizational hierarchy, and the exact character of the cosmopolitan realm he proposes. Yet, settling these questions is central for assessing the utility of Kant's framework to theorize cosmopolitanism today. If, as I argue here, Kant's critique of cosmopolitanism was part of his reflections about progress rather than his theory of justice, his insights are less usable for a cosmopolitanism that wants to take seriously the claims of subaltern actors as part of the pursuit of justice. Moreover, if racial and civilizational hierarchies remain in Kant's framework, we might be importing them into our theorization today (falling into the *problem of hierarchy*). This chapter offers a novel contextual interpretation of this essay with the goal of assessing its ability to contribute to a contemporary critical cosmopolitanism. Unlike existing studies, it highlights the importance of the political and economic context and the specific character of the colonialism he opposed to make the claim that the set of problems it came to solve bears little resemblance to our present problems (falling into the *problem of correspondence*). In particular, this chapter shows that Kant's theorization of cosmopolitanism was driven by a concern with intra-European colonial conflict in the colonies and its effect on intra-European equilibrium. This contextualized reading is necessary in order to then amend or discard this framework in our contemporary theorization of cosmopolitanism.

Scholars have provided enlightening contextual accounts of *Perpetual Peace*, but have so far focused on its internal intellectual context, i.e., his broader writings (Bernasconi 2003, 2011; Hedrick 2008; Kleingeld 2007, 2014a) or its external intellectual context, i.e., the dialogues he established with contemporaries (Cavallar 2014; Kleingeld 2012; Maliks 2014). This is to the detriment of the examination of the connections between his thought and the social and political world (Moyn 2016), which this chapter considers in order to reconstruct the particular problem space Kant addressed. At the time, colonialism and colonial conflict were central to Europe's political economy and its military strategy. Despite this, Kant scholars have analyzed his comments on colonialism in the third article of *Perpetual Peace*, as a stand-alone, anti-colonial critique that can be put to work to solve contemporary problems. Instead, I suggest the cosmopolitan section is an integral part of *Perpetual Peace*, and should be considered alongside his claims on republicanism and European international relations in the first and second articles of this essay. Scholars' narrow reading of eighteenth-century European politics (certainly narrower than Kant's own) has led interpreters away from a proper reconstruction of Kant's project, i.e., from what Kant was *doing*, as opposed to *saying*. As I show, a politically careful reading of Kant's comments on colonialism in *Perpetual Peace* can shed light on the meaning of central concepts in Kant's system (including colonialism, trade, and antagonism) and contribute to a more mindful and compelling borrowing from his framework in contemporary political theory.

This is not to say neo-Kantians are not attuned to the question of race and colonialism in Kant's thought. They are, but by not grounding this question in the sociopolitical and economic context of the era, they either misread *Perpetual Peace* as implying a shift in Kant's views on race in the 1790s, or implicitly consider his thought to be plausibly extricable from his hierarchical commitments. By contrast, this chapter shows Kant's cosmopolitanism is compatible with commitments to civilizational and racial hierarchy, which he likely maintained until the end of his life. Moreover, this chapter shows Kant likely developed his cosmopolitanism in response to a concern with Europe's ability to progress toward peace. These findings imply that the problems of hierarchy and correspondence in Kant are more pervasive than neo-Kantian scholars make them out to be because hierarchy persisted until the end of his life, on the one hand,

and because the political motivation of his cosmopolitanism was narrowly concerned with Europe, on the other.

Distinguishing between these two problems is important because it
shows that, even when Kant's framework is placed in an egalitarian
frame, its priorities and commitments are still determined by the particular problem space he constructed. This will result in disproportionate
attention being paid to European forms of international organization
and not enough engagement with the transnational structure of injustice
in which such organizations rested, a structure they also helped perpetuate. The implication is that Kant's thinking cannot be cleanly extricated as
a stand-alone analytical framework and put to work today by simply – to
adapt Virginia Sapiro's line about women (1998, 67) – "add[ing] [people
of color] and stir[ring]." Instead, we need to scrutinize his framework for
the ways in which the hierarchical motivations of his thought still permeate his conceptualization of cosmopolitanism and – if it is to be used –
reread expansively with an eye to attuning his principles to address our
contemporary problem space. In particular, it is important to ask of this
framework whether it can be expanded beyond Europe to highlight the
transnational counter-impulses that met Western imperialism, a task
I pursue in the next chapter.

Based on the historical reconstruction of the context of Kant's writing,
I make a twofold argument. First, Kant's anti-colonialism – as expressed
in *Perpetual Peace* – remains Eurocentric and partly motivated by a
concern with the effects of three features of colonial conflict (rather than
colonialism) on the prospects of republicanism and peace in Europe:
(i) European expansionism, (ii) intra-European colonial rivalry, and
(iii) the cruel and uncivilized practices characteristic of colonial conflict.
Second, while there is a moral critique of colonialism, it is focused on the
violence of the conquest and does not necessarily undo the racist and
civilizational beliefs that characterized Kant's beliefs before the 1790s.
Based on this, I conclude that Kant's cosmopolitanism – unmodified – is
ill-fitted to address questions of colonial and postcolonial unequal power
relations and to attend to the ways in which oppressed subjects understand their condition and act politically to contest it.

To develop these points, the next section introduces the debate on Kant
and colonialism and the related discussion on race. I then examine the
context in which Kant was writing by exploring the history of colonial
sites he mentions *by name* in *Perpetual Peace*, his correspondence, and
other contemporaneous essays. I argue that his primary concern was
Britain's expansionism and how it hindered republics from developing

and fueling progress toward peace. I move on to explain how the historical reconstruction depends on Kant's philosophy of history and the place of conflict within it, which he revisits after examining colonial conflict closely. I follow this by examining how Kant's transformed notion of teleology allows him to differentiate between different types of war. Finally, I consider my reading vis-à-vis Kant's system of Right, developed more fully in *The Metaphysics of Morals*, and his racial hierarchy. I conclude that Kant's cosmopolitanism and his anti-colonialism are *not* concerned with theorizing justice for colonial peoples and, in fact, advocate a retreat from the world that coexists with hierarchical views of race and civilization.

COLONIALISM, RACE, AND EUROPE

The definitive articles of *Perpetual Peace* introduce Kant's system of Right, composed of domestic, international, and cosmopolitan Right. Kant argues that republicanism is the ideal system of domestic government and traces an expected progression of European states toward peace through the leadership of republics and the formation of a voluntary federation of states. Regarding republics, he argues that "the civil constitution of every state shall be republican," a regime founded on the "*freedom* of the members of a society . . . the *dependence* of all upon a single common legislation . . . and their *equality*" (322, 8:249–350). The second definitive article establishes that "[t]he right of nations shall be based on a *federalism* of free states," a practical end because an "enlightened people can form itself into a republic," which, being naturally peaceful, provides a focal point for other states "to attach themselves to it" and gradually extend further and further" (325, 327, 8:354, 356). In contrast to previous accounts of cosmopolitanism in *Idea for a Universal History with a Cosmopolitan Purpose* (*Idea*, from now on) and the *Critique of Judgment*, where the cosmopolitan condition was achieved through the federation of states, in *Perpetual Peace*, cosmopolitanism appears as a separate realm regulating other types of relationships (Kleingeld 2014b, 68–71), notably European actions in non-European regions.

Kant had dealt with non-Europeans in his anthropology and geography, where he classified them as racially inferior to European whites. Scholars have noted two stages in Kant's racial theories: an early and less systematic stage, and the later stage – developed in the 1780s – when race takes a teleological character and is connected to Kant's critical philosophy (Bernasconi 2011; Larrimore 1999, 2008, 356). In particular, Kant tied racial difference to seeds that were triggered (not caused) by climate and slowly unfolded but eventually became permanent racial traits (Larrimore 2008, 344), resulting in a hierarchy with whites at the top and Native Americans at the bottom. Regarding the latter he argued in 1788, "their natural disposition has not yet reached a *complete* fitness for any one climate . . . too weak for hard labor, too indifferent for diligence, and unfit for any culture, still stands – despite the proximity of example and ample encouragement – far below the Negro himself," who otherwise held the lowest rung in the racial ladder (*UTP*, 48, 8:175–6). In his lectures of the 1780s, Kant asserted that only the white race contains all incentives and talents and even the "Hindus" who can be educated (and are thus superior to "Negroes") can be trained in the arts but not in abstract concepts (*RA*, 15:877–8).

Kant paired these assertions with uncritical discussions of Europeans' activities overseas, remarking upon the uses the different races should be put to, given their natural predispositions (*DHR*, 333, 2:438n). As late as 1792, Kant cited approvingly David Hume's statement that Africans had no claim to equality, and in the same lectures he contended that no freed Negro had distinguished himself with any skill (which is conducive to culture, according to Kant's *Critique of Judgment*) (Bernasconi 2011; Clewis 2015; Kleingeld 2014a). Moreover, in his early 1780s *Lectures on Physical Geography* (Doenhoff) (cited by Kleingeld 2014a, 46, 66) Kant argued that peoples from Hindustan would be "much happier" if "ruled by a European sovereign" and, in 1785, noted that unless visited by "more civilized nations," Tahitians would live in peaceful indolence forever (*RJGH*, 142, 8:65).[1]

In 1795, however, Kant published a critique of European powers' behavior in non-European regions (Kleingeld 2014a; Niesen 2007; Valdez 2012). The passages contain explicit and graphic descriptions of the violence performed by Europeans, contrasting the right to hospitality to the horrifying "*inhospitable* behavior of civilized, especially commercial states in our part of the world, the injustice they show in *visiting* foreign lands and peoples (. . . tantamount to *conquering* them)" (*TPP*, 329, 8:358). He continues by highlighting atrocities, in particular areas including "America, the negro countries, the Spice Islands, [and] the Cape," all of which were considered ownerless, "since [Europeans] counted the

---

[1] References to external rule as leading to improvement, it must be noted, stand uneasily with Kant's own account of racial difference as permanent.

inhabitants as nothing" (*TPP*, 329, 8:358). Kant then noted how these explorations spurred internal conflict, particularly in the East Indies, where foreign soldiers arrived with the excuse of "set[ting] up trading posts" but finished by oppressing the inhabitants and inciting Indian states to "widespread wars, famine, rebellions, treachery, and the whole litany of evils that oppress the human race" (*TPP*, 329, 8:358–9). After praising Japan's and China's restrictive policies, Kant noted the worst (or best, from the moral standpoint) aspect of this violence was that it was not profitable for commercial states, whose trading companies were on the verge of collapse. He offered the example of European actions in the Sugar Islands – site of the "cruelest and most calculated slavery" – which yielded no profit but served the intermediate and not very commendable purpose of training sailors to carry on wars in Europe (*TPP*, 330, 8:359).

How do we reconcile Kant's theory of racial hierarchy and his approving remarks of civilized rule before 1795 with the critique in *Perpetual Peace*? The connection between Kant's racial thinking and the status of colonialism in his system is contested in existing literature. For example, Anthony Pagden notes Kant's writings do not engage consistently with "colonies as such," and what he says is often "confused and contradictory" (2014, 19). Other scholars argue that colonialism (and hierarchy more broadly) is necessary in the trajectory of progress Kant envisioned, even if morally objectionable (McCarthy 2009, 171; Tully 2008a, 146–7). Yet, others claim Kant was simply unconcerned with colonialism, given that he considered non-whites "meaningless in the grand teleological scheme of things" (Larrimore 1999). In a recent exchange, however, Pauline Kleingeld (2007, 2014a) and Robert Bernasconi (2001, 2011) have argued that Kant's racial views led him to uphold colonialism on both paternalist and instrumentalist grounds. This view interprets *Perpetual Peace* as a change of heart, which Kleingeld attributes to unrecorded shifts toward racial egalitarianism and Bernasconi sees as leaving his racial inegalitarianism unchanged.

This debate is important to assess how – if at all – we should use Kant's thinking in theorizing cosmopolitanism. For this we would want to know what problems motivated Kant's 1795 critique of colonialism, how this critique relates to earlier statements on colonialism, and whether this critique was accompanied by a shift in his thinking on race or not. I argue that Kant inaugurated a cosmopolitan realm to complement *Perpetual Peace*'s overall argument about European republics, an international federation, and their role in the path to European peace. Kant *became* concerned about colonial conflict when he realized that, rather than necessary or meaningless, it was *detrimental* for progress toward peace. This explanation is internally coherent – vis-à-vis other arguments in the same essay – and externally coherent – vis-à-vis the political and economic context that has not been considered before, and so interpretatively firmer than existing accounts. Thus, the problem space that motivated Kant (reducing instability emerging from *intra*-European conflict *in* the colonies) bears little correspondence with the world-encompassing project cosmopolitanism must address today. It is true that Kant's condemnation of colonialism explicitly targets the injustice of these actions, which means Kant neither completely disregarded non-Europeans morally nor accepted the violent practices underlying European imperialism. As I will show, however, concern for non-Europeans and anti-colonialism are compatible with persistent hierarchical beliefs about race and civilization on Kant's part, a problematic implication if we wish to rely on Kant's thinking to theorize cosmopolitanism today.

WHAT COLONIALISM?

To understand Kant's position in 1795 we need to, on the one hand, explore the connection – if any – that exists between his earlier statements on colonialism, made in the context of his discussion about race, and his 1795 condemnation of colonialism, and, on the other hand, be cautious about interpreting his statements as being simply about the rightfulness of dyadic relations between colonizer and colonized. Instead, we must assess the critique of the violence of Europeans' actions in the non-European world contextually and on its own terms, before settling on its particular meaning and its place in Kant's overall system.

Existing literature on this topic has so far examined Kant's critique in light of conceptual histories of the notion of "colony" (Pagden 2014); as connected to evolutions of his thought on race (Kleingeld 2014a); associated with his growing appreciation of cultural diversity (Muthu 2014); or explained through Kant's discussion of international law (Niesen 2014, 173–7; Ripstein 2014, 146). Others have noted that Kant's changing notion of teleology explains both his reformed racial thought and his shift against colonialism (Storey 2015; Ypi 2014a). None of these scholars, however, scrutinizes the kind of colonial conflict Kant addressed in his critique, despite the fact that he explicitly mentioned six non-European locations in the article on cosmopolitanism. Nor does existing scholarship ask what purpose the critique of colonialism serves in an essay motivated by the Revolutionary Wars, which Prussia fought until it signed the Peace of Basel in 1795, removing itself from the confrontation for about a decade.[2] My interpretation concentrates on this background and shows that Kant's analysis of colonial conflict is tightly integrated with the discussion on republicanism and European peace occupying the rest of *Perpetual Peace* rather than constituting a self-standing critique of colonialism.

The cosmopolitan section of *Perpetual Peace* references the following geographic areas: the Cape (Cape of Good Hope, South Africa), the Spice Islands (Maluku Islands, Indonesia), the Sugar Islands (Caribbean Islands), the East Indies (South and Southeast Asia), the "negro countries" (West Africa), and America (North America). These locales were not simply sites where a European aggressor conquered and dominated natives, but places that witnessed intense strife involving two or more European powers in ways that were directly or indirectly connected to the American and French revolutions (Figure 1.1 provides a timeline of major events and Kant's writings).

If we organize the historical analysis around the American and French revolutionary wars, we can see that they resulted in important European infighting in the colonies (among European states, through trading companies, or native allies), especially in the six geographic areas explicitly mentioned in *Perpetual Peace*. During the American Revolution, France's support for the colonies and Holland's neutrality led to wars contemporary to the Revolutionary War: the Anglo–French War (1775–1783) and the Fourth Anglo–Dutch War (1780–1784). The fighting in these wars was not restricted to continental Europe or North America's surroundings: clashes between France and Britain took place in Southeast Asia, where France still had holdings (Malleson 2010). In particular, the Second Anglo–Mysore War was fought between the British East India Company and the Kingdom of Mysore, a French ally (Pradeep 2011, 29). Britain also attacked outposts of the Dutch East India Company, which lost Negapatam (Southern India), Ceylon, and other outposts of the Indian subcontinent, in addition to the Maluku Islands (Edler 1911, 245–6; Tarling 1958, 182). This led to the decline of the Dutch East India Company and its West Indian counterpart, which had been losing its West African slave trading posts to France and Britain during the eighteenth century (Furnivall 2010, 50–1; Rawley and Behrendt 2005, 78–9).

---

[2] Scholars mention the Peace of Basel as the motivating event for the essay, but do not interrogate its connection with Kant's discussion of colonial conflict (Kleingeld 2012; Wood 1998).

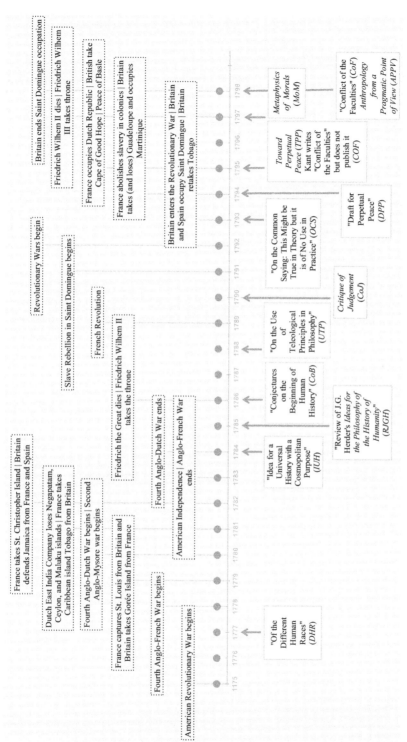

FIGURE I.I Timeline: Kant's works and historical events

Dominance in the slave trade was tightly connected to the power of the naval and merchant fleets available to European powers (Rawley and Behrendt 2005, 78–9). This did not escape Kant, who in his drafts of *Perpetual Peace* (from now on *Drafts*) linked the slave trade, naval power, and the capacity to fight more and more violent wars (222, 23:174). Because of the triangular structure of trade,[3] the slave trade was tightly connected to the trade in sugar, which was a prized commodity. Kant's contemporaries, like the Abbé Raynal, took "the labors of the colonists of the long-scorned islands [the Caribbean]" to "double perhaps triple the activity of . . . Europe" and the principal cause of the "rapid movement which stirs the universe" (Shapiro 2008, 72).[4] Trade restrictions imposed on Britain's North American colony, possibly devoted to undermining France's West Indies vis-à-vis British ones, led to North American discontent for the lack of access to trade with the thriving French possessions. In response, Britain partially legalized trade with the French West Indies, but contraband continued to thrive and disputes remained, becoming subsidiary causes of the American Revolutionary War. France's interest in protecting its West Indies possessions, in turn, was a prime reason for supporting Americans (Egnal and Ernst 1972; Rawley and Behrendt 2005, 104–5), with significant fighting between Britain and France taking place in the Caribbean (see Figure 1.1). In addition to these clashes, several slave trading posts in West Africa changed hands between France and Britain during the Anglo–French War (France took Saint Louis, in present-day Senegal, and Fort James, in Gambia; while Britain took Goré, in Senegal) (Rawley and Behrendt 2005, 105).

This reconstruction suggests that Kant's goal in naming those sites in *Perpetual Peace* was to highlight the harms brought about by Britain's naval dominance, its refusal to let go of its North American colonies, and the vast spatial reach of its warfare. European struggles were amplified into non-European space by enlisting trading companies and non-European man power for war. This imperiled European peace and the

---

[3] During the eighteenth century, the slave trade relied on the use of merchant ships for transporting – subsequently – European manufactures, slaves, and sugar. Intra-European rivalries were commonly about trade, control of strategic areas in West Africa and the West Indies, the regulation of access to slave markets (e.g., the "asiento," the Spanish's crown authorization to transport slaves to Spanish America, was particularly coveted), and sugar production (Rawley and Behrendt 2005, 101).

[4] In 1795, France and Britain were the greatest sugar producers and exporters in the world (Mintz 1985, 35).

development of the American Republic. Importantly, many of the rivalries around commercial interests and trading spots in the colonial locales were still playing out during the French Revolutionary Wars (i.e., the immediate context of Kant's writing), which I examine next. This analysis confirms that Kant's concern with intra-European conflict, British expansionism, and the fate of republics was a prominent impulse for the strongly worded critique of colonialism that appeared in the third article.

The War of the First Coalition (1792–1802) was the first part of the Revolutionary Wars in which allied Europeans fought Republican France. The Peace of Basel – which famously motivated Kant to write *Perpetual Peace* – brought a temporary pause to this war and was signed by Prussia and Spain in 1795, the same year in which France and Holland signed the Treaty of The Hague after Holland's defeat (Blanning 1996, 135; Dubois and Garrigus 2006, 30). Soon after the outbreak of the war, Spain and Britain invaded French Saint-Domingue, where conflict had been ongoing since the 1791 slave rebellion. This rebellion disrupted the sugar trade, benefiting Britain and Spain – also sugar producers – and gave way to feuds between France and the United States (Dubois and Garrigus 2006, 30). Britain and Spain – while committed to slavery in their possessions – supported rebellious slaves in Saint-Domingue (Geggus 1982). The 1795 peace treaty transferred the Spanish territory back to France, while the British capitulated in 1798. Additionally, Britain retook Tobago in 1793 – after twelve years of French rule – and invaded Martinique in 1794 (Laurence 1995, 7; Morgan 2007, 48). In February 1794, the island of Guadeloupe was invaded by the British (in coalition with anti-abolition French planters), only to be retaken by France in December (Morgan 2007, 48).

Conflict in West Africa had abated by this period. France never became self-sufficient in transporting slaves to its Caribbean colonies and Britain became dominant in the Atlantic slave trade, transporting over 50% of slaves between 1791 and abolition (Rawley and Behrendt 2005). Finally, Kant's reference to the Cape is aligned with the other examples. Given its strategic location on the route to India, Adam Smith deemed its "discovery" one of the greatest events of the era (Bell 2016, 3n) and it was at the center of Anglo–French maritime rivalry in the late eighteenth century (Turner 1966). In 1795, in particular, the Cape was a front in the Revolutionary Wars, when Britain took it over from the Dutch in retaliation for France's occupation of the Dutch Republic (Palmer 1954, 22). Interestingly, the example of the Cape appears only in the published version of *Perpetual Peace*, unlike the others, featured already in *Drafts*, which Kant started writing in 1794. This is perhaps because Kant decided to add this case only after hearing of the events of January 1795.

In sum, the non-European sites Kant mentions in his essays are quite diverse: West Africa, site of European slave trading posts without territorial control; the Caribbean, prime destination of slaves demanded by European planters who produced one of Europe's most prized commodities; America, likely its northern part, characterized by settler practices and the exploitation of natives; the Cape, strategic port on the way to India; India, site of struggle between trading companies, which controlled territory in alliance with local rulers; and the Spice Islands, site of competition among Europeans over access to spices. This variegated set of examples does not seem to amount to a coherent point about colonialism, unless the point is about European states competing viciously among themselves for colonial sites in ways connected to trade and intra-European wars.

This suggests Kant's claims on colonialism are an integral part of the project of European peace contained in *Perpetual Peace*, rather than a self-standing critique of colonialism. This was a response to Kant's frustration with expansionism, particularly on the part of Britain, which appears as the aggressor in a significant number of the examples he offers and was the dominant world power at the time. In other words, Kant was grappling with the character of colonial conflict in terms of its effects on republicanism and peace – which occupy the rest of the essay – rather than with the dyadic encounter between colonizer and colonized as a question of injustice. There is little continuity between this focus and the arguments in previous examinations of colonialism – concerned with non-Europeans as subjects who would benefit from external (civilized) rule, given their defective capacity for self-government or passivity.

Kant's claims in the cosmopolitan section of *Perpetual Peace* are also different from later discussions outlawing the establishment of colonies and bondage after war between states, located in the section on international Right of *The Metaphysics of Morals*, applicable to interactions among European states. Despite interpretations of Kant's anti-colonialism as resulting from international Right and – in particular – the regulation of war (Niesen 2014; Pagden 2014; Ripstein 2014), Kant consistently does not include any treatment of conflict with non-Europeans in the sections on international Right (in *Perpetual Peace* and *The Metaphysics of Morals*). This exclusion was not simply about the political status of these peoples, given that Kant explicitly considered some non-Western peoples to be states.[5]

War, Britain, and the Context of Writing

The previous section suggests Kant's problem space was the spatial extension of intra-European conflict beyond Europe and into the colonies, and the nonconventional character of this conflict. The dominant colonial power in Kant's time was Britain, and both of the wars examined had Britain at their center. If this was the case, why didn't Kant address the question of Britain's expansionism and belligerence more directly? In this section, I put forward complementary evidence suggesting that Kant may not have been able to criticize Britain directly. While scholars have noted that Kant's writings on religion were repeatedly censored during the reign of King Friedrich Wilhelm II (Wood 1996, xxvii), less has been said about how the war also made Kant hesitate to speak out openly about warfare and international politics, but this was clearly the case. For example, in 1793, he declined to republish his essay *Idea* with an addendum about "current affairs" because "the powerful of this world are in a drunken fit . . . one must strongly advise a pygmy who values his skin to stay out of their fight" (*LCS*, 456, 11:417).

Kant's hesitation in writing about the war was likely due to the participation of Prussia in the War of the First Coalition against France. Writing on republicanism or criticizing European powers' behavior would have been likely to upset the Prussian monarchy, as he confirmed in another missive: "the hand of the censor lies heavily" not only on religion but also on "public law [*Staatsrecht*] and international law [*Völkerrecht*])" (*LFTG*, 489, 11:531). In 1794, Kant wrote the first part of *Conflict of the Faculties* (from now on *Conflict*) for the *Göttingische Bibliothek der neuesten theologischen Literatur* but ultimately declined to publish. The journal, based at the University of Göttingen, in Hanover, a personal union with Great Britain, would shelter Kant from Prussian censorship ("the orthodox George III" would be sufficiently esteemed by the "equally orthodox" Friedrich Wilhelm II so that he would be shielded

---

[5] He refers to Indian "states" [*Staaten*] and to China as a "great empire" [*großes Reich*] in *Perpetual Peace* (329–30, 8:359–60). He arguably would have thought of Japan equivalently, given the long-standing political order in that region, which was "fully capable of resisting [Europeans'] demands" (Clulow 2014, 37–8), a feature Kant praises in his essay.

from the "hyper orthodox . . . in our locality" (*LCFS*, 491, 11:533)). This suggests, on the one hand, there was a special relationship between Prussia and Britain so that the sponsorship of a Hanoverian university would assuage the censors. On the other hand, it also suggests his critiques of Britain were likely to be particularly scrutinized.

Kant's critique of Britain would have hit close to home because of the deep political and familial connections between the Houses of Hanover and Hohenzollern, which ruled Britain and Prussia. Duke Karl Wilhelm Ferdinand of Brunswick-Wolfenbüttel (from the electorate of Hanover) was married to George III's sister, Princess Augusta, and commanded the allied troops of Austria and Prussia in the War of the First Coalition (Brown 2003; Krimmer 2008). He also lent his name to the 1792 manifesto,[6] which threatened the "complete ruin" of Paris if the French monarchs suffered any violence at the hands of their people (Fremont-Barnes 2001, 25). The future King Louis Philippe claimed this missive "inspired more enthusiasm in France for the defense of the fatherland than the patriotic appeals of the National Assembly and the revolutionary societies put together" (cited by Blanning 1996, 72).

This was the charged climate that surrounded Kant, which may explain why *Perpetual Peace* was published during the armistice keeping Prussia out of the war until 1806 and allowing intellectuals to consider the question of war (Krimmer 2008, 47). Yet, Britain remained at war and was belligerent in French-controlled areas such as the Cape of Good Hope and Saint-Domingue in 1795. Interpretively, this context suggests Kant may have been reluctant to explicitly criticize Britain, despite the fact that the status of Britain as the major slave trader, naval power, and France's archrival would have warranted it. Despite Kant's self-censorship, incorporating the historical context suggests he was concerned about Britain's expansionism, something that is confirmed by other works written around the same time but that went unpublished. For example, Kant did not publish *Conflict* until 1798 – after the death of Friedrich Wilhelm II and the end of the War of the First Coalition. This is unsurprising, given that the second part of this essay claims the British monarchy is "unlimited" because "everyone knows perfectly well that the monarch's influence . . . is . . . so certain that nothing is resolved by the Houses except what he wills and purposes through his minister" (305–6, 7:90). Even if it was not published, we know Kant was working on this

---

[6] Which was in fact authored by French émigrés (Blanning 1996, 101).

part in 1795 (Wood 1996, 276), which suggests these questions were in Kant's mind when he wrote *Perpetual Peace*.

While the critique is explicit in *Conflict*, it is possible Kant's comment about the Sugar Islands as a "stronghold of the cruelest and most calculated slavery" (*TPP*, 330, 8:359) was also directed against Britain, given that, by 1795, France had abolished slavery in the colonies.[7] Britain was also the only belligerent party left in the area, after Spain returned its portion of Saint-Domingue (Whitaker 1936). More specific language also appears in Kant's critique of Europe in *Drafts*, where he singles out for critique the "coastal people of the seas" [*Küstenvölker*] among the civilized states (221, 23:173).

Britain's expansionism threatened balanced European war, which Kant valued not because it led to a traditional balance of power, which he considered a "mere fantasy," but because of the "lively competition" or "productive resistance", which – along with political practices and institutions – could lead to an enduring and law-like peaceful balance (Muthu 2014; *OCS*; *TPP*).[8] This finding led Kant to a more fine-grained consideration of the role of antagonism in his philosophy of history. Such a reconsideration, however, depended on a shift in Kant's teleology that allowed for the examination and critique of man's free action in interaction with the laws governing nature, with the goal of making possible the realization of the highest end.

ANTAGONISM AND EQUILIBRIUM

Close attention to Kant's concern with colonial conflict is important for our purposes because it provides clues regarding the kind of intervention Kant was making in the third definitive article. In particular, antagonism and war play a central role in Kant's philosophy of history, i.e., the reflective assessment of the possibility of progress given the actual human inclinations and material background in which these operate. This is different from claims about morality, i.e., the determinative assessment of particular actions and political arrangements according to justice. The

---

[7] Following the request in February 1794 by three deputies from Saint-Domingue (one black, one mulatto, and one white) and against the strong opposition of the French colonists of the island (Gauthier 2014, 273–80).

[8] The distinction between the notion of equilibrium, or the "right to equilibrium" [*Recht des Gleichgewichts*] and "balance of power" [*Balance der Mächte*] in Kant is sometimes lost in English editions that wrongly translate the former as balance of power (*MoM*, 484, 6:346; *OCS*, 309, 8:312).

distinction is important for assessing the correspondence between Kant's goals in theorizing cosmopolitanism, and the uses to which we want to put cosmopolitanism today. If, as I argue, the bulk of the critique of colonialism is devoted to making the case that intra-European conflict is detrimental to the path of progress toward peace Kant had devised for Europe, the framework may be ill-fitted to support a normative project condemning colonialism and postcolonial legacies. This is the case even if we acknowledge that Kant did condemn colonialism morally, to the extent such condemnation is not the primary goal of Kant's system of Right and a consideration of the experience and political agency of those at the receiving end of colonialism is lacking, features that raise the problems of correspondence and hierarchy, respectively.

In order to categorize Kant's critique of colonialism as either reflective or determinative, it is necessary first to consider the apparent contradiction between the stark critique of conflict that appears in *Perpetual Peace* and the role antagonism and war had in Kant's philosophy of history. This contradiction dissolves once we realize that Kant's conception of antagonism shifted between *Idea* and *Perpetual Peace* to accommodate colonial conflict. Kant's new understanding of teleology, presented in the *Critique of Judgment*, enabled this reformulation. Early on, in *Idea*, Kant defines antagonism as resulting from men's asocial sociability [*ungesellige Geselligkeit*], or "[the tendency] to come together in society, coupled" with continual resistance that "constantly threatens to break this society up" (44, 8:21). Kant values asocial resistance reflectively because it transforms men's "primitive natural capacity for moral discrimination into definite practical principles" and compels them to come together under a civil constitution. The same logic applies to states in the state of nature, whose "natural capacities" cannot be developed until they overcome a stage in which commonwealths' resources are mainly devoted to armaments and the imperative of war readiness. The evil of war, however, "still ha[s] a beneficial effect" (*IUH*, 49, 8:25–6). Wars, military preparations, and the distress that follows them are "means by which nature drives nations" to prepare to take a step reason would have dictated without so many "sad experiences," to abandon a "lawless state of savagery and enter . . . a federation of peoples" where every state can derive its security and rights from a "united power and the law-governed decisions of a united will" (*IUH*, 47, 8:24). Thus, the path toward a federation need not be dictated by reason because nature employs the antagonism of men and of states as *means* to "calm and security" (*IUH*, 47, 8:24). The teleology of nature in *Idea* operates irrespective of men's intentions: the "intention of nature" fuels wars and destroys some states, dismembers others, and results in revolutions that will eventually result in a peaceful state of affairs (*IUH*, 48, 8:24–5). Certain civil arrangements, moreover, facilitate efforts on the part of commonwealths to educate their citizens and to allow them to mature morally. This process is neither intentional nor random, but guided by the "wisdom of nature" and need not lead to a "lapse into inactivity" but to a government of the actions and counteractions through a principle of equality (*IUH*, 49–51, 8:25–6).

In *Idea*'s account of antagonism, Europe is the site of progress, and wars and commerce occur among European states.[9] The strong language indicates Kant acknowledges the violent propensities of individuals and states, but trusts these dimensions to awaken the natural capabilities of men and – through the mere exhaustion and learning from the destructiveness of these events – encourage the establishment of a common constitution. These natural capacities, or germs [*Keime*] to be developed, are, according to his racial theory, differently distributed among different races, with only the European race being able to fully develop morally.[10] In sum, Kant's idea of cosmopolitan progress in *Idea* is Eurocentric, hierarchical, and potentially imperial, even if not particularly concerned with the specificities of the empires taking shape as he was writing.

A decade later, *Perpetual Peace* opens by warning readers about destructive war resulting in the "peace of graveyards" (317, 8:343). Kant offers a more critical view of war and trade and enacts specific regulations limiting and regulating violence, rather than expecting it to lead indirectly to peace, as in *Idea*. Relations between Europe and the rest of the world,

---

[9] Only in one passage does Kant mention other regions, when he argues that knowledge about them confirms the improvement of Europe's political constitutions, which "will probably legislate eventually for all other continents" (*IUH*, 52, 8:29). Kant is thus thinking about non-European regions as eventually somehow subsumed under the European imperial states that will join in a federation and form a cosmopolitan whole. This is consistent with Kant's assessment of non-white races as lacking (in different degrees) politically relevant capacities of self-government, magistrature, freedom, and virtue (Kleingeld 2014a, 46).

[10] While scholars have argued Kant's "impure" ethics play a role in his definition of moral nature and results in differential affinity between particular cultures and moral ends (Louden 1999; Marwah 2012), disagreement remains about the moral implications of Kant's developmental thinking for his moral thought (Bernasconi 2003; Hill and Boxill 2001; Kleingeld 2007; Larrimore 2008; Mills 2005, 2014). It should be noted, however, when Kant refers to "humanity" when discussing progress, this does not imply "whites and non-whites will equally contribute to and share in this process," as Kleingeld notes (2007, 582n). The whole may be progressing even if "some of them lag behind" as Kant noted in his *Reflections on Anthropology* (*RA*, 15:650, cited in Kleingeld 2007, 582n).

and between state and non-state actors (which had not concerned him in 1784), are now regulated by a separate cosmopolitan sphere. Despite these qualifications, the idea of war as beneficial does not disappear. Certain forms of conflict are still conducive to a civil constitution, but certain techniques of war, certain dyads, and wars in particular spaces are unconditionally condemned. The criteria by which antagonism is evaluated is connected to the question of equilibrium, a notion already present in *Idea*. According to this essay, antagonism leads to moral progress because it "compel[s] our species to discover a law of equilibrium to regulate the essentially healthy hostility which prevails among the states and is produced by their freedom." The cosmopolitan whole envisioned in *Idea* "reinforce[s] this law by introducing a system of united power [and] . . . political security" that – through *equality* – governs the actions and counteractions so states do not "destroy one another" (49, 8:26).

Equilibrium remains important in 1793, when Kant suggests that "it is not in the nature of the human being to relinquish his power by choice," but reason relies on the evil arising from the opposition of inclinations to one another to play freely and "subjugate them all and, in place of evil" establish the self-sustainable rule of good (*OCS*, 308–9, 8:312). This focus continues in *Perpetual Peace* in the appendix and in the first supplement "Guarantee for Perpetual Peace." In the latter, while discussing international Right, Kant contrasts healthy equilibrium and despotism. He argues that while "the *separation* of neighboring states independent of one another" is a condition of war (which could only be avoided by a federative union), this is better, in accordance with reason, than if these states were fused "by one [despotic] power overgrowing the rest." Here nature reappears, and "*wills* it otherwise:" while differences of language and of religion bring pretexts for war, "increasing culture and the gradual approach of human beings to greater agreements in principles" leads to understanding in a state of peace that "is produced and secured . . . by means of their *equilibrium* in liveliest competition" (*TPP*, 336, 8:367, my emphasis; see also *DPP*, 225, 23:187).[11]

---

[11] We see the indirect value of war in other portions of the "Guarantee," where Kant notes, "by war [nature] has compelled peoples" to both spread out in the world and "enter into more or less lawful relations" (*TPP*, 332–3, 8:363). War, he continues, "needs no special motive but seems to be engrafted onto human nature and even to hold as something noble" (334, 8:365). War, or the threat of it, also forces peoples "to submit to the constraint of public laws" given that "each people would find itself in the neighborhood of another people pressing upon it, against which it must form itself internally into a state in order to be armed as a power against it" (*TPP*, 335, 8:366).

The indirectly beneficial effects of antagonism in equilibrium appear already in the "Critique of Teleological Judgment" (*CoJ*, 233–95, 5:359–485), according to which the standpoint of scientific inquiry and moral conduct both rely on a conception of nature "as a realm governed by laws that make possible the realization of the ultimate object of morality" (Guyer 2005, 317), without conflating the two types of arguments (i.e., a step taken "toward morality" is not necessarily a "moral step" (*TPP*, 343, 8:376)).[12] It is notable, however, that, unlike the other definitive articles of *Perpetual Peace*, the cosmopolitan section addresses simultaneously questions of Right and realizability – to which Kant devotes most of the space, likely because this is the first time he considers seriously how colonial antagonism fits within his philosophy of history. Hence, he deals with both moral judgments (what is moral conduct, what is the highest end) and reflective judgments (how are these ends achieved given the natural constraints we face). Kant makes reference to the unprofitability of colonial violence, a fact that is welcome from "the standpoint of the moral judge [*moralischer Richter*]" (*TPP*, 330, 8:359). The purpose of colonial violence, Kant claims, is "mediate and not particularly laudable," in contrast to purposeful actions that lead to moral progress. In other words, Kant notes that, first, colonial violence is morally objectionable (a determinative argument); second, we can expect it won't persist, given the profit-seeking nature of human beings (a reflective argument); and, third, persistent conflict of this kind works against progress toward morality (a reflective argument).

This style of argument is consistent with Kant's "pragmatic anthropology," namely "the investigation of what [the human being] as a free-acting being makes of himself, or can and should make of himself" (*APPV*, 3, 7:119). In this scheme, nature contributes to morality by providing the conditions for the development of the cultures of skill and discipline, with the latter being particularly central to tame the "crudeness . . . of our animal inclinations and prepare man for a sovereignty of reason." Judgment's role, in turn, is to identify and criticize actions that are not harmonious with the maximum development of

---

[12] Kant's shifting teleology is also the focus of Lea Ypi's and Ian Storey's effort to understand his anti-colonialism. Ypi argues that in the 1790s Kant rejected trade and accepted only rightful war as mechanisms that would result in progress (2014a, 115–16, 22–4), but I suggest a more fine-grained reconceptualization of antagonism is at stake. Storey, in turn, notes that Kant's teleological shift makes judgments about race only subjectively valid (2015, 682, 6), but sees Kant's anti-imperialist arguments as evidence of a shift toward racial equality without, however, considering the explanation offered here.

human beings' natural predispositions and to devise institutions that can regulate our freedom (*CoJ*, 319–21, 5:431–3; Ypi 2014a, 114). Hence, teleology works as a heuristic device that guides conduct in two senses. First, it guides inquiry to discover laws of nature, and, second, it guides our moral conduct so that morality and human freedom can be realized within nature (Guyer 2005, 326–7, 9–31). Finally, our inquiry into the laws of nature can also work to assign responsibility for hardships and to adjust our conduct appropriately to remedy them (*CoB*, 231, 8:120–1).

A TYPOLOGY OF ANTAGONISM

The previous section establishes that equilibrium is a core condition for antagonism to work indirectly toward progress. Moreover, it shows how determinative and reflective arguments interact in the third definitive article. This discussion already hints at the fact that, from a moral standpoint, Kant condemned both European war and colonial conflict. In contrast, according to reflective criteria, and unlike intra-European conflict taking place in Europe, he found colonial conflict did not indirectly serve moral advancement. This means Kant needed to update his claims about antagonism in *Perpetual Peace*, which he did – as I explain – by differentiating between (a) intra-European conflict in Europe; (b) intra-European conflict in or about the colonies; and (c) conflict between European and colonial peoples.[13] In the process, I continue to distinguish between arguments that concern morality (determinative) and those that concern the discovery of laws of nature and their relation to moral progress (reflective), and discuss the consequences of these findings for the problems of hierarchy and correspondence.

War and Europe

Kant held Europe responsible for the unending conflict in the colonies, and differentiated this conflict from conventional intra-European war. This is already discernible in the *Critique of Judgment*'s contrasting

---

[13] Sankar Muthu proposes a binary distinction between resistance that seeks to achieve "equal worth" and "domineering unsocial sociability," where only the former involves productive resistance that benefits societies and cultivates capacities (Muthu 2014, 93–4), while the latter despotically asserts superiority. There are affinities between my distinction and Muthu's, but I argue the first kind of resistance depends on a preexisting equilibrium of forces and the distinction only emerges in *Perpetual Peace*, where Kant considered colonial conflict for the first time.

accounts of violent conflict. Here, Kant blames "man's own absurd *natural predispositions*" for getting himself in trouble and "[making him] put down others of his own species in great misery through oppressive domination [and] *barbaric wars*" that work "for the destruction of his own species" (*CoJ*, 318, 5:430, my emphasis). Only a couple of pages later, however, Kant describes war as "an unintentional human endeavor (incited by our unbridled passions)" but also "a deeply hidden and perhaps intentional endeavor of the supreme wisdom, if not to establish, then at least to prepare the way for lawfulness along with the freedom of states, and thereby for a unified system ... with a moral basis" (320, 5:433).

What distinguishes these excerpts is that "barbaric wars," referenced in the first passage, may end in destruction, while the conflict mentioned in the second passage remains the way of nature to develop man's aptitudes, keeping him away from "absurd predispositions" associated with passion and moving toward the regulation of states' unlawful freedom (*CoJ*, 320, 5:432). While destructive wars bring "oppressive domination" and barbarism, other wars are a hidden endeavor of supreme wisdom. No states are mentioned in the first excerpt, suggesting Kant may be thinking of colonial conflict, while the second extract specifies states, suggesting war among European states is preparatory for a lawful constitution.[14] Lest we expect "barbaric wars" to be indirectly conducive to peace, Kant notes after the first passage that nature's beneficence is insufficient to counter these predispositions. Instead, man must overcome them through skill and discipline because he is "the only being on earth that has understanding and hence an ability to set himself purposes of his own choice." While man's vocation is to be "the ultimate purpose of nature," he still "must have the understanding and the will to give both nature and himself reference to a purpose ... independent of nature, self-sufficient, and a final purpose" outside nature (*CoJ*, 318, 5:431).

Thus, understanding and man's ability to set himself purposes are now central to Kant's notion of progress, in the sense that certain forms of antagonism observed in nature need to be criticized publicly and ultimately avoided outright for progress to ensue. These are the wars that result from man's "absurd *natural* predispositions," not those constituting

---

[14] These examples are offered in the context of a discussion of human happiness in relation to nature's ultimate end and morality's final end (*CoJ*, 317–20, 5:429–33; Guyer 2005, 316–35). This discussion is part of the conceptualization of Kant's novel understanding of teleology and the place for different forms of antagonism within it.

"antagonism in accordance with principles of outer freedom," which can be conducive to lawfulness (*MoM*, 485, 6:347). Rather than an overall shift in his evaluation of antagonism in historical progress, Kant's departure from *Idea* is a refined understanding of antagonism that distinguishes between different forms of conflict in terms of their indirect teleological role.

Kant's view of war is also concerned with its effects over character. This appears in the first part of *Critique of Judgment*, when Kant asserts there is something sublime in war when "it is carried on in an orderly way" and it respects "the sanctity of the citizens' rights." He claims that the "way of thinking of a people that carries [war] on" is as sublime as the dangers they face and the courage they show, vis-à -vis the "selfishness, cowardice, and softness" of the commercial spirit of peacetime (122, 5:263). If the honor and courage Kant associated with certain wars was particularly attuned to awakening the skills and discipline required for men to devise and follow through self-imposed purposes, the excessive violence associated with colonial wars may be too unbridled and prone to produce the wrong kind of affect.

If we connect these reflections to the historical and textual evidence from previous sections, it is evident the two dimensions of colonialism highlighted in Kant's assessment (the quest for expansionism and its brutality) have no affinity with progress toward peace. This is because progress requires a virtuous process of friction among equals that will develop men's predispositions. Similarly, while some forms of conflict activate men's courage and drive for honor and advance culture, others awaken their basest passions for evil, making men unfit for citizenship and states unfit to qualify as "a person in the relation of states" (*MoM*, 485, 6:347). *Drafts* confirms this: colonial wars upset the progression toward peace fueled by civilized war among Europeans by – among other things – accelerating wars rather than leading to the gradual abandonment of aggression, and by facilitating the expansionism of states that "recognize no limitation to their presumptions except whatever their own powerlessness prevents them from doing," treating "the person of the foreigner" as nature-given booty (*DPP*, 221-2, 23:173). Kant's concern with expansionism is such that "the menacing increase in another state's power" is one of the few grounds he takes to be legitimate, in the state of nature, to initiate war (*MoM*, 484, 6:346).[15] Of equal concern to Kant is

---

[15] In *The Metaphysics of Morals*, he terms this "a right to equilibrium" [*Recht des Gleichgewichts*] (*MoM*, 484, 6:346, amended translation).

the multiplicative character of conflict in the colonies. Yet, both of these concerns emerge because of their effects fueling more war in Europe, a relatively narrow problem with little correspondence to the cosmopolitanism we want to theorize today. In later sections, I provide more evidence of the European focus of his critique and also provide insight into two connected conceptual issues: his reconsideration of trade as potentially destructive and the connection between his anti-colonialism and his hierarchical understanding of the world.

Multiplication and Trade

The multiplicative character of colonial conflict and its effects on Europe is a recurring theme in *Drafts*, where Kant notes that Europe's position "in *reciprocal trade*" means gains or losses from around the world "are . . . felt very sensitively in Europe, which receives new and *never diminishing material to expand and perpetuate this continent through war* rather than peace" (*DPP*, 23:174, my emphasis). Thus, Kant came to see trade as a negative force in the quest for European progress. Compare this with his assessment of trade as "another mechanism that unwittingly contributes to the plan of nature" in *Idea*, where Kant still believed trade interests would force states "by their own insecurity" to arbitrate and prepare the way for an institution that will arbitrate in the future (*IUH*, 51, 8:28). The reversal may have to do with Kant's consideration of the actual shape of colonial "trade." In *Perpetual Peace*, he asserts that European trading posts were excuses for the subjugation of natives. Most "trade," at least in Asia in the eighteenth century, was conducted by state-chartered corporations, which recruited armies and had quasi-sovereignty over territory. In the case of the British East India Company – which was dominant in Asia by 1778 vis-à-vis the Dutch and French companies – trading interests took its army well beyond the confines of East India and into commercially strategic regions, often alongside the British army (Bowen 2005, 45–7). The slave trade was also conducted by trading companies (in the case of Britain, the Royal African and the South Sea companies), which operated in West Africa, typically without territorial control (Morgan 2007, 53–60). The close connection between war and trade in trading companies underlies another mechanism of conflict multiplication: the accumulation of sea power and sailors/soldiers that results from the growing trade operations of these companies. As Kant notes, trading companies in the Caribbean train "sailors for warships and so, in turn, carrying on wars in Europe" (*DPP*, 23:175; *TPP*, 330, 8:359).

Another example of this phenomenon appears in the second definitive article on international Right, where he argues, "the difference between the European and the American savages" is that the latter eat their enemies, while the former "know how to make better use of [the] defeated . . . and would rather increase the number of their subjects," and use them as instruments for more extensive wars (*TPP*, 326, 8:355). This excerpt is significant because it is the only mention of non-European peoples in the section on international Right, confirming Kant was concerned about how the problem emanating from engagements in colonial areas affect an otherwise virtuous intra-European antagonism.

Multiplication and Hierarchy

Not only does *Drafts* problematize the multiplicative effect of overseas conflict because of its effects in Europe, it also does so in a way that seems compatible with a hierarchical assessment of the world. For example, Kant notes, "overstepping the borders of hospitality" brings ills to the human species but also to Europe, which originally brought this commerce to all people of the earth, "under the tutelage of [its] most active part." He also notes, Europe "finally brought *upon itself* ", the wars it waged upon others, which, "with the awakening of commerce" may become "*more and more frequent and to follow faster upon one another*" (23:173–4, my emphasis). This passage's reference to "the tutelage of the most active part of the earth" echoes another in *Conflict*, which Kant also wrote in 1795. There he argues – in the context of calling human beings "a trifle" vis-à-vis omnipotent nature – the "*sovereigns of* [human beings'] own species" treat man as such a trifle by "burdening him as an animal, regarding him as a mere tool . . . or exposing him" in their internal conflicts to have him massacred. This is no trifle, he concludes, but a subversion of the *final end* of creation itself (305, 7:89, my emphasis).[16]

Colonial violence is evaluated as purposeless in the scheme of moral progress, it is a "self-inflicted evil" that must be overcome (*CoJ*, 318–20, 5:431–2; *OCS*, 301, 7:84);[17] it provides endless grounds to perpetuate

---

[16] This excerpt does not explicitly mention colonial conflict, but its wording echoes the discussion of the effects of intra-European conflict in the colonies over natives in *Perpetual Peace* and the *Drafts* (*DPP*, 23:174; *TPP*, 329, 8:359).

[17] This condemnation, however, seems compatible with the hierarchy evident in the assertion that European states are "the sovereigns" or "the most active part" of the species, a question I go on to discuss at greater length.

war – rather than peace – in Europe, magnifying the repercussions of faraway conflict in Europe. Again, *Drafts* provides illustration, noting: "a spark of violation of human rights suffered in another continent," given the flammability of the thirst for power in human nature, and particularly its leaders, "lights the flame of war that *reaches the region where it [originated]*" (*DPP*, 223, 23:175, my emphasis).

These excerpts are concerned with the backlash of colonial conflict on Europe, and are continuous with four other statements in *Drafts*, which claim Europe has not only waged war upon others, but has "finally brought it upon itself" (222, 23:173–4); "trade in negroes," an offense against black peoples' hospitality, will be "even worse for Europe in its consequences;" the internal wars Europeans provoked have finally reached their own territory (222, 23:174); and Europe's position in reciprocal trade means it receives new and never diminishing material that expands and perpetuates war in Europe (223, 23:174). This concern makes sense of Kant's understanding of the cosmopolitan realm as a "supplement" [*Ergänzung*] of the other two realms. The acceleration and never-ending material for conflict that results from colonial conquest means rightful regulations at the domestic and international (European) level are insufficient to appease the "thirst for power" and regulate the unconventional actors who appear in this period, needing to be complemented by cosmopolitan regulations. This means Kant's scathing critique of colonialism in 1795 is necessary for the coherence of his project of perpetual peace in Europe and this – interpretively – explains the treatment of colonial conflict in *Perpetual Peace*.

This supplementation is particularly necessary when we read Kant's colonial critique alongside his support for a republican constitution (theoretically, in *Perpetual Peace*, and politically, in his support for the French Revolution). Through the examples, Kant highlights wars that pit Britain against the nascent republics in the United States and France,[18] noting how the establishment of rightful civil constitutions were impaired by colonial conflict, and criticizing actions that hinder a society from "providing itself with a civil constitution, which appears good to the people themselves," in a statement condemning the Revolutionary Wars directly (*CoF*, 302, 7:86). Kant also considered war detrimental to the pursuit of civic education and other valuable domestic projects characteristic of a republican constitution – by nature the least bellicose – dampening the

---

[18] On Kant's sympathy for these revolutions, see Beck (1971) and Ypi (2014b).

development of the culture and institutions that would otherwise work toward peace, making conflict indirectly multiplicative (*CoF*, 304, 7:88; *TPP*, 323, 335, 8:350, 365).

Sense and Sensibility

So far, I have argued that Kant differentiated between intra-European conflict – which was indirectly virtuous[19] – and intra-European conflict taking place in the colonies – which led to expansionism and multiplied conflict in Europe. Yet Kant worried about the effects of colonialism in Europe also because of the particularly debased practices of European armies in their interactions with natives; he feared their effects on the European character and, as a consequence, progress toward enlightenment.

Evidence of Kant's concern with the conduct of war appears in the preliminary articles, which proscribe "dishonorable stratagems," including the use of assassins or poisoners, which corrupt the morals of those who perform them, making them unfit for citizenship (*TPP*, 320, 8:347). I believe this same principle is behind Kant's concern with the barbaric practices prevalent in colonial conflict, as expressed in the passage on the Sugar Islands, which focuses on "the cruelest [*allergrausamste*] and most calculated slavery" (*TPP*, 330, 8:359). Elsewhere in *Perpetual Peace*, Kant comments on other manifestations of evil in the East Indies where soldiers arrived with the excuse of setting up trading posts but instead "oppress[ed] the inhabitants, incite[d] . . . Indian states to widespread wars, famine, rebellions, treachery, and the whole litany of evils [*Übel*] that oppress the human race" (329, 8:358–9, amended translation).

Unlike Kant's discussions of asocial sociability, these excerpts are not coupled with reflections on how conflict between evil – regardless of the will of actors – will result in the eventual establishment of a common law and/or peace. Neither does Kant pursue his idea that "the history of freedom begins with evil" (*CoB*, 227, 8:115; *OCS*, 308–9, 8:312). Instead, I argue that Kant's concern about the excessive cruelty at play in colonial conflict emerges partly from his assessment of cruel acts as

---

[19] Note that this does not mean Kant believed remaining in the state of nature is acceptable for European states. Instead, it means intra-European conflict, if allowed to continue in the state of nature, and as long as the contending powers are relatively equal, is bound to subside eventually and lead the warring parties toward gradual agreement to enter a civil condition (i.e., a federation). This logic degenerates when European states also compete for colonies in a way that multiplies conflict.

deviations from the economy of feeling he expects to result in the cultivation of humanity and progress toward culture. This process requires making "headway against the crudeness and vehemence of . . . inclinations that belong to us primarily as animals," which may not make man "morally [*sittlich*] better for [life] in society, but still civilized [*gesittet*] for it" and prepared "for a sovereignty in which reason alone" dominates (*CoJ*, 321, 5:433).

Antagonism, Judgment, and Teleology

In sum, Kant's writings on colonial conflict set out to clarify the role of antagonism in his philosophy of history, which had not been concerned with colonialism before. The virtuosity of conflict depends on certain equality among the contending forces, which holds within Europe but is threatened by the unbridled expansionism facilitated by the space of the colonies. Among the three forms of antagonism Kant conceptualizes (intra-European conflict in Europe, intra-European conflict in the colonies, and conflict between Europeans and native peoples in the colonies), only the first kind of conflict is consistently considered indirectly conducive to progress.

Moreover, it is possible Kant saw violent conflict in the colonies and the cruelty involved in conquest as eroding trust in the plausibility of progress toward peace and morality and undermining men's beliefs in and actions toward such a project, because the "mixture of good and evil in [man's] predisposition" makes it difficult for humankind to assess the possibility of moral progress for the whole species (*CoF*, 300–1, 7:84). Accordingly, Kant's intervention offers the right standpoint to assess this question and answer it affirmatively: that "the human race has always been in progress toward the better and will continue to be" (*CoF*, 304, 7:89), and what could be "an accelerated fall into baseness" is surmountable because of the capacity of human beings to use reason and act freely.

Thus, Kant's concern with the evil of colonial violence is rooted in his interest in reflectively establishing a path to peace in Europe, despite the abundant evidence of barbaric violence in European colonial wars. This account is necessary to motivate actors to act morally, a question that looms large in Kant's public philosophy. For example, he argues that actors' motivation is strengthened particularly by the "feeling of self-inflicted evil, when things disintegrate altogether," which leads them to make things "even better than they were before that state" (*CoF*, 300, 7:83). While research on the role of history and experience on Kant's theory of progress has focused on the French Revolution as an occurrence demonstrating humanity's moral tendency (Nicholson 1992; Ypi 2014b), evil acts must also be put in the proper perspective to avoid finding human affairs senseless, making us turn away in revulsion and despair (CoF, 300, 7:83, IUH, 53, 8:30). Kant was interested in devising the right position from which to regard the course of human affairs and predict the outcome of free actions (CoF, 300, 7:83–4), including evil acts. What is clear so far, however, is that the emphasis on intra-European conflict and the evident concern with European progress toward peace, make Kant's cosmopolitanism ill-fitted to theorize the injustice of colonialism and consider paths toward justice that aim to bring justice to the world beyond Europe.

NOT PHILANTHROPY, BUT RIGHT

I have so far established that the consequences of colonial conflict on the possibility of European peace and the character of Europeans fueled Kant's critique of colonialism in *Perpetual Peace*. However, I have not yet considered two connected questions that have implications for the problems of correspondence and hierarchy: first, what is the relation between Kant's teleological consideration of colonial conflict and the arguments of Right he makes in *Perpetual Peace*? Second, what is the link between Kant's (moral) condemnation of colonial conflict and his race beliefs?

Perpetual Peace and *The Metaphysics of Morals* take the steps of: (a) characterizing a realm of cosmopolitan interaction that was novel and analytically distinct vis-à-vis Kant's previous works and its connection with other realms and the trajectory toward peace; and (b) condemning morally the annexation of non-European territory. This chapter so far has been concerned with the first point in *Perpetual Peace*. Regarding the task of evaluating the morality of European actions outside of Europe, Kant announces at the outset that cosmopolitanism is concerned with "Right," rather than philanthropy. Following this statement, as noted earlier, Kant characterizes the actions of Europeans outside of Europe as "cruel" (slavery in the West Indies), displaying "injustice" (their visits, which are truly conquests), and "oppression" (in the West Indies) and resulting in "the whole litany of evils that oppress the human race" (i.e., the incitement of Indian states to wars, famine, and rebellions). These condemnations focus on violations of the right of hospitality and on actions that follow from this violation (i.e., the cruelty of slavery in the

West Indies and the oppression of East Indian natives and states driven to internal wars).

These two tasks, importantly, are accomplished separately in *The Metaphysics of Morals*. On the one hand, the destabilizing effect resulting from expansionism and unending colonial conflict is no longer covered under cosmopolitanism. Instead, it appears in the section on the right of nations, which theorizes rightful antagonism. In this section, Kant defines: (a) a "right to equilibrium" [*Recht des Gleichgewichts*] among contiguous states; (b) a principle of outer freedom that allows the preservation of states' belongings but not new (and threatening) acquisitions; (c) conduct of war that is outlawed because it would make subjects unfit for citizenship, states unfit for entering relations with other states, or destroy trust requisite to achieve future peace (*MoM*, 484–5, 6: 346–7). These statements are in line with *Perpetual Peace* in condemning conduct incompatible with equal freedom, convergence, and equilibrium, namely, those actions that reveal "a maxim by which, if it were made a universal rule, any condition of peace among nations would be impossible and a state of nature perpetuated" (*MoM*, 487, 6:349).

On the other hand, the section on cosmopolitanism (§62) is narrowly concerned with establishing the injustice of settlements in non-European lands (this time specifying the protection of nomadic peoples and using only the examples of the "Hottentots," the Tungusi, and "most of the American Indian nations").[20] In this section, Kant rejects "specious reasons" offered for settlement/conquest and claims they "cannot wash away the stain of injustice" of the forceful means used (490, 6:353). Kant's condemnation of settlement in *The Metaphysics of Morals* is clear and contains substantive innovations vis-à-vis his less systematic pre-1790 reflections on colonialism, which were associated with his writings on racial and civilizational inferiority and, it should be noted, never went as far as authorizing violent conquest and the oppression of natives. In particular, non-Europeans were recognized as contracting agents, with a right to exclude, whose nomadic lifestyle established possession. Yet, it is important to note that Kant's condemnation focused on the means.[21] This

---

[20] When discussing property rights, he adds "the inhabitants of New Holland" to these examples (*MoM*, 417, 418, 6:266–7).

[21] Muthu's work focuses on this very point but argues that Kant's anti-paternalism, which understands different cultures as incommensurable, precludes a "duty to civilize others" and thus also condemns the ends (Muthu 2000, 25n, 40). As Inder Marwah notes, however, Kant valued culture because of its role as a "transitory move" that pushes humanity toward the perfection of moral capacities, an end that preserves inequality

is not to say that the protection of natives was indirect, but to say these condemnations were compatible with civilizational hierarchy, that is, Kant's belief that populating these countries with civilized peoples would potentially be more conducive to progress, even if he knew in the particular juncture when he is writing, this could not happen without violence, and was thus impermissible. For example, in the section on property rights (§15), he concludes, a "veil of injustice . . . would sanction any means to a good end" (418, 6:266). The same rationale informs the closing argument of §62, which claims "supposedly good intentions cannot wash away the stain of injustice in the means used for them" (490, 6:353). While Kant was skeptical of the intentions being genuinely good, his language is clear in attributing the injustice to the means. He concludes this paragraph by comparing these claims to the arguments revolutionaries use to justify force, that is, a more just system can be established. We know, of course, Kant favored the kinds of governments revolutionaries wished to establish, but opposed the means to their establishment, and his arguments against colonial settlement seem to contain a parallel claim.

Claims about civilizational hierarchy are connected to claims of racial hierarchy in Kant's system, since only certain races develop the proper predispositions to attain culture and develop morally (Larrimore 2008). Moreover, the establishment of a unified system of Right is in line with Kant's long-standing concern with achieving unity in multiplicity, in which race played a central role. Hence, Kant's unified system of Right, rather than implying the abandonment of beliefs about hierarchy and difference, could have followed from his postulate of unity in difference – "first an article of moral faith, and then a project for human beings" (Larrimore 2008, 348, 56). In fact, it is the difference (i.e., relative weakness) of non-European peoples that requires these protections, because it prevents an engagement in conditions of equality with Europeans, making the logic of antagonism – which regulates European states' relations – fail. In other words, protections of Right are extended in order to prevent violence and oppression, but also to accommodate inequality, rather than as a recognition of equality. Ergo, in contrast to Mark Larrimore's (1999) claim that Kant considered non-Europeans inferior and meaningless in the grand scheme of progress, I argue Kant likely came to consider them far from meaningless, and perhaps even a

---

because it privileges European culture that "prepare[s] [humanity] for a sovereignty in which reason alone is to dominate" (CoJ, 321 5:433; Marwah 2012, 386–7).

central obstacle to progress toward peace, because of their inability to stand up in "lively competition" against European conquerors.

We can think of this form of incorporation in parallel to that of women, who, as feminist critics of Kant have noted, Kant considered naturally inferior to men and unfit for the public sphere, even while he accorded them respect and a role in men's education (Kleingeld 1993; Kofman 1997).[22] Just as a belief in gender inequality is compatible with a concern with the well-being and general standing of women, incorporating non-Europeans into Kant's system of Right did not require an incorporation on equal terms (Bernasconi 2011, 292), that is, a retreat from Kant's commitments to racial hierarchy. Differently put, condemning violence against non-European groups and the violent means of conquest does not in and of itself require an acceptance of those groups as racially equal or their civilization as comparable to Europe's. The permanence of Kant's racial and civilizational thinking receives support from a later claim, from the 1798 edition of his anthropology lectures:

This much we can judge with probability: that the mixture of stems [Stämme] (by extensive conquests), which gradually extinguishes their characters, is not beneficial to the human race – all so-called philanthropy notwithstanding.

(*APPV*, 415, 7:320)

CONCLUSION

Examining the historical context of the non-European locales that appear in the third article suggests that, for Kant, a leading concern of Kant's anti-colonial critique was the detrimental effect of colonial conflict (both intra-European and between Europe and native peoples) on the progress of Europe toward culture and civilization. Kant's examples suggest that his critique is directed at Britain, the dominant empire, slave trader, and naval power, and the historical rival of France. Kant's ability to communicate this was complicated by the close ties between the Prussian rulers and the House of Hanover and the wartime atmosphere. Kant's intervention can be understood as a plea to European monarchs to retreat from their colonial entanglements and allow for France's republican

---

[22] There is disagreement in this literature; some commentators claim Kant's views on women do not impact his moral ideals or that other places in Kant's works grant women rational moral agency (Mikkola 2011; Varden 2017).

constitution to progress and lead Europe toward peace. This examination shows Kant's problem space was the question of progress toward peace in Europe and his criticism of colonialism neither negates the permanence of his racist and civilizational beliefs nor constitutes a full-fledged normative account of colonial injustice. Instead, most of Kant's critique of colonialism is devoted to a reflective assessment of the role of this form of antagonism in Europe's trajectory toward peace. Kant's moral condemnation of colonialism is brief and centered on the violence of the means of conquest and the hypocrisy of the conquerors who claim to want to improve the condition of natives.

These findings mean there is little correspondence between the problem space that motivated Kant's cosmopolitanism and the normative goals that a cosmopolitanism must serve today, to theorize (in)justice in a deeply unequal world bearing the marks of European imperialism. Ironically, the role of Kant in theorizing contemporary cosmopolitanism may prompt a redemptive reading of his anti-colonialism. In other words, the "retrospective significance" (Skinner 2002, 72–3) of his work might lead scholars to understand Kant's text to be saying something that he – I argue – could not have accepted as a fair account of what he was doing (Skinner 2002, chapter 4). Yet the central role of Kant in contemporary cosmopolitan projects should instead make us mindful of blind spots in our interpretation in order to avoid transferring Eurocentric and hierarchical notions to our contemporary thinking. For example, Kant's idea of a world federation was devised for a group of relatively equal actors, putting in question its suitability to structure contemporary multilateral organizations whose members are deeply unequal. Moreover, Kant's framework, uncorrected, is also ill-fitted to counter racialized narratives of civilization that he helped construct and whose legacies still mark the international sphere (Anghie 2006a). Absent the engagement of cosmopolitan scholarship with anti-colonial intellectuals who critically engaged with these institutions during the post–World War II period, their ability to conceptualize normative critiques of international organizations and racialized dynamics might be weakened. Incorporating these writings would, moreover, extend the cosmopolitanism of this scholarship from its subject matter to its mode of inquiry, by productively historicizing and denaturalizing some of its conventions (Godrej 2011, 38).

This is the project I pursue in the rest of the book, for which this chapter has set the stage by pursuing the interpretive task of contextualizing Kant's cosmopolitanism in the political motivations that pushed him to theorize about it. This contextualization shows hierarchies remaining in Kant's framework and a motivating problem space with little correspondence with the problems we must face today. My task in the rest of the book is to further examine the way in which hierarchy and lack of correspondence often unwittingly remains in contemporary neo-Kantian accounts of cosmopolitanism and how that – as well as the substance of Kant's principles – affects the productivity of neo-Kantian framework for our times. To anticipate, from this assessment I conclude it is crucial to move beyond Kant and consider W. E. B. Du Bois, a global thinker and political actor who can redirect and radicalize our theorization of cosmopolitanism in transnational and emancipatory directions. Such an amendment will allow for the reconsideration of the question of racial injustice as it appears in diverse imperial instantiations and for informing normative theorizing based on the political action by those that struggled against these structures. This task differs substantially from simply superimposing egalitarian assumptions over Kant's framework. This project is thus more than an amendment of Kantian cosmopolitanism; it is an effort to redirect attention to Du Bois as an irreplaceable interlocutor in the literature on cosmopolitanism.

2

Vertical and Horizontal Readings of Kant's Principles

The previous chapter reconstructed the social and political context in which Kant wrote *Perpetual Peace*. It argued that when Kant wrote this essay, he was most interested in the effects of colonial conflict on Europe. In particular, it was the expansionism and the multiplicative character of conflict resulting from colonial conflict that troubled Kant. He saw these features as an obstacle to European balanced conflict, which he expected would eventually lead to a peaceful federation that would pave the way for progress toward civilization and morality. Moreover, the chapter suggested Kant's hierarchical understanding of civilization and race remained compatible with his cosmopolitanism, and may have remained unchanged until the end of his life. Given this evidence, I contend that Kantian cosmopolitanism does not model the form of equal concern, that would allow us to consider the problem of cosmopolitanism from the ground up.

The present chapter expands this argument by examining the ways in which the Eurocentrism and narrow concerns of Kantian cosmopolitanism persist in contemporary approaches to cosmopolitanism indebted to Kant. This is what I identify as the interpretive task of deconstruction. I do not mean the Derridean type of "deconstruction," but the interpretive practice of identifying how hierarchical strands of a framework may resurface in approaches indebted to it. Interpretively, this means not taking the framework's egalitarianism at face value, but unpacking the particular practices of theorization and their substantive effects on the cosmopolitan substance of the inquiry or lack thereof. This interpretive step of deconstruction is necessary because a simple update of Kant that embeds his framework in a liberal egalitarian understanding of world politics but retains practices of theorizing connected to his problem space is insufficient to rid the framework of the three forms of Eurocentrism outlined in the introduction. Namely:

(a) *Federative Eurocentrism.* Kant did not theorize imperial domination as an instance of injustice *per se* or as the negation of freedom, or in order to put in question Europe's status as the superior race and civilization. Instead, imperial domination concerned Kant because it was a form of unconventional conflict that was derailing the trajectory of European progress by upsetting the natural progression of conflict and wrongly shaping Europeans' selves. His response to this danger was to advocate a retreat from colonial exploration and a renewed focus on federative organizations that could – under the leadership of republics – lead a set of relatively equal states toward peace. When this framework is repurposed to think about the present without giving proper weight to the problem space that we are facing, scholars may end up rediscovering an international realm that is not ours. Such a sphere is more indebted to Kant's sketch of the perils and possibilities of the late eighteenth century (Walker 2010, 35) than to the questions of transnational solidarity, emancipation, and unequal sovereignty, which guide non-Westerners in their consideration of cosmopolitan projects. In this case, Europe is centered because the institutions that served to solve its problems are offered as a solution for the wider world.

(b) *Unworldly Eurocentrism.* The neo-Kantian literature retains the Eurocentrism of Kant also because it does not engage with anti-colonialism as a political practice and an intellectual tradition, i.e., with thinkers of color who attempted to conceptualize questions of racial and imperial domination that they saw as exceeding the nation.[1] While this is characteristic of much of political theory in the Anglo-American world, cosmopolitan political thinkers, invested as they are in devising a theory to guide the world toward

---

[1] It should be noted that authors like Amy Allen (2016) and James Ingram (2013), who contest Enlightenment notions of progress and universality, respectively – and thus go some way toward addressing the first and third forms of Eurocentrism – still stay within the bounds of canonical thinkers. In other words, while their normative orientation is to signal the productivity of the constant contestation and revision of notions of progress, they do not engage with those non-Western thinkers that have been engaged in precisely that task (see also Singh 2016).

justice, have much to gain from the intellectual tradition and emancipatory politics that nurtured solidarity beyond the nation and contested global institutions that supported empire.[2]

(c) *Ahistorical Eurocentrism.* The federative focus in Kant's cosmopolitanism and the lack of attention to non-Western political thinking and practice is facilitated by a selective historical genealogy in the cosmopolitan literature. This genealogy predominantly limits its focus to the Western projects of internationalism of the twentieth century (the League of Nations, the United Nations [UN], and the European Union), which it incorporates as precursors of the cosmopolitan sphere. While this engagement is critical, this critique does not center on the fact that the League of Nations and the UN, founded as they were by imperial countries, shied away from contesting colonial domination. Similarly, the reliance on the European Union as the standard to follow worldwide reveals a particular strategy to "solve" the problem of injustice. This strategy replaces hierarchy with an assumption of sameness, rather than making the problem of hierarchy and the political road to overcome it the core of the theorization, as this project suggests. A focus on the imperial origins of these institutions, moreover, would direct the attention of political theorists to the alternative internationalisms that raised objections against these institutions during the twentieth century.

These limitations notwithstanding, neo-Kantian scholars have been proactive in theorizing transnational forms of politics and have variously amended Kant's framework. However, these frameworks often obscure the full range of horizontal forms of solidarity that operate transnationally, or attempt to reinsert the forms of politics they uncover into the domestic or international realm of politics, rather than making transnationalism their central feature. Transnational cosmopolitan politics encompass exchanges and forms of identification connecting marginalized groups that are differently located in the West and the

---

[2] This is not to say that colonialism is not theorized *at all* (see, for example, Valentini 2015; Ypi 2013a; Ypi et al. 2009). Instead, it is to say that it is not theorized by considering the writings of intellectuals who conceptualized colonialism from a condition of oppression or the political practices of actors who contested colonial domination, a practice that I show entails a theoretical and normative loss. An exception to this trend is Katrin Flikschuh's recent engagement with African philosophy, which she puts in dialogue with the political philosophy literature on global justice (Flikschuh 2017a).

non-West and who see each other's plight as shared (although not homogeneous). These forms of exchange sidestep both domestic and the international sites of politics, and often emerge precisely because they are not recognized as political subjects in those realms. Recognizing these instances of political craft is important for grounding cosmopolitanism as a project of justice at the level of the cosmos that is constructed from below.[3]

In other words, the important efforts by neo-Kantian scholars to theorize the post-national constellation are curtailed when reconstructions remain centered on Western institutions and on imagining the extension of these spheres to the rest of the world. These practices miss an opportunity to retheorize cosmopolitanism from the ground up by attending to the alternative models of subaltern transnationalism that flourished in the past and continue to exist in the present. Without these intellectual resources, this literature tends to theorize cosmopolitanism as a subsequent step taken after (predominantly Western) domestic justice is attained, which supposedly makes Western citizens' orientations more cosmopolitan and ready to lead the world toward justice. This form of interconnection, interestingly, does not exhaust the possible readings of Kant's complementarity, which could entail, for example, the emergence of dynamic cosmopolitan exchanges by those excluded from Western democracies and Western-led international political spaces. To anticipate, such a reading sets the stage for the Duboisian transfiguration of hospitality, discussed in the next chapter, which contributes to the project of attuning cosmopolitanism to the challenges in our current global order, alleviating the problem of correspondence.[4] The proposed reading of Kant's cosmopolitan principles of complementarity and hospitality does not attempt to rescue his cosmopolitanism by suggesting that there are alternative exegetically plausible and more democratic readings,[5] but instead it offers a creative and disloyal reading of Kant against the grain of his Eurocentrism, which could advance efforts to theorize the transnational.[6] The reading I offer attempts to transform cosmopolitanism by

---

[3] While I focus on both text and practices of politics that contested domestic and international fora "from below," I am indebted to Gayatri Chakravorty Spivak's discussion of the practice of "using the Enlightenment from below" (Spivak 2004, 565n).

[4] To recapitulate, the problem of correspondence emerges when we adopt a framework of analysis attuned to a set of problems that is different from those we face today.

[5] As I have, in fact, suggested in the past (Valdez 2012).

[6] Thus, my project differs from those of Onora O'Neill (2000, 74) and Katrin Flikschuh (2017b, 365), who are also interested in highlighting that there are various plausible

letting contemporary challenges guide our normative and political theorization and orient us toward disloyal readings of Kantian principles that–in combination with subaltern thought and action–allow us to genuinely embrace equal concern.

In the rest of this chapter I support these claims. The next section critically examines the recent neo-Kantian literature on cosmopolitanism, noting how – in different ways – its attempts to conceptualize transnational politics carry over some Kantian limitations. The section titled 'A Horizontal and Reciprocal Reading of Kant's Spheres of Right' proposes creative and more expansive readings of two key principles of Kant's cosmopolitanism: complementarity and hospitality, and examines neo-Kantian approaches that have also moved in this direction.

NEO-KANTIANS' COSMOPOLITANISMS

Neo-Kantian scholarship is diverse and borrows to different degrees and in different forms from Kant's corpus in general and his political writings and his cosmopolitanism in particular. These theorists do not homogeneously diagnose the contemporary problem space nor do they emphasize the same aspects of Kantian cosmopolitanism in their theories. Moreover, while they all fall to some extent into one or more of the three forms of Eurocentrism specified earlier, which thwart their impulse to incorporate transnational forms of politics. In this section, I start by engaging with the work of Jürgen Habermas. I then consider how James Bohman, Seyla Benhabib, Pauline Kleingeld, and Lea Ypi[7] have sought to conceptualize the transnational through amended neo-Kantian frameworks.

Jürgen Habermas's approach to the question of global governance tackles the mismatch between the transnational reach of markets and the still territorially limited character of legitimate political authority. In his exploration of the "post-national constellation," Habermas explicitly invokes Kant's project and supports an update of this project based on the hindsight acquired in the two centuries that have elapsed since *Perpetual Peace* was published. Habermas's engagement is not uncritical; he acknowledges the legitimation deficit of supranational institutions and the problem of Western hegemony. Moreover, he is ambivalent about the

---

readings of Kant's principles but still locate the authority of these readings on their exegetical plausibility.

[7] I deal with Flikschuh's work in a subsequent section.

possibility of realizing democratic ideals through all-encompassing institutions such as the UN (Fine and Smith 2003, 473–4; Habermas 2001, 106). In fact, these reasons lead him to suggest institutional reforms to address this problem. However, in so doing, he bypasses transnational forms of solidarity and will formation that are not aligned with the forms of vertical integration he proposes. In particular, Habermas suggests that a more legitimate global domestic politics depends on progressively extending "the channels of democratic legitimation . . . 'upwards' from the level of the nation-state to the level of continental regimes" (2006, 141). This structure ignores the entanglements between the local and the transnational affecting democratic polities in ways that cannot simply be solved at the domestic level in the gradual process of upward integration, but which need to be addressed conceptually on their own (Lu 2018b). Two forms of injustice in particular are deflected in this conceptualization. First, the fact that the lack of a democratic global sphere allows for deeply unjust forms of interconnection, which hampers the ability of dependent polities to deepen their democratic character.[8] Habermas does not consider this problem and instead assumes states will independently deepen their democratic regimes to give rise to more legitimate mid-level organizations, which will produce a legitimate global sphere. Second, Habermas does not recognize the centrality of racial injustice in Western democracies and its connection to an imperial past and attendant processes of racialization that, in Du Bois's terms, "belt the world."[9] Absent a joint consideration of these problems, the process of upward democratization risks maintaining a deficit in the representation of racialized citizens and adjudicating responsibility for lack of democratization exclusively on individual states, so preventing these questions from being conceptualized as questions of (transnational) cosmopolitanism.

Habermas's proposals for meeting the Kantian project "halfway" are particularly telling. For example, he proposes that other regions of the

---

[8] For example, conditionality imposed by international multilateral institutions like the International Monetary Fund or the World Bank restricts the availability of resources that could be devoted to universalistic social policy, which can both guarantee a minimum level of well-being while being consistent with egalitarian notions of citizenship. Rainer Forst centers these questions in his account of transnationalism, which I analyze later (Forst 2001, 2015).

[9] In other words, the continued racialized hierarchy that characterizes the world (Anghie 2006a, 2006b) is not independent from the racialized process of formation of settler and slave-holding societies, which is in turn related to hostile reception of migrants and refugees of the Global South in the West.

world integrate and democratize along the lines of the European Union in order to negotiate and implement transnational compromises at an intermediate level (2006, 177–8). According to Habermas, the present obstacles for the emergence of this forum are the lack of concreteness and democratic form of these arrangements beyond Europe, where projects of political integration are still "in their infancy" (2006, 177–8). By privileging the European Union as a leader in the cosmopolitan project with which the rest of the world must catch up, Habermas both returns to Kant and forgets one of his main lessons. He returns to Kant by putting his hopes for peace in a European federation and considering democracies leaders in the path toward peace. Yet he forgets Kant's damning (even if civilizational) critique of Europe in *Perpetual Peace*, which could translate in a critique of the role of Europe in establishing the pervasive hierarchies that organize multilateral fora (Pouliot 2016), or the disproportionate power of certain states within the European Union, which became all too evident in the wake of the 2007 financial crisis. Moreover, this account incorporates the non-West as an empty receptacle for European forms of governance and filters out from view the instances of non-Western transnational organization and processes of will formation, which in fact further his goal of public legitimation at the global level. Historically, these forms included alliances between racialized subjects in the West and anti-colonial activists in the non-West, which I reconstruct in the next three chapters. At the time of writing, moreover, they consist of transnational social movements that oppose neoliberal globalization, grassroots environmental movements, and different forms of coalition making among labor groups within and outside the West. This is important because these more variegated forms of transnational coalitions are a response to the legitimation gap that so worries Habermas, and, without considering them, "additive" solutions of upward democratization and regional integration are bound to be insufficient to close the gap. Hence, Habermas seems to fall into precisely the problem of functionalism he criticizes in accounts of the European Union, which confuse institutionalization and legitimation (2006, 67–8). By contrast, a substantive consideration of the character of transnational questions would consider other forms of organization as vital for the achievement of legitimacy. For example, the Caribbean Reparations Commission could be a forum worth expanding to include African Americans in the United States and other Afro-diasporic communities in South America in order to more powerfully bring up the question of reparations in the global public sphere. Similarly, while Habermas mentions the World Trade Organization (WTO) and positively remarks on its recent incorporation of human rights provisions as part of its rules, the elimination of globally regressive agricultural subsidies by the Organisation for Economic Co-operation and Development countries would also mean a substantial improvement in the livelihood of millions of peasants and agricultural businesses in the non-West, something that has been championed by the counterpublic formed by Brazil, India, and China within the WTO (Hopewell 2015). These two examples are cases of contentious politics in the global sphere that target transnational injustice, which Habermas misses because he privileges a vertical understanding of democratic legitimation and a formal understanding of institutionalization.

This formal outlook emerges from an update of Kant's argument that republics are less belligerent than non-republics. In Habermas's version:

> [T]he idea that a democratic order tends to foster nonbelligerent conduct toward other states is not completely false. . . .. To the extent that the universalist value-orientation of a population accustomed to free institutions also influence foreign policy, a republican polity does not behave more peaceably as a whole; however, this orientation does change the wars it conducts. The foreign policy of the state changes according to the motivation of its citizenry. The use of military force is no longer exclusively determined . . . by an essentially particularistic *raison d'état* but *also* by the desire to promote the proliferation of non-authoritarian forms of state and government.
>
> (1997, 120–1; see also 2000, 172–3)

While this optimism is somewhat tempered in his post–9/11 accounts of the Kantian project, given the turn US hegemony takes in that period, Habermas still believes that "[c]itizens of a democratic political community sooner or later become aware of cognitive dissonances if universalistic claims cannot be squared with the particularistic character of the obvious driving interests" (2006, 185). As in this instance, Habermas often connects leadership in universalist values with the West. Whenever non-Western countries enter the discussion, it is so that Habermas can highlight their burdens (civil war, ethnic fragmentation, or authoritarianism), which puts them at a disadvantage from the West, where states are better located to harmonize their national interest with "normative claims established by the United Nations" (1997, 132; 2000, 152–3). The strategy of placing Western democracies and, in particular, their citizens, in the role of a moral leader in the spread of universalist values, operates to obscure the fact that these states are responsible for hierarchical world orderings that benefit from, and at least partially explicate, political and economic developments in the non-West. Similarly, this strategy obscures the fact that various anti-hegemonic forces and fora exist outside the West or in marginal quarters of the West, and imagining institutional arrangements that could amplify their voice and their access to realms of authority might be normatively promising.[10]

The limited range of view that Habermas brings to his theorization also follows from the particular historical genealogy implicit in his work. This genealogy traces the experiments of the League of Nations, the UN, and the European Union as limited but nonetheless instructive starting points for our theorization of cosmopolitanism today. His deflection of the supporting role these organizations played in sustaining imperialism and the anti-colonial fora that emerged to contest these institutions is particularly puzzling because of his otherwise perceptive concern with public memory in the German context. In one intervention on the question of memory in Germany, for example, Habermas argues that the work of memory is at its best when it shakes trust in traditions and fosters a "critical attitude toward one's own particularity" (1996, 28–9). This work is necessary because, he notes, the "singular crime" of the Holocaust was "issued from the very midst of our collective life," thus requiring subsequent generations to engage in public history in order to:

bring about some clarity concerning the cultural matrix of a burdened inheritance, to recognize what they themselves are collectively liable for, and what is to be continued, and what revised, of those traditions that once had formed such a disastrous motivational background.

(1996, 31)

There are echoes between the process of *Vergangenheitsbewältigung*, as described by Habermas in the cited excerpts, and the work needed to assess the burdens of the West in world society, given the centrality of imperial violence, exploitation, and dehumanization of colonial subjects

---

[10] Habermas has more explicitly engaged with Eurocentrism in his work on the post secular age, which puts into question the Weberian assumption that development is accompanied by secularization and conceptually opens the public sphere to religious argument (2008, 2009; for a critique see Rees 2017). While this work is not directly connected to cosmopolitanism, it is notable that Habermas's most explicit effort to decolonize his political theory is devoted to incorporating religion into it. While I agree that this is a necessary endeavor (Valdez 2016), the assumption of secularism is by no means the only way in which political theory remains Eurocentric.

to the project of global governance.[11] Yet, the "burdened inheritance" and the need to revise traditions are not brought up or theorized when Habermas sets his sights on questions of cosmopolitanism and international organizations.

The aforementioned critique does not imply completely discounting the positive valence of the ideals of republicanism and peace that motivate Kant's writings, which Habermas updates through a belief in the cosmopolitan effects of Western democracies and European integration. Revolutionary France and the enthusiasm it created throughout Europe was central in Kant's thought because it was evidence of the opening public spheres of deliberation that could further the project of Enlightenment that he championed. But in order to make this celebration normatively valid for a cosmopolitan project, a separate investigation of how newly republican regimes in Europe and the United States related to the rest of the world or to its internal racial others is necessary. In this sense, a desire to have the French revolutionary project contribute to a universal project of cosmopolitanism would require engaging with the revolution's normative assessment of external and internal others. For example, it would be important to engage with the alternative ways in which French revolutionary thought sought to address the question of slavery and empire (Fischer 2004), or with internal critiques of American "democracy" that conceptualized the racist character of its founding and development as a liberal hegemonic power (Du Bois *CDCP*). Regarding projects of European or Western peace, their importance is beyond doubt against the background of historical rivalries and bloodshed that characterized this continent. However, the normative value of these institutions for a cosmopolitan project depends on whether they served to contest or reassert forms of imperial domination in the rest of the world, an area where their record is mixed. This experience should foster a healthy skepticism over the promise of multilateral federative institutions as fora conducive to properly institutionalizing political responsibility and justice in the world sphere. Hence, the problem is not the reliance on these particular examples as internally valuable within the European tradition, but the effort to build a universal project relying solely on them, without

---

[11] Interestingly, and to anticipate the discussion in Chapter 3, what Habermas finds so troubling (that the genocide of Jewish people emerged "from the very midst of . . . collective life") was precisely what Du Bois pinpoints as a particular feature of modern imperialism: that it is Western "democracies" that are the exploiters (*ARW*, 709).

making a specific case for them based on a reciprocal communication with others encompassed by the project. Instead, I argue that the ability of cosmopolitanism to face forms of injustice and foster loyalty and coalition making requires looking beyond the traditional realms of the domestic and the international, and requires exploring the transnational. Other neo-Kantian scholars have brought light to precisely these processes, which I examine in turn.

Conceptualizing the Transnational within Cosmopolitanism

Neo-Kantian scholars often echo Habermas's privileging of Western cosmopolitan leaderships when they conceptualize cosmopolitanism, even if other aspects of their work, particularly their efforts to theorize transnational phenomena, often push against this move. Pauline Kleingeld's theorization of cosmopolitan patriotism is a case in point. In her reconstruction of Kant's cosmopolitan patriotism, Kleingeld argues that complementarity implies there is no inherent conflict between patriotic and cosmopolitan duties because improving one's own republic may involve making it more just in its dealings with other states (2012, 33). She resorts to the same Kantian principle of complementarity Habermas cites: republics are naturally more peaceful, making the citizens' work on behalf of their republic contribute to the achievement of world peace (2012, 33). In this example of cosmopolitan patriotism, the compatibility of patriotism and cosmopolitanism depends on privileging the domestic sphere of politics over the cosmopolitan one and downplays other forms of interaction. This is in contrast to other possible scenarios in which actions stem primarily from a cosmopolitan commitment, a situation in which virtuous effects on republics result from actions in the cosmopolitan realm, or a case in which republics behave viciously toward other peoples. Despite Kleingeld's nominal commitment to a *reciprocal* notion of complementarity of realms, the examples she offers are restricted to the way in which virtuous republics become more just in their dealings with other state and non-state actors. In addition to placing cosmopolitanism (and the international sphere) as simple beneficiaries of domestic-bound processes, this interpretation also depoliticizes these other realms, whose conflicts and divisions and the specificities of their public spheres are therefore not theorized.[12]

---

[12] In other work, Kleingeld goes beyond Kant's hospitality by arguing that physical harm – rather than just death – could justify a right to admission, and argues further that certain

Lea Ypi's notion of cosmopolitanism, posited as dependent on domestic political processes, partly echoes the unidirectional understanding of Kant's complementarity that characterizes Habermas and Kleingeld. Ypi follows Kant and Rousseau in arguing that "justice is realized through citizens' participation in collective political practices of deliberation, through the exercise of popular sovereignty coupled with civic education" (2012, 30). She continues:

It is *very important not to undermine this process and instead build on its strengths whilst attempting to bring about political transformations. Ius cosmopoliticum* represents a necessary '*supplement* to the unwritten code of the right of a state and the right of nations'; it indicates the emergence of a new normative interpretation of the function and purpose of shared institutions whilst at the same time acknowledging the relevance of existing political obligations. It constitutes the condition of development of the *ius gentium* but it neither leads to an exercise of power with juridical rule – which is always statual or inter-statual – nor does it require a substitution or vertical dispersion of sovereignty.

(2012, 30, my emphasis)

Ypi's interpretation of "supplement" in this excerpt has two dimensions. First, cosmopolitanism is not juridical, in contrast to international Right or civil Right. Second, cosmopolitanism is sequentially secondary, in the sense that the "exercise of popular sovereignty" and "civic education" must be consolidated before we can turn our sights toward the other realms. This interpretation does not recover the potential for less unidirectional relations between realms of politics that could be disloyally read in Kant against his Eurocentrism, nor does it capture the transnational character of injustice and the instances of transnational political action that are yet to be encompassed by juridical rule today. In particular, Ypi's account does not consider the possibility that popular sovereignty and civic education may not develop in cosmopolitan directions unaided by external contestation. In this regard, Ypi's notion of "avant-garde political agency" is more promising. Avant-garde political movements "elaborate concrete projects for the emancipation of society by occupying the empty space between the critique of existing institutional practices

grounds to deny admission – such as "discriminatory rules" based on "skin color" – should simply be outlawed (Kleingeld 1998, 77). In this case, Kleingeld identifies shortcomings in the ways in which republics deal with foreigners and acknowledges the need to contest the grounds established by imperfect Western democracies but does not trace the origin of these complaints to transnational activists who contest admission norms from outside the polity.

and normative interpretations in need of being contextually recognized" (Ypi 2012, 163). Thanks to their actions, proposals that at first seemed "odd or unacceptable" to a polity, progressively become popularized and adopted by broader sectors (2012, 164). At the cosmopolitan level, the notion of avant-garde political agents includes:

> All those individuals and social groups who appear distributively affected by current globalization processes and whose experience of conflict in particular societies forces us to rethink understandings of the function and purpose of existing political arrangements.
>
> (2012, 167)

Cosmopolitan avant-gardes, according to Ypi, promote inclusion and solidarity with foreigners in their own countries and support cooperative, rather than exploitative, global institutions (2012, 168). Ypi identifies pro-migrant movements, transnational human rights networks, and the environmental movement – among other groups – as examples of cosmopolitan avant-gardes. Yet, ultimately, Ypi's framework truncates the full transnational character of movements struggling against global injustice. This is for two reasons. First, Ypi's examples focus on Western efforts to support the plight of others, be they migrants, landless activists in South America, or human rights activists in repressive regimes. While she recognizes that part of the goal of these activists is to highlight the role of Western governments in supporting unjust global arrangements, her framework is less aware of the continuities between the injustices in the Third World and those of marginalized citizens in the West.[13] Second, and as a consequence, the focus of Ypi's reconstruction of cosmopolitan avant-gardes is less about recovering the spaces of politics created by the transnational entanglements of the *avant-guarde*, than about their role "persuading fellow citizens to endorse emancipatory political projects" (2012, 156). In other words, the cosmopolitan avant-garde simply continues "the democratic struggle for the expansion of progressive interpretations of the function and purpose of political institutions" (Ypi 2012, 156).

In this way, Ypi opens up the field of politics to consider transnational political action, only to close it again by making these experiences merely serve a persuasive function in the domestic realm of politics. The fact

---

[13] In this, she echoes other scholars in the global justice literature, as I argue elsewhere (Valdez 2019).

that she identifies her treatment of cosmopolitan avant-gardes as the book's "case study" (2013b, 126) also suggests these instances of transnationalism are not intended to be taken up theoretically to move beyond Kant. Moreover, even the descriptive engagement reveals a somewhat limited account of cosmopolitanism. This is because the particular groups highlighted are predominantly foreigners (migrants, citizens of authoritarian regimes, landless activists in South America). These subjects are interesting to Ypi because they are affected by and thus conscious of the transnational character of injustice and can serve to enlighten Western publics without putting the theoretical preeminence of the domestic sphere in question. But this conception of transnationalism is limited. To understand why, consider how defining migrants as an avant-garde group persuading domestic publics distracts us from an understanding of migration as a node of a transnationalized, political economy that needs to be conceptualized. In other words, migration to the United States cannot be understood apart from the effects of the North American Free Trade Agreement (NAFTA) on Mexican agriculture and internal migration. Moreover, this trade treaty should also be understood as connected to the destabilized access to US manufacturing employment and the dislocation of American working-class communities. These forms of interconnection pose theoretical challenges to a statist framework. This is why anti-colonial intellectuals who – during the twentieth century – considered the question of race-based injustice a transnational force, and imagined and performed new forms of politics, can contribute theoretically to cosmopolitanism. The Duboisian transnationalism that I begin to sketch in the next chapter locates Western democracies as enforcers of the injustice that operates globally, something that Ypi acknowledges but – because of her statist framework – can not theorize. The framework I propose centers the theorization on the particularities of this injustice and the horizontal associations among marginalized groups in the West and the non-West that challenge the primacy of the domestic.

The attention to realms of politics beyond the domestic and their potential to democratize the cosmopolitan project is something that appears prominently in James Bohman's neo–republican-inflected Kantian account of transnational democracy, one of the fuller and more political understandings of transnationalism among neo-Kantian cosmopolitans. Bohman offers a promising notion of mutual interaction across domestic, international, and transnational spaces of politics and argues that it is in the differentiation and multiplication of polities that we can see the powers of citizenship realized. In his words:

> The guiding principle here is not just that democracy promotes such active powers of citizens, but also that such rights and powers are best protected and promoted when there are differentiated and overlapping institutional locations for their exercise.
>
> (2007, 186)

Importantly, Bohman explicitly acknowledges hierarchy in the international sphere and the possibility of subordination of democracies to other democracies. His response to hierarchy is to offer a conception of humanity as a moral property related to "the status of membership in a political community," which can operate as a horizon in democracies and orient them to "do justice to others" (2007, 104–5). In practical terms, Bohman's framework requires the "dispersal of power," which is in part about multiplying the venues in which citizens can "initiate deliberation" and in part about the "constant interaction among institutions and publics" in which these two constructs become fully reciprocal and co-constitutive" (2007, 105, 191). However, whenever Bohman's account turns from the abstract character of humanity to the practical question of historical and contemporary examples, he turns to the UN and – most prominently – the European Union, which he describes as:

> a sufficiently complex and differentiated institutional structure, as well as a novel set of institutions and practices that are responsive to appeals made by those whose rights have been violated.
>
> (2007, 134)

While Bohman acknowledges that the European Union is a far from ideal structure, he, as Habermas, returns to Kant and at once forgets one of Kant's main lessons. In so doing, he misses the opportunity to highlight the role of Europe in establishing and maintaining hierarchies in the international sphere (see also the section titled "A Reciprocal Complementarity"). His account, moreover, obscures other actors and spheres of contestation that may have more radically contested extant notions of membership and initiated deliberation on topics silenced in Western-led institutions. Finally, and somewhat at odds with his overall framework, Bohman's account still privileges vertical forms of interconnection, in which citizens "outside the zone of the democratic peace" are expected to benefit from transnational spaces where they can establish "social ties that may become the basis of democratization through communicative interchange and mutual claim making" (2007, 187). In doing this, he posits the need to "learn" democratic norms from Westernized spaces and discounts both the hierarchical practices that Western countries uphold in the world,[14] and the more democratic and horizontal practices that emerge from ties connecting groups fighting transnational injustice in the West and non-West.

Among neo-Kantian approaches, Seyla Benhabib puts forward a cosmopolitan model that carefully theorizes the interconnection between the cosmopolitan realm and domestic democratic polities. She readily recognizes that Kant's motivations were far from those that occupy us today (2004, 37, 40), but nonetheless values the way in which he conceptualizes the contradictions between universalist and republican ideals, which constitute what she calls the "paradox of democratic legitimacy" (2004, 43–8). She complements Kant's framework with an Arendtian account of political action, which illuminates the paradoxes emerging at the intersection of the national and the international, and centers the political process through which polities make sense of these encounters. In particular, she adopts Frank Michelman's notion of jurigenerativity in order to capture the particular way in which democratic politics shape and particularize the meaning of principles of rights and the way in which the incorporation of outsiders as "hermeneutical partners" contributes to this process (2004, 169). In Benhabib's framework, the practice of political agency by insiders and outsiders mutually transforms and shapes their identities and the meaning of rights (2004, 168–9).

In this way, Benhabib provides a much richer account of democratic politics and the way in which it operates vis-à-vis the realm of cosmopolitanism. Her model of political action makes it clear that cosmopolitan rules influence domestic struggles and transform actors' identities through the process of political engagement, thus giving particular content to rights. This is the work of democratic iterations, i.e., moral and political dialogues, through which constituencies of "all sizes" reappropriate and reiterate global principles and norms. In this framework, "concerns for global justice can . . . become guiding principles of actions for democratic peoples themselves" (Benhabib 2004, 113). Yet, despite Benhabib's challenge of the twin ideas of a unified demos and that of a self-enclosed and autochthonous territory over which that *demos* governs, her defense of democratic self-determination ultimately narrows her focus on the

---

[14] Here one may ask why these social ties are supposed to result in the diffusion of democratic practices, rather than in the co-optation of developing countries' elites by Western elites that serve to facilitate domination, as noted by Forst (2001, 173–4).

democratic public itself.[15] This public, she argues, can "reconstitute itself by enfranchising groups without voice or by providing amnesty for undocumented immigrants" (2004, 218–20). A similar approach informs her treatment of the status of international law and transnational legal agreements vis-à-vis democratic sovereignty. She argues that cosmopolitan norms such as human rights require "local contextualization, interpretation, and vernacularization by self-governing peoples" (2009, 692).

While I am sympathetic to this project,[16] it has the undesirable consequence of depoliticizing the realm of cosmopolitanism by identifying it as a realm of norms that are vernacularized exclusively in domestic polities, the ultimate sphere of political legitimation. Instead, the framework could, first, consider in depth the publics that formed outside international and domestic spheres, and in oppositional conversation with them. Second, and relatedly, this framework could acknowledge that, historically, "global principles and norms" were deeply hierarchical and racist, and, rather than vernacularized, they had to be radically contested politically. In this case, it was the spheres of politics inaugurated by marginalized groups throughout the world that did the work of contestation as well as the work of imagination of alternative transnational arrangements.

A HORIZONTAL AND RECIPROCAL READING OF KANT'S SPHERES OF RIGHT

In the previous section I examined neo-Kantian approaches to cosmopolitanism and argued that their frameworks have offered productive ways of conceptualizing the transnational character of contemporary cosmopolitanism. I also noted, however, that they do not always theorize these formations as inherently cosmopolitan but end up subsuming them into domestic politics (Ypi and Benhabib); or that they still privilege Western democracies and federative European-led institutions as the starting point of cosmopolitan projects (Habermas, Kleingeld's recent work, and

---

[15] This is not to say that a defense of self-determination is misguided, particularly in the context of the problematic uses to which globalism and human rights can be put, including justifying sanctions and military invasions, as Jean Cohen notes (2008). It is to say, however, that parallel attention must be paid to other realms that also politicize questions of global justice, often because they face a hostile reception domestically.

[16] In particular, the careful theorization of democratic agency and identity and the way in which they operate and become constituted through political action at the intersection between cosmopolitanism and sovereignty, a topic to which I turn in Chapter 4.

Bohman); and that their historical genealogies miss important instances of transnational political association that emerge from horizontal forms of coalition making between groups affected by colonial and semi-colonial power (all of those previously mentioned). In this section I return to Kant's works in order to show how the principles of complementarity and hospitality can be read in more horizontal and reciprocal ways, and engage with the neo-Kantian approaches of Rainer Forst, Brian Milstein, and Katrin Flikschuh who have moved in this direction. I note, however, that these readings still need to be complemented by an examination of the transnational structures of injustice that limit cosmopolitan projects and the forms of relationality that can facilitate the struggle against them.

A Reciprocal Complementarity

My reading of complementarity in Kant starts with his cosmopolitan patriotism – concerned as it is with the compatibility of domestic and cosmopolitan duties and political action. In her book, *Kant and Cosmopolitanism*, Kleingeld reconstructs Kant's cosmopolitan patriotism. She traces Kant's notion of patriotism, not yet associated with the nineteenth-century meaning that we commonly attribute to it today, and reconstructs an older tradition. This tradition highlights "citizens' commitment to or love for their shared political freedom, and the institutions that sustain it." This notion of patriotism is "synonymous with 'public spiritedness' and commitment to the common good" (Kleingeld 2012, 21). In Kant, Kleingeld notes, patriotism is opposed to the "national delusion that one's own nation is superior to others" and connected to "citizens' commitment to or love for their shared political freedom, and the institutions that sustain it" (2012, 21, 6). This commitment requires the individual to engage in civic activity on behalf of the political community and its members (Kleingeld 2012, 21).

Kant's patriotism develops in tandem with his republican ideal and applies to the state as well as to citizens (Kleingeld 2012, 28). For the state, patriotism implies treating citizens as co-legislating members rather than property (*NaF*, 19:511, cited in Kleingeld 2012, 28). Given this structure, much of politics could be properly understood as the struggle to make the state patriotic by demanding the acceptance of all citizens as co-legislating members of the state. Thus, the public-spirited action of citizens, in Kant's republican understanding, is properly patriotic. As Kleingeld notes, just republics simply could not come about if it was not for the duty of citizens to devote some of their time to the public affairs of their own community, including its preservation, and flourishing (although not at the expense of others) (2012, 31–2). However, she argues, patriotism must be properly understood as an imperfect duty, namely, a duty to adopt a maxim that may coexist with other maxims, such as helping those who are in need in other countries (2012, 32). In this way, Kleingeld dissolves the tension that could exist between patriotic and cosmopolitan goals. This finding is not too surprising when considered in the context of the conceptual importance of complementarity in Kant's system of Right. However, when illustrating this complementarity – as already noted earlier – Kleingeld focuses predominantly on the way in which the improvement of one's polity may result in it dealing with other states in a more just manner. This is a strategy common among Kantians and is based on Kant's own reflections on the peaceful character of republican government (*TPP*, 323, 8:350–1) and his actual interests at the time, but it is not – strictly speaking – the only available reading of complementarity in his work. Indeed, in a less noted reflection on the interconnection between republics and war, Kant suggests a different direction:

Nowhere does human nature appear less lovable than in the relations of entire peoples to one another . . . The will to subjugate one another or to diminish what belongs to another always exists, and arming for defense, which often makes peace more oppressive and more destructive of internal welfare than war itself, can never be relaxed.

(*OCS*, 309, 8:312)

In this extract, the origin is not in the domestic sphere, but in a dysfunctional international peace (one that does not completely eliminate the possibility of war) that results in the regression of domestic regimes because of the oppressive nature of militarism at home. While the example focuses on vicious complementarity, the same logic suggests that a genuinely peaceful international sphere will give republics the resources and space to devote to welfare rather than warfare. This dynamic underlines that republics are dependent on factors that are not fully under their control and that their virtuosity may not always be the defining feature in ensuring international and cosmopolitan justice, but may instead depend on it.

An understanding of complementarity of this kind, however, disappears from view in the approaches outlined in the previous section, particularly when they privilege domestic spaces of politics and implicitly or explicitly highlight the leadership of Western democracies in projects of cosmopolitanism. This interpretation, moreover, also runs against some explicit statements by Kant in *Perpetual Peace*, in which the international and cosmopolitan realms stand in mutual relationship to the domestic realm, potentially contributing or imperiling its process of enlightenment. In his famous essay, moreover, Kant's skepticism regarding the capacity of domestic processes of civilization alone to produce citizens with a cosmopolitan orientation is evident. In fact, the rhetoric about uncivilized European states pervading *Perpetual Peace* seems to be devoted precisely to overturning the notion that considering only the domestic character of government is enough to assess the virtue of states:

If one compares with this the *inhospitable* behavior of the civilized, especially commercial, states in our part of the world, the injustice they show in *visiting* foreign lands and peoples (which with them is tantamount to *conquering* them) goes to horrifying lengths. When America, the negro countries, the Spice Islands, the Cape, and so forth were discovered, they were to them, countries belonging to no one [*die keinem angehörten*] since they counted the inhabitants as nothing.
(*TPP*, 329, 8:358)

While this passage has been interpreted primarily as a critique of the behavior of European states in colonial locales – which it is – it is also a claim about how the level of civilization of European states (about which Kant was moderately optimistic (*MPC*, 221, 27:470–1)) did *not* guarantee civilized behavior when these states interacted with non-European states or peoples. The passage highlights that virtue within a country cannot accurately serve as an indicator of the cosmopolitan orientation of its citizens; the civilized character of European states is not apparent in their relations with subjects they encounter abroad. Moreover, their own civilization might in fact be providing reasons to deny recognition to native claims of ownership or sovereignty of their territory because of their sense of superiority regarding their property arrangements, a question that Kant addresses specifically in the *Metaphysics of Morals*, although without considering the way in which his own earlier writings on race and civilization contribute to this problem.

In other words, even if the previous chapter makes clear that the space of Europe is the leading concern in Kant's conceptualization of a cosmopolitan realm, the forms of interaction he theorizes do not necessarily locate the cosmopolitan realm as sequentially secondary. In fact, quite the opposite is true; while Kant did see republics as particularly oriented toward peace, and potential carriers of a cosmopolitan orientation that would contribute to peace, this is only because the decision to go to war would be evaluated by the citizenry, which, out of self-interest alone has incentives not to engage in war. Moreover, this is just one of the linkages or interconnections singled out in his system of Right. In this sense, one may think of Kant's claim that cosmopolitanism is a supplement (*Ergänzung*) as something more than a step that is subsequent to the other realms of Right. Instead, it could be productively considered something that is necessary to correct a deficiency, a way of addressing the incompleteness of an existing system. In this case, cosmopolitanism must be understood as a realm in its own right that is meant to address the failings of the joint work of civil and international Right and contribute to justice in these other realms, rather than being the realm to turn to *once* republics have consolidated. In other words, the failings of domestic and international Right follow because their regulations do not cover forms of interaction between states and non-state actors and so cannot prevent certain injuries from taking place. These injuries are widely felt but cannot be addressed with the laws provided by republics and the institutions that organize states. In Kant's words:

Since (the narrower or wider) community of the nations of the earth has now gone so far that a violation of right on *one* place of the earth is felt in *all*, the idea of a cosmopolitan right is no fantastic and exaggerated way of representing right; it is, instead, a *supplement* to the unwritten code of the right of a state and the right of nations necessary for the sake of any public rights of human beings and so for perpetual peace; only under this condition can we flatter ourselves that we are constantly approaching perpetual peace.

(*TPP*, 330–1, 8:360, my emphasis)

This excerpt suggests that there is a mismatch between the deeds of peoples and the law that regulates them. As noted in the previous chapter, cosmopolitanism is required to restrain European citizens' conduct in war, or to limit the actions of trading companies in their dealings with natives and other European corporations. Even with a republican government, or a working international organization of European states, events happening outside their legal purview impinge on the capacity of European states to govern themselves and to coordinate relations among them. In sum, while cosmopolitanism's legal status is not equal to that of the other two realms in Kant, the relations between happenings in each of these spheres is nonetheless reciprocal.

This mismatch between deeds and laws has motivated a dynamic literature on transnational and global justice (Fraser 2009; Goodhart 2005), but it already concerns Kant and underlies his often overlooked critique of sovereignty. Scholars have argued that Kant grants priority to sovereignty and therefore declines to endorse a world state capable of coercing individual states. In particular, Katrin Flikschuh argues that a coercive world state would compromise the moral personality states have by virtue of the public will they represent (2010, 479–80). Other scholars cite the limited right to hospitality that he offers, which merely grants peoples the prerogative to regulate visits, as further evidence of his privileging of sovereignty (Benhabib 2004; Kleingeld 1998). What is notable, though, is that in the Third Definitive Article, Kant was particularly keen on granting non-European peoples the right to regulate visits; an attribute of sovereignty that was not recognized for these peoples at the time (Kleingeld 1998; Muthu 2000). This move, moreover, was a radical restriction of what European countries considered *their* sovereign right, to the extent that it delegitimized the way in which Europeans had seen, and would continue to see, the non-European world as a territory to be controlled, annexed, and disputed with other European powers.[17] It was also a departure from his own earlier view that Europe would eventually legislate "for all other continents" (*IUH*, 52, 8:29). In other words, Kant's conceptualization of a limited right to hospitality both strengthens the sovereignty of non-European peoples and restricts the sovereignty of Europeans. If one thinks of Kant's audience, European leaders and intellectuals, the most salient part of this essay was probably the curtailment of European sovereignty he was proposing. Kant saw the unlimited extension of sovereignty (over other territories and other peoples) as dangerous to his project of republicanism and international peace in Europe. In the context of thinking on natural law, his proposal involves a significant restriction on the authority that Europe was starting to claim over the rest of the world. When compared with arguments that used the principle of hospitality as a free-for-all right to conquer and exploit other lands and with a general consensus that non-European countries could not claim sovereignty, the recognition of non-Western countries' ability to restrict visits may be the closest thing to the imposition of coercion in the realm of cosmopolitanism (Meckstroth forthcoming; Valdez 2012). It would be somewhat paradoxical for Kantians to remain wedded to Kant's

---

[17] This binary view of sovereignty as belonging to European peoples only and including the prerogative to occupy the rest of the earth, subject only to the restriction of other European powers, would still be true over half a century after Kant wrote, when Italian nationalist Giuseppe Mazzini could defend "the right [of a nation] to fashion its own life," self-determination, and association with other peoples at the same time that he hoped Italy would not lose out in the spread of European colonies and trade "across the Asian continent" (Mazzini 2009, 233, 238).

view of sovereignty when his own intervention radically contested the view that was prevalent in his time. In other words, when the choice is between maintaining his particular assessment of sovereignty or adopting instead the critical spirit of his intervention, which claimed that the particular understanding of sovereignty and hospitality in his time was failing and needed reconsideration, I suggest that we must adopt the latter insight.[18] This is particularly urgent for our assessment of the contemporary global condition, in which a world of formally equal states interconnected through a myriad of bilateral and multilateral treaties and organizations coexists with deep asymmetries in economic and political power. Staying with Kant's defense of sovereignty is not only unwarranted – if one reads his intervention as curtailing sovereignty – but also unduly privileges exegetical loyalty over attunement to the particular challenges that we face today. This reading instead suggests a productive way of thinking about sovereignty beyond the Westphalian paradigm: to consider sovereignty (and thus, rightful coercion) as an institution to be modulated according to cosmopolitan goals. While in Kant the overarching goal was to prevent dysfunctional colonial conflict and its effects in Europe, the principle of modulation can be redeployed to consider whether guaranteeing justice globally may require a different intensity of sovereignty in particular areas of policy, or even different sovereignty regimes for different actors in the international sphere.[19] Far from claiming that Kant envisioned such a world, my argument is that a regulatory principle of modulation of sovereignty might be a productive way to think about transnational politics in the present time. In other words, a contemporary creative reading could highlight the emancipatory character of restricting Western overreach in the name of sovereignty and its critical purchase to address the question of unequal self-determination in the world today.

This is a path that some neo-Kantian scholars have taken. Notably, Rainer Forst's work brings out these dimensions through his conceptualization of "transnational contexts of justice." A context of justice, for Forst, obtains "wherever relations of political *rule* and *social cooperation exist and* wherever forms of *domination* exist, whether or not they are

---

[18] This is particularly the case if we are interested in relying on Kantian insights to inform contemporary challenges and want to allocate interpretive weight accordingly. I propose such reading for the case of immigration elsewhere (Valdez 2012).

[19] This way of thinking about sovereignty is particularly important given the potential vicious affinities between cosmopolitan projects and neo-imperial humanitarian endeavors that have been rightly highlighted (Cohen 2004, 2006, 2008).

legally institutionalized" (2015, 100, emphasis in the original). In making contexts of justice dependent on the *existence* of rule, domination, or cooperation, Forst explicitly departs from Kant's focus on legal coercion, as well as from global justice accounts based on sanctioned relations of association and cooperation. Forst's right to justification, which conceptually grounds his contexts of justice, is based on his reconstruction of the Kantian categorical imperative (Forst 2012, 2). The right to justification implies "a qualified veto right against any norms and practices which cannot be justified reciprocally and generally" in a public sphere (2001, 169). Forst's approach starts from the "dignity of human beings as agents," who should not be subject to power that is beyond their control, in order to characterize the realm of the transnational as currently "very much in need of justification" (Forst 2012, 249–50). Yet, Forst is agnostic as to the ultimate institutional shape of the realm of transnationalism. Instead, in another departure from Kant, he acknowledges the open-endedness of the politics of justice, which will determine "with a view to the situation that is supposed to be transformed" what form of regulation of domination is to be established (Forst 2015, 104–5).

Forst's transitional contexts of justice go a long way beyond some of the Kantian features I find most confining. This approach is grounded, to the extent that it starts from the examination of relations of domination, rule, and cooperation. This approach is also transnational, rather than centered on the domestic and the international or, alternatively, the global. Finally, Forst allows for the dialectical character of emancipation struggles to take precedence over the impulse to theorize a predetermined institutional formation that satisfies certain normative requirements as an endpoint of cosmopolitanism. Yet, Forst's theorization is sometimes ambivalent regarding the particular mechanisms through which contexts of justice emerge and operate vis-à-vis each other. On the one hand, he clearly acknowledges the way in which transnational alliances of the kind Du Bois established are central theoretical building blocks, arguing that:

> transnational mechanisms of domination can also be uncovered and denounced through transnational critical alliances that constitute a politically relevant demos in virtue of being subjugated under specific structures of domination.
>
> (2015, 104)

At the same time, in other portions of his work, Forst seems to privilege the domestic sphere, arguing that the primary political context where moral rights turn into a basic political right to justification is "the context of a particular, 'domestic' society and its basic structure" (2001, 172).

Elsewhere, Forst argues that the domestic sphere of "fundamental (minimal) justice" as a starting point of procedural justice will then allow the pursuit of transnational (i.e., 'full (maximal)') justice (2015, 92). Forst is aware of this tension and he quickly complements this claim with the acknowledgment of a broader story, in which democratic regimes benefit from unjust relations with other states and weaker countries' democratization prospects are limited by their insertion in an international regime that obstructs these attempts (2001, 173).

However, the tension remains, to the extent that he privileges the domestic context, "into which (in the normal case) persons are born as citizens, that is, where they find themselves situated as members of a historically situated political community and order" (2001, 172). But what about the *ab*normal case? What about subjects who are born in a domestic sphere that declares them colonial subjects, property, second-class citizens, or members of a group ignored or devalued by historical narratives? If we were to judge from the portions of the world population subject to each kind of regime, normality would veer toward the experience of subjects who cannot politically exercise a right to justification in the domestic realm. In this regard, an understanding of the domestic realm as the primary realm of politics could be further relativized. Moreover, Forst's individualist understanding of democratic politics as a "practice of reciprocal and general justification [whose] task . . . is to secure the political autonomy of those who are supposed to be both subjected to and authors of binding norms" (2015, 98) could also be usefully complemented. Forst wishes to extend this model to transnational contexts, but this extension is not possible without centering other aspects of experience, which need to be understood relationally through the consideration of constructed group identities that both solidify racial practices of exclusion and motivate emancipatory forms of solidarity countering exclusion. Forst is theoretically attuned to relationality to the extent that his right of justification appears politically in the "relational freedom of being a codetermining agent of justification within the normative order that bind us" (2015, 98). But this relationality remains concerned with attaining autonomy rather than with studying the forms of heteronomy that characterize injustice and the creative forms of relationality that must be established beyond the nation-state in order to contest them.

To consider the question of relationality in a way that exceeds the realm of the domestic, scholars working within the Kantian tradition have resorted to the notion of hospitality, which I examine next.

Hospitality

The main orienting principle of the cosmopolitan realm is the right to hospitality:

> *hospitality* (hospitableness) means the right of a foreigner not to be treated with hostility because he has arrived on the land of another . . . What he can claim is not the *right to be a guest* . . . but the *right to visit*; this right, to present oneself for society, belongs to all human beings by virtue of the right of possession in common of the earth's surface . . . this right to hospitality does not extend beyond the conditions which make it possible to *seek* commerce with the old inhabitants.
>
> (*TPP*, 328–9, 8:357–8)

In principle, Kant's grounding of the right to hospitality on the "possession in common of the earth's surface" is promising. This community makes them:

> stand in a community of possible physical *interaction* [*physischen möglichen Wechselwirkung*] (*commercium*), that is in a thoroughgoing relation of each to all the others of *offering to engage in commerce* with any other.
>
> (*MoM*, 489, 6:352)

The possibility of seeking society and establishing commerce (*Verkehr*), which constitutes the right to hospitality, has been understood more broadly as exchange and communication. Sankar Muthu, in particular, argues that Kant's use of the Latin term *commercium* means that "the concept of a right to visit also more widely refers to any possible interaction among individuals of different peoples" (2000, 36). However, for the relationality of such an exchange to be reciprocal and egalitarian depends on the goal of these exchanges and the relative standing of the parties in the exchange. Regarding the latter, as I note in the previous chapter, and as Muthu himself acknowledges, Kant's critique of the *means* of European imperialism in his political writings is compatible with inequality among peoples, i.e., a lack of recognition of the value of non-European cultures on equal terms (Muthu 2003, 199–200; see also Bernasconi 2003; Marwah 2012, 2015; Meckstroth forthcoming; Wood 1999).

Regarding the goals of hospitality, on the other hand, we know that *Perpetual Peace*'s goal was to stabilize, likely through reducing, exchanges between Europe and the rest of the world. This is acknowledged by Brian Milstein's work on commercium, which notes that Kant counted on this principle to consolidate the world in separate states, rather than integrating it further (Milstein 2015). In this context, it makes sense that Kant's notion of hospitality is rather minimalistic. For example, in the *Doctrine of Right* Kant characterizes cosmopolitanism as having to do "with the possible union of all nations [*die mögliche Vereinigung aller Völker*] with a view to certain universal laws [*allgemeine Gesetze*] for their possible commerce" (*MoM*, 489, 6:352). In other words, cosmopolitan right is simply the condition of possibility for further exchanges, which, judging from the examples that appear in his cosmopolitan texts, have to do with economic trade with the colonies. The goal of the right to hospitality, then, was likely meant to counter the way in which trade was intimately tied with war and unsanctioned violence at the time he was writing (Meckstroth forthcoming). Kant's praise of China's exclusionary policies and Japan's restriction of all communication between foreigners and locals is consistent with this view: the banning of Europeans or their restriction to a particular space sought to avoid the destructive forms of exchange that characterized Europeans' economic dealings with the rest of the world.

Hence, on the one hand, it is true that Kant amply justifies the need for theorizing interaction and devising ways of regulating it because "individuals and states" stand "in the relation of externally affecting one another" and must therefore be treated as "citizens of a universal state of mankind (*ius cosmopoliticum*)" (*TPP*, 322, 8:349–50). But, on the other hand, it is also true that he was not concerned with subaltern resistance (beyond mentioning the cases of China and Japan) or the challenges of organizing a widely heterogeneous and unequal world. Rather, he was interested in maintaining stable forms of interaction among European states, i.e., relatively equal actors in a relatively restricted realm of interaction.

Despite these limitations, there is in Kant's cosmopolitanism a clear curiosity about how to tackle the question of relationality and loyalties beyond borders. In an excerpt from his *Lectures on the Metaphysics of Morals*, recorded by Vigilantius, we get a suggestive version of this interest:

Just as the cosmopolite views the nature round about him in a practical light, for the exercise of his well-wishing towards it, so the otherwise distinct *cosmotheoros* [student of the world] busies himself with nature only in regard to that knowledge thereof in a theoretical sense, which needs to be increased. This by no means coincides in a moral sense with dutiful global and local patriotism. Both are proper to the cosmopolite, who in fealty to his country *must* have an inclination to promote the well-being of the entire world.

(*MoMV*, 406, 27:673–4)

The cosmopolitan subject in this excerpt is not devoid of loyalty to his own country. Instead, this very loyalty necessitates a cosmopolitan sense. The balance and logical connection of loyalties is central to Kant's account. As Muthu notes, Kant is equally concerned about patriots whose attachments could be detrimental to their love of humanity and by cosmopolitans who, because of the generality of their attachment to "humanity," lose any adherence to individuals (*MoMV*, 406, 27:673; Muthu 2000, 23). The double commitment to the global and the local, in turn, depends on a hospitable engagement with others and the complementarity between these engagements and those that exist at the domestic level. In this interpretation, the notion of complementarity and the mediating role of hospitality in exchanges between realms can be repurposed to consider forms of relationality not envisioned by Kant, so that this notion can give rise to more radical and political versions of communication and action.

In other words, my claim is not that Kant intended the principle of hospitality to be an encompassing political notion of communication and exchange, but rather that agreement that such a "bridge" concept is needed and frustration with the limitations of the Kantian version can fuel a creative process of reconceptualization of a concept that can connect realms in more political and transformative ways. This would require theorizing political interaction without leaving aside how relations of power shape them and how struggles for emancipation emerge, so radically transforming the concept of hospitality. The normative claims that would emerge from such an exercise would be more responsive to a critical engagement with the problems they serve to solve, even if this involves a misinterpretation of the principles as originally articulated. This is consistent with the anachronism I defended in the introduction, in which contemporary preoccupations fuel our engagement with historical texts in a way that results in creative misinterpretation of original texts that, while not faithful to these texts, could not have come about autonomously (Leslie 1970).

Some recent work by neo-Kantian scholars has focused precisely on this project, i.e., making the question of hospitality and commercium work for our time. Milstein, for example, hopes to rescue the notion of "thoroughgoing interaction," which he traces back to Kant's *Critique of Pure Reason*, to provide a cosmopolitan methodology. His approach offers a promising way of conceptualizing how the diversity of human existence is inescapably situated in interaction with one another (2015, 19). Moreover, Milstein also aims to investigate how the full range of this interaction is frustrated by "forces, structures, and institutions [that] emerged out of our own historical struggles to share the earth in common" and eventually "acquire[] an objective, quasi-natural character" (2015, 21). In illuminating this historical process, Milstein aims to show the converse, namely, that the status of boundaries is always contested because it depends on how "participants . . . constitute, reproduce, and transcend modes of identification, community, and boundaries" (2015, 17, 8).

In this framework, cosmopolitanism is a global community of standpoints on community emerging from subjects' participation in thoroughgoing interaction. This participation "generates, renews, and transforms lifewordly relations of community with one another by means of continuous negotiation and renegotiations of social boundaries" (Milstein 2015, 25). In this view, cosmopolitanism is defined by participants' efforts to assert "collective and reflexive control over the global complex of relations through which we share our lives on earth in common with one another" (Milstein 2015, 17). This account usefully redirects our view to really existing instances of political action and remains agnostic about the realms of politics and the shape of institutions that will constitute cosmopolitan arrangements. Moreover, it contains a critique of the state, whose "reified logic compels participants and their communities to adjust to *its* imperatives instead of the other way around" (Milstein 2015, 21). Yet, Milstein's account could be complemented by addressing existing forms of power that are properly transnational, like the "international color line" and the imperial system it sustained. These are relations of power and forms of exclusion that operate beyond the state and also within it, and stand in the way of the "thoroughgoing interaction" from being genuinely reciprocal. Finally, Milstein does not engage with those instances of reciprocal interaction among subaltern actors that take place in defiance of the reifying logic of the state and provide important insights to the potential pathways toward a cosmopolitan condition.

Katrin Flikschuh's work with Martin Ajei is another example of a creative repurposing of the right to hospitality in contemporary theories of global justice. In particular, the pair considers Kantian hospitality as a right to communication that must be initiated by the visitor and presupposes equality (Ajei and Flikschuh 2014). Based on this conceptualization, Ajei and Flikschuh consider whether the contemporary literature on global justice is rightly oriented toward horizontal communication or – instead – maintains a certain colonial mentality preventing such communication (2014, 238). What I find most productive about this approach is that it gets to the core of the performative contradiction of cosmopolitan thought, i.e., the attempt to theorize justice at the global level without being mindful of the hierarchies this thinking contains or the alternative cosmopolitan formations that emerge from subaltern thinking and action. In this exercise, however, they do not always maintain enough interpretive distance from Kant, whose thinking was central in establishing developmental thinking – a target in their critique of the global justice literature (Ajei and Flikschuh 2014, 243).

Interpretively, Flikschuh's more recent work increasingly tends to ask less of Kant and to find more often that he is frequently at "the end of his road," suggesting we see such a situation as an opportunity to put certainties into question and to start the inquiry afresh by listening to those for whom Kant cannot/does not speak (Flikschuh 2017b, 366). This reading gives less authority to Kant and more to the project of reconstructing a form of communication that is genuinely open to the other, while partly abandoning the concern with what "Kant *himself* 'really' thought or intended" (2017b, 365, emphasis in the original). It is this ambivalence that I find most fruitful, along with Flikschuh's acknowledgment that, at some point, Kant is no longer of help. This is because these moves facilitate a theorization oriented toward the present and concerned with the concepts and theories that can provide the most critical purchase *today*. I do still believe that we should at times care about what Kant "really" thought, if only to acknowledge the productivity of his thinking or to consider critically the echoes of his racist, civilizational, and developmental thinking in our current practices of theorization and thus to better contest and rethink those portions. The task of contestation, however, needs to proceed by expanding our realm of substantive concern toward what those whom the West encountered had to say and did in response to those confrontations, a task to which I turn in Chapter 3.

CONCLUSION

In this chapter I have examined neo-Kantian approaches to cosmopolitanism, paying attention to how they theorize transnationalism. I argue that these approaches are limited because they privilege the domestic realm as the primary space of politics. I propose more reciprocal and horizontal readings of Kant's notion of complementary, and address neo-Kantian thinkers that have relied on these dimensions to theorize transnational domination and more reciprocal forms of interaction. In line with these readings, I examine the notion of hospitality as a promising "bridge concept" that can be helpful to conceptualize transnational forms of communication that may be politically consequential for cosmopolitan projects. This examination takes Kant's writings seriously in order to find openings that can be used against his own narrow concerns with European peace. When reading in this way, the authority emerges both from the textual sources *and* from the ability of the readings – however exegetically unfaithful – to plausibly and productively assist us today. This rereading, however, needs to be further enriched by a characterization of the kinds of transnational communication ignored by Kant, enacted by those that contested the bounded realms of the domestic and the international in times of colonialism.[20] In this sense, hospitality could be more radically rethought as a tool to build transnational alliances to contest the hard boundaries of exclusion built along racial lines, which structure domestic and international politics.[21] For this task, Chapter 3 turns to conceptualize transnational cosmopolitanism and a transfigured notion of hospitality based on W. E. B. Du Bois's anti-imperial writings and political action. Transnational cosmopolitanism and the radical hospitality proposed offer notions of identity, solidarity, and public will that depart from existing formations. Transnational cosmopolitanism, in other words, emerges from the juxtaposition between Kant's notions of complementarity and hospitality and the intellectual sources and political practices of subaltern subjects, which remind us to retain "a double-edged attitude to the European Enlightenment" (Spivak 2004, 565n).

---

[20] Kant is, for example, silent on the Haitian Revolution, which was also contemporary to the writing of *Perpetual Peace*.

[21] This is not a prescriptive claim, i.e., a claim that this is the only or the "ideal" form that a transnational cosmopolitanism can take. Instead, it is an effort to open the normative conversation to consider ways in which central power structures associated with race and imperialism were contested. In so doing, we can enrich the available scripts that exist to contest global injustice and advance our normative account of the way in which relational notions like racial identity and solidarity figure in supporting these projects.

3

Du Bois and a Radical,
Transnational Cosmopolitanism

For us [Du Bois] is the originator of the Pan-African movement both in theory and in fact and it is astonishing the number of subjects and the spheres of the intellectual organizational activity in which Dr. Du Bois was 25 years ahead of all other persons in the United States and a good many elsewhere.

C. L. R. James (1973)

The previous chapter engaged with neo-Kantian efforts to theorize the transnational and traced the legacies of the Kantian framework that can still be detected in their approaches. It argued that neo-Kantian scholars have – in different ways – offered promising though ultimately limited ways to consider transnational politics, including Lea Ypi's "cosmopolitan avant-gardes," James Bohman's "overlapping institutional locations," and Seyla Benhabib "jurisgenerativity" (Benhabib 2004; Bohman 2007; Ypi 2012). The chapter also engaged with thinkers like Rainer Forst and Brian Milstein, who have gone beyond Kant by recognizing the centrality of transnational realms of politics for cosmopolitan projects, in particular to counter relations of domination in the international sphere. The previous chapter proposed that a more reciprocal and horizontal reading of Kant's principles is possible – even if it may be creative or disloyal. This chapter implements such a reading but enlists the actors and historical fora that contested the legitimacy of European associations and conceptualizes the particular role of race and empire in shaping power relations transnationally. Rather than merely going "beyond" Kant, this reading "transfigures" (Benhabib 1986, 41–2) the notions of complementarity and hospitality. This means to break radically and qualitatively with the Kantian forms of interconnection that arbitrate between the national and the international and instead center the novel transnational cosmopolitan sphere of politics where the voices excluded can speak and the justice of sanctioned spaces can be put into question.

As I show in this and subsequent chapters, transnational cosmopolitanism transfigures Kantian cosmopolitanism in three ways. First, it involves a transformation in consciousness that allows racialized subjects to reenvision themselves as part of a transnational collective and exit the dynamics of misrecognition of the domestic sphere. Second, this transformation is enabled by the inauguration of a public relying on ties of solidarity and a common sense of imperial temporality as bloody and radical regress, rather than progress. Third, these twin realizations, in turn, feed into new disruptive forms of politics, which upend sanctioned existing spaces of politics. The focus on this chapter is on how W. E. B. Du Bois's hospitable engagements with African, Afro-diasporic, and Asian subjects aesthetically alters subjects' self-understanding and possible communities of cooperation, rather than simply facilitating a smoother interaction between sanctioned realms of politics, as in Kant. Thus transfigured, communication and exchange with foreigners and loyalty in the pursuit of justice domestically can cohere and result in the creative use of alternative spaces and alliances to further justice, which is transformed and reconceived as a transnational problem in the process. Even if domestic political struggles continue, they are partly the product of the strength domestic actors gain from transnational alliances, including a refined understanding of the shape of injustice they face.

A transfigured principle of hospitality no longer serves as a minimalistic form of communication that can further progress toward a republicanism at home and an ordered federation. Instead, a transfigured hospitality puts in question the foundations of that project as imperial and racial and retraces ties of solidarity to inaugurate new spaces of politics, which can politicize and counter imperial relations of domination. A transfigured hospitality transforms a simple right to initiate communication with strangers into the starting point of a politically and normatively productive set of exchanges. This is *because* it shows the dramatic epistemic and political consequences that ensue when excluded groups throughout the world communicate and associate with each other with the purpose of emancipation. These associations do not aim to realize the Enlightenment vision of progress but depart from it by illuminating its harsh imperial face and imagining alternative formations.

I further these claims through an engagement with Du Bois's political craft represented by three events he spearheaded between 1919 and 1947. Transnational cosmopolitanism's focus on these subaltern encounters gives radically new content to the principle of complementarity and redefines the goals that cosmopolitanism pursues. This focus on a cosmopolitanism "of color" is by no means a retreat to the vernacular or an "applied" cosmopolitanism. Instead, it is a necessary complement to theoretical accounts of Western modernity, an incorporation of Afro and other modernities with their own "rhythm, flux, reflux, advances and setbacks" (Gooding-Williams 2011; Hanchard 1999, 267). This examination leads to radical revisions of notions of progress, subjectivity, and publics in ways that deliver on cosmopolitanism's commitment to equal concern. This commitment comes to life in the process of reconstructing these struggles and reconceiving our normative priorities and dominant forms of conceptualizing. This form of attention is what transnational cosmopolitanism is about: highlighting the entanglements between overarching forms of power and local social and political formations in order to faithfully theorize the shape of injustice and the forms of resistance and emancipation that contribute to diverse forms of institutionalization of cosmopolitanism.

In the rest of this chapter I support these claims. The next section engages with Du Bois's writings on empire, colonialism, and radical internationalism. Through these writings, which I explore further in Chapter 4, I reconstruct Du Bois's shifting conceptualization of the transnational toward the definition of the common threads of injustice behind slavery, colonialism, and neocolonialism – a color line that "belts the world." This mature transnationalism, I argue, operates aesthetically over politics, a claim I support through the examination of three events he spearheaded. These actions transform black consciousness and expand the reach of political solidarity toward the transnational. These events creatively combine resources in different realms of politics to disrupt spaces of white diplomacy and advance causes of racial justice in the American polity and colonial spaces. Based on this reconstruction, the last substantive section puts forward a notion of transnational cosmopolitanism that conceptualizes interconnected realms of politics and multiple loyalties in ways that contrast with existing accounts of cosmopolitan patriotism.

PROGRESS IS REGRESS

A nation with a great disease set out to rescue civilization; . . . that disease of race-hatred and prejudice hampered its actions and discredited its finest professions . . . On the other hand, there is not a black soldier but who is glad he went – glad to fight for France, the only real White democracy; glad to have a new, clear vision of the real, inner spirit of American prejudice

W. E. B. Du Bois, "An Essay Toward a History of the Black Man in the Great War," (*ETHBM*, 921–2)

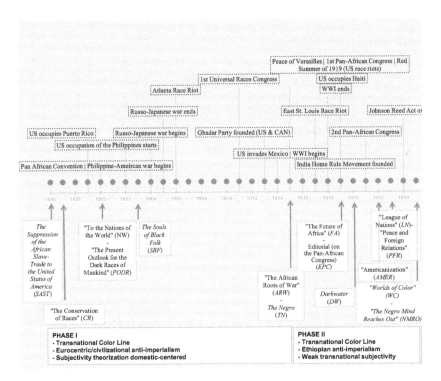

FIGURE 3.1. Timeline: Du Bois's works, stages of imperialism, and historical events

Transnational cosmopolitanism is built upon the transnationalism of W. E. B. Du Bois. Yet, Du Bois's early internationalism – despite containing a critique of the racial foundations of the international order – still contained a liberal developmentalist notion of progress that could "civilize" the worlds of color once their equality was acknowledged.[1] We can see traces of Du Bois's civilizational thinking in his remarks at the first Pan-African Congress in 1900 (see Figure 3.1 for a timeline of historical events, Du Bois's works, and the stages of his anti-imperialism). In this speech, coauthored with other Pan-African leaders, Du Bois appealed to the conscience of the United States and requested it grant the franchise to African Americans. Referring to Britain, "the first champion of Negro freedom," he pleaded for it to continue the work of abolitionists by granting rights of responsible self-government to black colonies (NW).

---

[1] In this, Du Bois's thought echoed imperial critics from Africa and India, who saw avenues of reform within "liberal imperial ideal[s]" but shifted toward more radical critiques when these avenues became more constrained (Mantena 2016, 303).

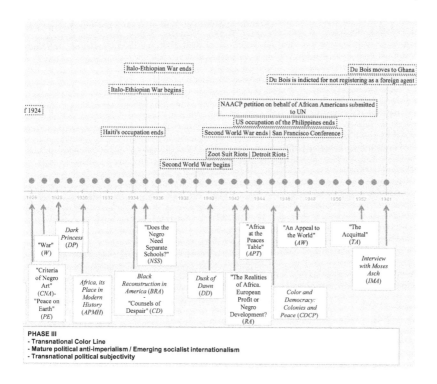

These earlier interventions reveal his trust in the civilizing power of the West, which is also present in his address to the American Negro Academy that same year in which he celebrated the expansion of British imperial possessions in Africa, because "the plain fact remains that no other nation – and America least of all – has governed its alien subjects with half the wisdom and justice that England has" (*PODR*). So, Du Bois's interest at the time was less in self-determination or transnational justice than in fostering "responsible government" in the colonies, which, often times, was reduced to requesting a "gradual transition" to self-government. Du Bois's developmental understanding of world history is tied to a hierarchical view of Africans as uneducated peoples requiring guidance, which Du Bois initially expected would come from Britain and, later on, from African Americans themselves.

Thus, Du Bois's early writings give us no original, radical anti-colonial position, but instead fall into some of the tropes of Eurocentrism I specify in the previous chapters. Du Bois's early developmental thought, in particular, argued for the gradual incorporation of Africans, as a people, or – in the early language of international relations – as a race, as full members of the international regime. The kind of historical genealogy that he espoused either does not grant Africa a place in world history or conceives of its entry to world history as needing guidance. Finally, and relatedly, the teleological character of his civilizational notion of progress led him to de-emphasize – at least in his internationalism – the more nuanced conceptualization of the politics of transnational racial justice and consciousness that characterizes his writings on democratic thought as well as his later transnational thinking.

Throughout the first decades of the twentieth century, Du Bois gradually reconsidered the place of Africa in world history, a shift he associated with his encounter with the work of Frantz Boas. Boas – one of the most influential anthropologists of his time – in a commencement speech at Atlanta University, "awaken[s] [Du Bois] to the complexity, creativity, and historical importance of African civilizations and the need to place African American experience within this frame" (Briggs 2005, 84). This reconsideration expanded Du Bois's scholarly endeavors into the study of African history, geography, and politics (*ARW, ETHBM, RA, APT, APMH,* and *TN*), and motivated a project to assemble an African Encyclopedia. This new intellectual path paved the road for a transnational account that reversed his earlier developmentalism. The full extent of this reconsideration, however, took place only after the World War I.[2] In fact, just before the Great War Du Bois advocates for the participation of African Americans in the war, with the expectation that racial inclusion could follow the detachment of African Americans from their laborer status and their display of courage on the world stage. This effort still betrays some hope that African Americans can find a "place" on the world stage through a supportive alliance with civilized Western powers, a hope that would disappear as African Americans returned from the battlefield to a worsening context of racial violence. A parallel hope that the war would result in an opening toward a colonial government responsive to Africans and Afro-diasporic colonial subjects was also dashed by the League of Nations trusteeship policy, which did little more than transfer former German colonies to other European powers. The postwar context was also characterized by the continued colonial orientation of US foreign policy and frantic debates about the menacing strength of

---

[2] The importance of this event is reflected in his plan to write a history of "the Black Man in the Great War." Du Bois traveled to Paris in 1919 partly with the goal of collecting material for this manuscript, for which he tirelessly, and with little success, sought funding after the war (Keene 2001, 136).

Asia in the international sphere during the first decade of the century (Aviator 1908; Lake and Reynolds 2008; Pearson 1894). Western anxiety about Asian power also appeared domestically in the nativist panic and restrictionism in response to Asian migration to the United States (Higham 2004), a panic also directed toward anti-colonial activists, such as members of Indian nationalist parties relocating to the United States (Sohi 2007), as well as non–Anglo-Saxon European migrants. This particular juncture brought into relief the multiple points of intersection between US racial formations and imperialism and was likely an important impulse in the development of Du Bois's thinking.

Hence, the relevant shift was not in his assessment of the problem as local or transnational, but in the way in which he envisioned the transnational struggle against racism in relation to Western internationalism and Western civilization. The shift was not complete. Some of Du Bois's civilizational hierarchies persisted into the period of his more radical anti-imperialism, like his privileging of African-American leadership on the road to African self-governance. However, we do witness a substantial transformation in Du Bois's outlook on Western civilization, which resulted in the articulation of a radical, racial, and Marxist critique of Western internationalism, which also articulates a political project of emancipation led by the non-West (Mullen 2015, 25).

This shift in tone becomes apparent in the writings during and after the war, which engaged with many of the arguments of imperialism scholars such as John Hobson and Rosa Luxemburg, but more systematically reflected on the role of race prejudice in this phenomenon and the interconnected character of racial injustice at home and abroad. This is clear, for example, in Du Bois's understanding of the connections between modern imperialism and slavery, and between both of those structures and racism:

[T]he Congo Free State . . . differed only in degree and concentration from the tale of all Africa in this rape of a continent already furiously mangled by the slave trade. That sinister traffic, on which the British Empire and the American Republic were largely built, cost black Africa no less than 100,000,000 souls, the wreckage of is political and social life, and left the continent in precisely that state of helplessness which invites aggression and exploitation. 'Color' became in the world's thought synonymous with inferiority, 'Negro' lost its capitalization, and Africa was another name for bestiality and barbarism.

(*ARW*, 708)

Du Bois sees African "bestiality and barbarism" as a wreckage brought about by the traffic in slaved Africans. Moreover, he sees this devastation as leading to the helplessness that would set the stage for colonialism. In other words, slavery produces the barbaric African that racist ideologies see as characteristic of blackness. These racist categories, in turn, support imperial and capitalist profit: "Thus the world began to invest in color prejudice. The 'Color Line' began to pay dividends" (*ARW*, 708).

Importantly, Du Bois sees the development of imperialism as closely connected with developments in Western domestic polities, in a way that cannot be captured by traditional frameworks of democracy and popular sovereignty. He argues that "starvation wage and boundless exploitation of one's weaker and poorer fellows at home" was waning because of what "[w]e called Revolution in the eighteenth century, advancing Democracy in the nineteenth century, and Socialization of Wealth in the twentieth" (*ARW*, 708–9). As a consequence, Western polities cannot be considered fully democratic, not as long as they oppress darker peoples abroad. Instead, he terms this type of regime "democratic despotism:"

[T]he white working man has been asked to share the spoil of exploiting 'chinks and niggers.' It is no longer the merchant prince, or the aristocratic monopoly, or even the employing class, that is exploiting the world: it is the nation; a new democratic nation composed of united capital and labor.

(*ARW*, 709)

Thus racism allowed for the odd pairing between capital and labor, in opposition to oppressed darker peoples at home and abroad. Here the reversal in Du Bois's developmentalism is complete, to the extent that he pairs progress in the West with exploitation abroad.

Transnational cosmopolitanism's attention to grounded forms of domination unearths dynamics that pose a theoretical challenge to existing frameworks. The dynamics Du Bois described as central organizing forms of imperial modernity are opposed to the neo-Kantian view of Western democracies as enlightened leaders of cosmopolitanism. Instead, growing political enfranchisement in the West relies on and requires imperial exploitation. Modernity (i.e., "Revolution . . . Democracy . . . Socialization") within the West is securely tied to despotic relations toward the rest of the world. This not only questions the universalizable character of these advances, i.e., their ability to exist without a dark side, but it establishes an alternative temporality, that of violence and regress, that requires novel languages of emancipation. Notable among the distinct character of the anti-colonial emancipatory struggle is the need to contest the terms established by dehumanizing racist narratives that organize oppression within Western societies and in Western imperial territories, a question that calls for an aesthetic response.

AESTHETICS AND POLITICS

Transnational cosmopolitanism can benefit from attending to the aesthetics of politics because it aims to defamiliarize practices of cosmopolitan theorizing to redirect their focus toward non-sanctioned realms of politics and because it must contest the racialized narratives that organized – just as they do now – domestic and international politics. Appropriately, just as Du Bois's post–World War I political thinking was developing toward the transnational, it also became more explicitly aesthetic in ways that were meaningfully connected. These twin developments were tied to other transitions in his life, notably his move from academia to the National Association for the Advancement of Colored People (NAACP), which he cofounded, becoming the founding editor of its magazine *The Crisis*. During this time, Du Bois noted repeatedly that the persistence of racial prejudice meant that concentrating on the production of social and historical knowledge about African Americans was unlikely to result in a substantial transformation of the political status of blacks in the United States (*IMA*; Lewis 1993, 385). Instead, he argued there was a need to turn to action and propaganda, i.e., to aesthetically reconsider his understanding of the struggle against racial injustice. In this period he theorizes the power of artistic production to shape the perceptions of African Americans in the United States and, in particular, to counter the negative effect of demeaning images in novels, science, and political discourse upon the intellectual resources available to conceive of change:

> The attitude of the white laborer toward colored folk is largely a matter of long continued propaganda and gossip. The white laborers can read and write, but beyond this their education and experience are limited and they live in a world of color prejudice. The curious, most childish propaganda dominates us, by which good, earnest, even intelligent men have come by millions to believe almost religiously that white folk are a peculiar and chosen people whose one great accomplishment is civilization and that civilization must be protected from the rest of the world by cheating, stealing, lying, and murder.
>
> (*NMRO*, 407)

Hence, propaganda operates through a variety of discourses that solidify and legitimize forms of racial exclusion associated with capitalism and imperialism. The sources that proclaim the "myth of mass inferiority of most men" are many ("poet and novelist, the uncanny welter of romance, the half knowledge of scientists, the pseudo-science of statesmen") and put the white worker "absolutely at the mercy of its beliefs and prejudices" (*NMRO*, 407).[3]

Thus, Du Bois's writings on imperialism (further analyzed in Chapter 4) trace the configuration of a world color line that is grounded and sustained by a society of Western democratic regimes that are despotic toward its racial others within and in the colonies. This regime is underpinned by a careful process of construction of racialized others that resulted from the material devastation produced by the slave trade and reinforced by a series of literary, pseudo-scientific, and political narratives that sustain the "myth of mass inferiority" of non-whites. The robustness of this formation and its foundation on the inclusion of non-whites as inferior others is what requires a transfiguration, i.e., the imagination of an alternative regime that qualitatively departs from the current one, rather than a mere request for inclusion. Importantly, imagining such an alternative regime required transforming the common sense of those oppressed, opening avenues for thinking otherwise, a task that Du Bois increasingly saw as associated not with knowledge, but with propaganda, that is, aesthetics.[4] Aesthetics were, for Du Bois, centrally concerned with "truth and goodness" and vital to the construction of an ideal of justice for the "great fight we are carrying on" (*CNA*, 324). He considered art, moreover, "one true method of gaining sympathy and human interest" and altering deep-seated beliefs (*CNA*, 327–8). Du Bois's 1926 essay "Criteria of Negro Art," concerned with the aesthetic as a tool in the struggle for justice, considers the role of the aesthetic in the project of developing an alternative script oriented toward the future. He finds American ideals of strength and possessions somewhat "tawdry and flamboyant" and devoid of the beauty and joy of a "splendid future" that African Americans can devise if they acquire a "new will to be"

---

[3] See also "Of Work and Wealth" (*DW*, 47–59).

[4] The 1920s was a moment ripe for this project. As the editor of *The Crisis*, Du Bois was reaching a sizable black readership, fostered by literacy and town living fueled by the Great War. The mobilization of the war effort had also resulted in a more cosmopolitan orientation among blacks by exposing those who joined the effort to alternative racial formations, and gave way to an intellectual production highlighting blacks' patriotism and their hopes for social and political advancement in recognition of their sacrifices (Whalan 2011, 287). Du Bois sought to capitalize on this moment by redirecting the focus of African Americans and social democratic reformers more broadly away from Europe and the United States.

(*CNA*, 325–6). Moreover, the privileged perspective into imperialist propaganda available to African Americans granted them a central role in the task of debunking the myths of white supremacy, which prevent white labor from seeing capitalist and imperial exploitation for what it is:

White labor is beginning dimly to see this. Colored labor knows it, and as colored labor becomes more organized and more intelligent it is going to spread this grievance through the white world.

(*NMRO*, 408)[5]

In other words, Du Bois's remapped black imagination in ways that made the US polity seem confining – although not obsolete – to their struggle, both in terms of the forms of identification it offered and because the relations of injustice to be countered exceeded such a realm. This move, however, required a wider aesthetic remapping that can be understood through Rancière's "politics of aesthetics," and "aesthetics of politics," examined in the next subsections.

The Politics of Aesthetics

Jacques Rancière defines "the politics of aesthetics" as the way in which aesthetic experience disrupts the distribution of the sensible when subaltern actors upset established meanings and tasks associated with the confined places given to them (2009, 5). Rancière focuses on the ability of subjects to escape certain experiences (like bodily experiences in the case of labor) as the only ones appropriate to them and instead participate in imaginative activities (2009, 7–8). Rancière's work is not attentive to race, but his insights can help articulate the way in which political practice can facilitate black subjects' escape from the places of slave, laborer, and criminal they had been granted by the American polity.

There are three parallel moves in Du Bois that unsettle black subjects' assigned places in US society. First, as editor and commentator of *The Crisis*, Du Bois positioned himself as a visible actor in the debates about African-American participation in World War I. His enthusiasm in this

---

[5] Du Bois's mature conceptualization of exploitation is indebted to Marxism, although – as Joel Olson notes – amended by considering how racial alliances, i.e., the sharing of white privilege across classes, undercuts the potential of the proletariat as a universal class. This situation leaves the "dark worlds" to fulfill the role of the universal class (Olson 2005, 122–5). This role becomes all the more important because of the strength of white solidarity, which makes the political question of grouping together the "worlds of color" a priority in Du Bois's work.

instance was closely associated with the possibility of African Americans exiting their laborer status and earning recognition as warriors, a distancing of the always readily available association of African Americans with slavery and forced labor (*ETHBM*; Du Bois 1919; Keene 2001). Second, after the war's end, Du Bois positioned himself and his Pan-African associates as direct interlocutors of Woodrow Wilson and the Allies congregating in Paris to discuss the question of trusteeships and the founding of the League of Nations. In so doing, he refigured himself and the association of Afro-diasporic subjects that made up the Pan-African Congress as statesmen, a status clearly denied to them at the time.[6] Finally, as a commentator in debates about the crisis of the West that took place before and after the war, Du Bois highlighted the significance of the rise of Japan as an empire and its defeat of the Russian Empire in 1905. The feeling of Western anxiety only deepened after the ravages of World War I further put into question the achievements of Western civilization and, with it, the white race. Du Bois welcomed these events from a world historical perspective, valuing in particular their ability to shatter the common sense of Whites' unquestionable dominance of the world sphere advanced by scientific racism. On the occasion of the Russo–Japanese war, for example, he noted that "a great white nation has measured arms with a colored one and been found wanting," something that will surely be followed by the "awakening of the black and brown races" (Du Bois 2005 [1906], 33–4).

These three examples concern the politics of aesthetics because they distance racialized subjects or peoples from their assigned "place" and problematize the status of the West as the superior civilization. In intervening in these debates and highlighting these events to his black readership, Du Bois expanded the range of experiences that racialized subjects could lay claim to and opened the way for their political voice. Not all of these shifts are equally promising in terms of allowing racialized subjects to attain political subjectivity, or at least not directly so. One may see Du Bois's desire to see black soldiers fight for the United States as an instance of closure, given their recruitment into a project of aggression and militarism. Yet again, as the epigraph to this section suggests, army service not only allowed African American to be soldiers, it also made them travelers and nascent cosmopolitans, something that – given mobility for African diasporas was either forced or limited, but never free – is

---

[6] See the next section for a fuller account of this event.

highly significant. If we focus on the ability of soldiers to partake of the world of the traveler, not just the soldier, and thus to become familiar with European metropoles, new languages, and alternative forms of race relations, the shift in position suddenly appears politically more productive. Moreover, Du Bois trusted their participation in the war to create the conditions for political openings for reforms upon their return. A similar critique could be raised at Du Bois's celebration of Japan's victory over Russia, which fits well with his earlier developmental thinking that values the ability of the worlds of color to partake in military aggression. Yet again, it is clear in Du Bois's thinking that world power status is not a purely militaristic attainment, it is rather a process that is deeply enmeshed with narratives of Western cultural and political superiority underpinning white supremacy. In this sense, the promise of the Japanese military victory operates as a threat to the supposedly invulnerable hegemony of the white race.[7]

Highlighting these events allowed Du Bois to make the case that colonial and racial domination is never complete. This is also a reason why he focused on the existence of independent or rebellious African states and other experiences of anti-colonial resistance ("insurgent Morocco, independent Abyssinia and Liberia" [*NMRO*, 389]). When discussing English imperialism he recounted the demands of Indians in Kenya and their alliance with native workers resulting in "a yielding by England to the darker world" and an acknowledgment that "the common demand for a measure of representative government will in the long run prove irresistible" (*NMRO*, 405–6). Second, he called for experiences of rebellion to tempt "other black and subject populations" to agitate for freedom and autonomy (*NMRO*, 389), i.e., to be considered political resources and be rightly claimed to become part of their political imagination.

These moments and spaces in which excluded groups occupy new roles and successfully address sites of power are the ones toward which theorizing is reoriented in a transnational cosmopolitan framework. These moments alert us theorists to the inadequacy of existing institutions to host these views and suggest potential reconfigurations of these institutional structures.

---

[7] As Robert Vitalis has noted, international relations emerged as the discipline of race relations. Relatedly, the journal *Foreign Affairs* was born the *Journal of Race Development*, reflecting the "constitutive role of imperialism and racism in bringing an academic discipline in the United States into existence" (Vitalis 2010, 2015).

The Aesthetics of Politics

The second dimension of transfiguration that I wish to highlight is the "aesthetic of politics," i.e., the task of "configuring the sensible texture of the community for which . . . laws and constitutions make sense," including the question of which objects are common and which subjects are included in the community (Rancière 2009, 8–9). When Du Bois denies the exceptional character of the United States and aligns its history with the slave trade and European imperialism (Balfour 2011; *SAST*), and later further reconfigures the experience of black oppression in the United States as a particular instantiation of colonial domination (*NMRO*) he makes visible and intelligible a structure of domination obscured by particular sensible world contained in American exceptionalism:

> But one thing is sure and that is the fact that since the fifteenth century these ancestors of mine and their other descendants . . . have suffered a common disaster and have a long memory . . . But the physical bond is least and the badge of color relatively unimportant save as a badge; the real essence of this kinship is its social heritage of slavery; the discrimination and insult; and this heritage . . . extends through yellow Asia and into the South Seas. It is this unity that draws me to Africa.
>
> (*DD*, 117)

The "unity" between African Americans, Africa, and Asia originated in a "common disaster" but went beyond it. In order to activate these affinities, Du Bois fully immersed himself in networks of communication and exchange with other groups struggling against racial and colonial domination and relayed this experience to a black audience. Du Bois's goal here was to foster a hospitable orientation among African Americans toward other struggles against the color line, so that they came to see their own plight as shared with those of Africans, the broader African diaspora, and other colonial subjects. Moreover, his call extended to reformist intellectuals and social scientists interested in emancipation, who also failed to see the way in which their agendas dovetailed with the colonial question:

> [I]s it not possible that our research is not directed to the vital spots geographically? Our good-will is too often confined to that labor which we see and feel and exercise around us, rather than to the periphery of the vast circle, where unseen and inarticulate, the determining factors are at work. And may not the continual baffling of our effort and failure of our formula be due to just such mistakes? . . . At least it will be of absorbing interest, to step within these distant world shadows and, looking backward, view the European and white American labor problem from this wide perspective.
>
> (*NMRO*, 385–6)

This excerpt announces Du Bois's project of centering colonial subjects' struggles of emancipation and challenges the consideration of the problem of "labor" in isolation to the question of colonialism. The essay containing these lines – "The Negro Mind Reaches Out" – is a deeply aesthetic call to shift perspectives on emancipation, to look at the problem "backwards" by attending to "unseen and inarticulate" factors. The lack of theoretical interest in colonial peoples made evident the limited character of progressive common sense and political imagination and produced a mistaken picture of the politics of emancipation, from which Du Bois radically departed. Du Bois's interest in joining the question of emancipation with the anti-imperialist struggle also contrasts with the lack of interest in the emancipation of peoples of color or the outright support for their dependent status, which characterized the emergent discipline of international relations. About this field, Robert Vitalis notes that no white scholar argued "for the restoration of black citizenship rights, the dismantling of Jim Crow in the United States, and self-governance, let alone independence, for the colonies" (2015, 10–11). But beyond criticizing his contemporaries in the political arena and in the academy, Du Bois was interested in the aesthetic task of bringing to life a transnational community. "The Negro Mind Reaches Out" contributed to this goal by "likening and contrasting each land and its far-off shadow," meaning European countries and their colonial possessions. The essay contains detailed accounts of the character of colonial domination as well as instances of resistance taking place in different areas. Du Bois was interested in highlighting commonalities, like when he notes that "the characteristic of all color-line fights" is the "tearing apart of all rational division of opinion." He illustrated this by referring to the boycott of Sao Thomé cocoa – where "[l]iberalism, anti-slavery and cocoa capitalism [fought] Toryism, free Negro proprietors and economic independence" (*NMRO*, 388). For Du Bois, the localized and specific character of colonial oppression around the world could not obscure the commonalities that characterize "all color-line fights."

These moves are inherently transnational *and* aesthetic because they highlight that the obvious forms of community – the American polity or US blacks – are not quite squared with the character of injustice, and redirects attention toward the political community that is relevant in the fight against racial injustice, whose members are variously located throughout the world. Hospitality is therefore transfigured because communication and a receptive stance toward actors and events beyond the confines of the US polity inaugurates a new community made up of rebellious Haitian slaves, black intellectuals in European metropoles, African Americans struggling for racial justice, and anti-colonial activists. This hospitality does not mediate between realms so that they can remain intact but interact peacefully. Instead, the goal was to contest the benevolence of both the American experiment and Western cooperation, as well as to denounce sovereignty as an institution that obscures the marginalized from domestic and international realms and allows for the maintenance of imperial domination.[8]

Transnationalized Cosmopolitanism

The framework of transnational cosmopolitanism I propose focuses on the pursuit of racial justice by allied actors who are differently located but whose fates are determined by the color line and/or other forms of power operating transnationally. The compatibility of multiple loyalties that simultaneously advance the betterment of domestic polities and reform in other spheres emerges from the hospitable embrace of others' struggles. This embrace follows from the recognition of linked political fates and common sources of injustice and exclusion from formal realms of politics. This commonality is realized and furthered through transnational opportunities for communication, understanding, and political association, which come from the hospitable reception of others. The transnational cosmopolitanism that emerges does not require subjects to abandon group identity (that of "dark Americans," in Du Bois's words) in favor of a different one, but rather that they are able to reconstruct commonalities emerging from history and a shared experience of injustice, which can ground their multiple identities and orient them toward different arenas of politics and different forms of coalition through which they can advance toward emancipation. The next section recounts three events in which Du Bois performs such an understanding of politics.

---

[8] While the notion of hospitality might seem inadequate because of its reference to a visit, which in turn seems temporary, I aim for the term to reflect the openness to new encounters that can then develop into more long-standing communication, coalition making, and the formation of counter-publics. Thus, the transfigured hospitality signals the importance of the original moment of openness to the other that may in turn result in productive political action that aims for radical transformation.

DU BOIS AND THE EVENT

As Du Bois was reconceptualizing his understanding of racial injustice, emancipatory politics, and black subjectivity in his writing, he was also enacting radical new ways of doing politics in a transnational cosmopolitan way. These actions combined loyalty to the cause of racial justice in the United States with an understanding that such a cause was intimately entwined with other forms of emancipation pursued by actors abroad and needed to be pursued tactically in several realms at once. His political craft shows the possibility of doing politics beyond the spheres of the domestic and the international in ways that both highlight their exclusionary character and contest their status as the natural *loci* of politics. Access to these spheres was restricted for him as an African American and for colonial subjects, but by tracking his actions we can see him inaugurating alternative networks of communication, which resulted in novel forms of affiliation and made clear the limitations of Western "democracy" and "peaceful internationalism." His actions thus upset traditional spaces of white diplomacy that closed off anti-imperial critiques. Attention to these instances of political craft is valuable for the theorization of transnational cosmopolitanism because it zooms into the struggles that emerge in reaction to global currents of injustice, which would otherwise be lost in traditional accounts.

This reconstruction shows that the concept of sovereignty underlying both our conception of democratic politics and its formal separation from the realm of international politics was challenged by the actions of a set of intellectuals and activists who saw them as limitations to their projects of emancipation. The work of transfiguration by transnational cosmopolitanism makes intelligible a problem that Western political thought had not sought to conceptualize but that is needed to contest the organizing ideology of sovereignty and international society. This move is theoretical even if it follows from the examination of how activists (in this case, black and brown colonial intellectuals and activists) were and are involved in political action based on political affinities that did not emerge out of national communities. Conceptualizing these struggles exclusively as movements of self-determination or democratic inclusion, as statist cosmopolitans do, obscures the rich cosmopolitan currents that intersect with, and make intelligible, these different scripts of emancipation. The political craft involved in each of the three events described next shows that multiple loyalties are compatible and emerge organically from the day-to-day political work, the obstacles that are encountered domestically, and the possibilities that result from a hospitable engagement with actors and institutions exceeding the realm of the domestic. This claim is connected to the entwined character of injustice, but it is also distinctly political: it shows the particular way in which actors affected by common threads of injustice find each other, communicate, and act in concert.

In the rest of this section I discuss Du Bois's organization of the 1919 meeting of the Pan-African Congress, his domestic and international advocacy on behalf of the colonies, and his interaction with the United Nations (UN) on behalf of African Americans. We see in these events Du Bois invested in propaganda, pursuing a transformation that requires upsetting common ways of doing things by making salient "unusual or difficult" questions in ways that call for reflective engagement or deliberate focus (Rogers 2012, 189; Hopf forthcoming, 3). Du Bois attained this through creative action that connected isolated spheres of politics and combined loyalties to different but overlapping groups engaged in the struggle against racial injustice.

The Pan-African Movement

In 1919, Du Bois found himself in Paris as a newspaper correspondent at the Peace Conference meeting, where European powers came together to discuss the postwar settlement. The January issue of *The Crisis* asserted that Du Bois had traveled to Paris in a threefold capacity, including reporting on the peace meeting as a correspondent of *The Crisis* and collecting material that would go into the "History of the American Negro in the Great War." The third goal of this trip was:

> ... bringing to bear all pressure possible on the delegates at the Peace Table in the interest of the colored peoples of the United States and the world.
>
> (*FA*, 111)

Thus, Du Bois sees the lack of representation of peoples of color under colonial rule and that of "colored peoples of the United States" as parallel events. By summoning a Pan-African Congress in Paris at the same time the victorious powers were meeting at the Peace Conference, Du Bois aimed to call attention to the questions of internationalization of the former German colonies and the claims of blacks throughout the world (*EPC*, 112). At the time, Du Bois's program for the mandates system – which he had also sent officially to President Woodrow Wilson – aspired only to a "partial self-determination." In it, he proposed that decisions about the fate of German colonies should be left to a "public opinion" composed of the "chiefs and intelligent Negroes, natives of the German colonies in Africa," the "twelve million civilized Negroes of the United States," the "educated persons of Negro descent in South America and the West Indies," and the educated classes among the Negroes of French and British colonies (*FA*, 119). In this document Du Bois makes explicit a notion of public opinion that does not coincide with the domestic or international realm of politics but nonetheless possesses enough coherence and critical purchase to claim to be a legitimate representative of the former German colonies. What is notable in this plan – which did not progress – is the claim to legitimate authority, representation, and self-determination it contained.[9] Du Bois's claim suggests an affinity among transnationally located African and Afro-diasporic subjects that makes any decision on the fate of the colonies simply illegitimate without them.

The gathering of a group of "educated Negroes" in the same metropole where Western states were congregating put the question of their exclusion in stark relief, showing that the white diplomatic spaces, which were taken for granted, could no longer function unopposed. The presence of Africans and Afro-diasporic subjects, their knowledge of the issue, and their willingness to participate, prevented business as usual. Those who were excluded from the Western forum because of their status as "subject peoples" performed the role of statesmen in a parallel forum, hence disproving the very claims that denied them the capacity to self-govern and altering the distribution of the sensible. This goal of disruption and the push to reconsider the makeup of the community of concern was quite overt, as Du Bois noted:

A conference held to consider the disposition of the German colonies in Africa will serve, perhaps, better than any other means that could be taken, to focus the attention of the peace delegates and the civilized world of the just claims of the Negro everywhere.

(*EPC*, 112)

Unsurprisingly, the United States and other colonial countries explicitly opposed the meeting and denied visas to those who attempted to attend, and France officially denied the event was taking place (Contee

---

[9] It is important to note that the anti-colonial scripts providing the context for Du Bois's writings in the post–World War I era were broader than the request for self-determination that we have narrowly come to associate with anti-colonialism, as has been recently noted by scholars (Getachew forthcoming; Lawrence 2013; Wilder 2015).

1972, 16; Marable 1986, 101; *PAM*, 15). Du Bois went against these warnings and Paris's martial law in his efforts to organize the congress. Through the Senegalese Commissaire-Géneral in charge of recruiting native African troops he managed to obtain Premier George Clemenceau's approval ("Don't advertise it . . . but go ahead") (*PAM*, 15).

The material inauguration of this public and its aesthetic effects of transfiguring the existing regime of domestic and international politics was evidence of the existence of a collective political actor with a "place in the world" and an emerging consciousness, the product of mutual hospitality, communication, cooperation, and past joint actions. As in the case of any political venture, this was not always a harmonious one, but it had emerged from the realization of the common racial roots of the injustice faced by "the Negro everywhere" (*EPC*, 112). It was also an attempt to disrupt tightly staged international politics – along with its intention to dispose of the world by attending exclusively to the goals of European well-being and stability – by highlighting the lack of peace or justice at the core of European empire and American democracy. These claims, which by definition belonged neither in the international realm nor the domestic one, were a cosmopolitan intervention in the sphere of international politics, faithful to Du Bois's commitment to furthering racial justice in multiple realms.

The resistance to these meetings persisted until the 1921 Pan-African Congress, which Du Bois also organized, and about which he noted:

That aroused the colonial powers . . . they thought I was trying to start a revolution in Africa, which I wasn't at all. All I was trying to do is to get educated Africans in all parts of the world to come together and know each other, and talk to each other, and see what kind of program could be laid out for the future emancipation of Africans in their own country.

(*IMA*, 3:40)

The domestic character of the struggle – i.e., the fact that Africans' emancipation would take place in "their own country" – does not negate the cosmopolitan character of the recognition of a common fate and the political process through which this emancipation eventually came about. The mutual hospitality that made possible the acquaintance and communication among educated Africans and Afro-diasporic subjects was the condition of possibility for emancipatory projects to take off in diverse locales. Moreover, the communication itself was revolutionary in its ability to sidestep the exclusionary structure of the international sphere and reconceive of dispersed subjects of empire as sharing a common fate and able to oppose race-based oppression, however differently institutionalized. This political intervention thus attempted to reconfigure the community that was expected to partake in the governance of the world.

The Founding of the UN

Du Bois's work on behalf the colonies was not restricted to his involvement in the Pan-African Congress. In 1945, as Western powers defined the shape of the postwar international sphere, Du Bois campaigned tirelessly for the representation of colonial countries in the UN, calling for the US government to act as advocate (Du Bois 1978a [1945], 6; Lewis 2000, 503–5; Matthews 1945). He timed the publication of his book *Color and Democracy: Colonies and Peace* to coincide with the San Francisco conference (Yvi 1945), and supported – unsuccessfully – the inclusion of an article in the UN charter that would recognize the undemocratic character of colonial government and the right of self-determination, a position supported by China and Russia (Du Bois 1978b [1945], 11–12; The Chicago Defender 1945a). The visibility of Du Bois's actions was increased when he was granted access to the San Francisco Conference as one of three consultants from the NAACP, one of the forty-two nongovernmental organizations given access to meetings with US delegates during the conference (William 1998; *PAM*) . After the conference, Du Bois publicly condemned the lack of US support for the clause of self-determination in the charter (The Chicago Defender 1945a) and spoke at the Senate Foreign Relations Committee to this effect (The Chicago Defender 1945b). His inquiries – widely covered by black newspapers – made evident the muted exclusions that plagued the construction and eventual shape of the UN.

In this manner, Du Bois along with a few anti-colonial activists present at the San Francisco conference, and the official delegations of Ethiopia, Haiti, and Liberia, brought the voice of colonial peoples to the same arena where their imperial masters were defining their fate. The effort of the US government to reach out to civil society in the hope of legitimizing the internationalist project of the UN had the effect of bringing out domestic dissident voices, which pointed out the wrongs that would mark the origins of this institution. The hospitality of Du Bois – and the NAACP – to the anti-colonial cause and the past linkages established between them and anti-colonial intellectuals and activists, broke with the commonsensical exclusion of "subject peoples" by incorporating an anti-imperial critique that would otherwise have been absent from the forum. Du Bois once more operated over the politics of aesthetics, exiting his expected role – in this case that of a "member of U.S. civil society" – to adopt the perspective of colonial peoples excluded from the forum. The strength of the critique depended not only on the (symbolic) democratic opening in the domestic arena, but also on the United States' international stature and its self-conception as a liberal world power. While Du Bois had no illusions about the benevolence of the American leadership, he still relied on this trope to highlight how "America's democratic ideals were compromised by the government's 'alliance with colonialism imperialism and class dictatorship'" (Marable 1986, 169). The political meaning of this (ultimately unsuccessful) move exceeds the end point of granting representation to colonial countries. In the medium term, as Du Bois knew well, the recognition of colonial countries in the international sphere would prove complementary in yet another way; as an asset in the potential international support for the African-American struggle within the United States.

Moreover, Du Bois's advocacy on behalf of the colonies, along with his own writing on the postwar meetings, had the further effect of reaching a broad African-American readership through newspapers like *The Chicago Defender*, the *Baltimore Afro-American*, and the *New York Amsterdam News*, among others, which covered the discussions about colonialism to a larger extent than mainstream media (see also Chapter 5). In this sense, the critique of world powers and American leadership was also part of an ongoing conversation about transnational, racial injustice within this subnational public, whose allegiances beyond the national could only be strengthened by these events. The extensive publicity of these actions in black newspapers solidified linkages of solidarity and transnational community between African Americans and colonial subjects. This move expanded critical awareness of the duplicitous character of US liberalism, in this way reconfiguring the shape of the community that was intelligible to African Americans from the domestic toward the transnational, and operating over the aesthetics of politics.

An Appeal to the World

In 1947, under the auspices of the NAACP, Du Bois led a group of researchers in the preparation of "An Appeal to the World," a report describing the dire conditions of black Americans to be presented to the UN (*AW*). The grievances described and criticized included underfunded public schools, lynching, and political disenfranchisement. The report defines these ills as human rights violations and solicits UN intervention on behalf of African Americans. The preparation and presentation of this report followed in the steps of India's filing of a complaint to the UN regarding the mistreatment of Indian workers in South Africa and a number of petitions of US black organizations regarding "systemic practices of segregation, discrimination, and racial violence" (Roberts 2014, 155). In fact, when Du Bois presented the idea to the NAACP president Walter White, he emphasized his desire to join other countries in presenting petitions, and saw the situation of black Americans as "not merely parallel but . . . part of a broader anti-colonial politics" (MacKinnon 2019, 65). The presentation of this report was opposed by many, including human rights and civil rights advocate Eleanor Roosevelt, who was a member of the NAACP board. While Roosevelt had earlier facilitated the access of the NAACP delegation to the San Francisco conference, this time she saw the event as an embarrassment to the United States and an issue that would be seized upon by the Soviet Union (Lewis 2000, 503; Marable 1986, 169). The complaints regarding racial violence and disenfranchisement were indeed taken up by the Soviet delegation in order to argue for the inclusion of a nondiscrimination clause in the UN Covenants, which were also under discussion in 1947. Without such a clause, the Soviet Ambassador in Paris claimed that "the lynching of negroes would continue" (Economic and Social Council 1947, 10–11; cited in Roberts 2014, 168). These events were covered widely by black newspapers, as well as in the mainstream national and international press, but the UN responded by acknowledging its inability to do anything on behalf of the petitioners and the sanctioning of the Covenants was famously postponed until 1966.

This event again powerfully enacts principles of transnational cosmopolitanism through an aesthetic intervention that upset diplomatic spaces where United States hegemonic power was taken for granted. In this case, however, domestic injustice was furthered through the mobilization of a cosmopolitan public opinion. While the UN was a union of states, rather than individuals or other groupings, Du Bois's intervention continued in a series of efforts by subaltern actors to disrupt this arena and – with it – the dominance of Western powers in it. Du Bois's goals were many, including contributing to the reconfiguration of this forum as one where issues that were not exclusively interstate could be raised. Despite the UN's refusal to take up the Indian complaint or the NAACP petition, this forum amplified the claims of African Americans, brought into relief the limited enforcement capabilities of the institution that was supposed to uphold human rights, and illuminated the United States' role in blocking a more capacious human rights regime. Du Bois's intervention upset common ways of doing things in the international sphere by washing the United States' "dirty laundry" in a global forum and thus tarnishing its democratic credentials.[10] In so doing, and in alliance with supportive non-Western countries and publics of particular countries, notably India (Krishna 1947), he relocated the moral authority and identification with human rights to the non-West while at the same time placing the West under scrutiny.

In this case, the cosmopolitan sphere was deployed in order to correct, or at least highlight, the failed character of American democracy, and Du Bois once again engaged strategically with the United States' stature abroad by exposing its poor record of racial democracy. Aesthetically, on the one hand, Du Bois contested the sensible structure of the international by challenging the legitimacy of the nascent US liberal hegemony. On the other hand, the move also relied on an alternative political community available to US blacks by requesting solidarity from other dark peoples in the international arena. Luis Cabrera identifies this forum a "global institutional imaginary" (2018) and Emma MacKinnon sees it as a "a kind of declaration of rights" that stages the "messiness of the overlapping categories of state, nation, and people (2019, 65) My own approach re-grounds the global and goes further than noting the overlap of political categories by highlighting that transnational interconnections are persistent features of world politics. This persistence means that, rather than simple messiness of state, nation, and people as categories, transnationalism is an alternative political realm, which emerges because those categories' exclusions of subjects and occlusions of relations of responsibility push subjects to find political openings elsewhere. This is a point that I sustain further through the examination of solidarity and the anti-colonial counter-public in Chapters 4 and 5. Moreover, unlike neo-Kantian political theory work that privileges Western domestic spheres as particularly virtuous and oriented toward cosmopolitan feeling, this case illustrates how resistance to racial domination had to occur

---

[10] As several scholars have noted, this disconnect troubled US government officials because of the limits it imposed on its diplomatic Cold War strategy and its ability to make a case for representative government abroad (Anderson 2003; Dudziak 2011; Roberts 2014, 162–4).

outside this space, i.e., creatively inaugurate an alternative one, which was used to publicize the injuries suffered at the hands of a world power and delegitimize its world standing. Moreover, the contrasting behavior of Du Bois and Roosevelt, who privileged the standing of the United States as a liberal leader in opposition to communist Russia over racial justice, reveals the different forms of loyalty that can be enacted and their different relation to cosmopolitan justice. By requesting UN intervention, Du Bois purposively demoted the United States to the position of a polity whose internal affairs warranted international concern. In contrast, Eleanor Roosevelt's followed her condemnation of such a move with a threat to resign from the NAACP board and a refusal to continue granting the institution access to the UN (Roberts 2014, 169–70). Roosevelt's intervention privileged loyalty to a narrative of exceptionalism at odds with domestic justice and went further by closing-off paths to the creative and strategic use of alternative arenas characteristic of the transnational cosmopolitanism I propose.

Finally, this event highlights conceptually that the cosmopolitan actor may not be the individual who seeks to combine loyalty to her own country with the maxim of helping others in need in other countries – these being goals potentially in tension – but rather a marginal actor who shows that in loyalty to justice in one's own country she may have to exceed the domestic realm of politics at times. This is the political dimension of transnational cosmopolitanism and yet another facet of the radical complementarity of realms enacted by Du Bois. Transnational cosmopolitanism, far from resulting from the actions of virtuous Western democracies, brings into focus how pockets of exclusion within these regimes result in solidaristic coalition-making with other localized struggles to denounce entangled domestic and international exclusions.

TOWARD A RADICAL HOSPITALITY

The previous sections engaged with the writing and political action of Du Bois to recover a transnational cosmopolitanism that acknowledges the interconnected character of realms by conceiving of imperial injustice as inherently transnational and prescribing emancipatory political action that straddles traditional realms of politics. This reconstruction transfigures the notions of communication and hospitality that are central in Kantian and neo-Kantian accounts of cosmopolitanism by giving new meanings and new goals to the notions of communication and exchange at the heart of hospitality. In particular, it shows that differently located groups suffering connected forms of injustice can – through a hospitable engagement – jointly pursue emancipatory political action through the creative use of existing and newly inaugurated spaces of politics. This exchange is no longer devoted to easing a stable transition toward an ordered world of sovereign states, but breaks from the liberal narrative of progress by indicting spaces of diplomacy as spaces where imperial domination is sanctioned, and performing new forms of loyalty and community.

These coalitional practices disrupted diplomatic milieus, which upheld and policed boundaries between the domestic and international, as well as those between the self-governing peoples and "dependencies." Diplomatic spheres – an "array of socially organized and meaningful ways of doing things in the international stage" (Pouliot and Cornut 2015, 299; Sending et al. 2015) – were a perfect target of concerted action by colonial and neocolonial subjects invested in contesting questions of jurisdiction, authority, and (mis)representation playing out in those spaces. If diplomatic practices "bring the world into being" and thus legitimize and rationalize traditional ways of doing things (Pouliot 2016, 11, 53), transnational cosmopolitanism uncovers actors and actions that delegitimize claims to representation by Western powers and throw into relief the unjust exclusion of certain groups from international governance decisions.

This discussion also highlights the aesthetic character of the transfiguration of hospitality and the contrast between this notion and the Kantian transactional form of exchange or communication.[11] On the one hand, these events shows marginal political subjects taking new places and performing new, disruptive, roles not given to them willingly

---

[11] The notion of transfigured hospitality I put forward, however, does not imply a claim that this hospitality is absolute or devoid of hierarchy, conflict, or tension. Here it is pertinent to bring up Derrida's insight regarding the duplicitous character of the Latin *Hospitalität* and the German *Wirtbarkeit*, terms that contain traces of hospitality/hostility and host/patron, respectively (Derrida 2000, 4). The second opposition is particularly pertinent in the case of Du Bois, who at times offered himself, or African Americans as a whole, as patrons of other subjects around the world in need of emancipation. Conceptually, I am interested in the openness of the concept of communication that underlies transnational cosmopolitanism, an openness that allows for notions of progress to be disrupted and revealed as tragically narrow. In other words, I expect the transfigured hospitality to remain a realm where new arrangements remain subject to contestation, with emerging forms of hierarchy or patronage continuously contested, rather than resulting in an ideal and harmonious form of communication.

(e.g., non-white countries as world powers, US blacks as cosmopolitan soldiers, US blacks and anti-colonial leaders as statesmen, US blacks as representatives of the colonies in the San Francisco Conference, and subjects in need of UN protection). On the other hand, these actions also reconfigure the community both in terms of the formation of new groups of kindred subjects and the vision of Western domestic polities that prevails (that of exceptional democracies to lead the world toward cosmopolitanism or that of colonial and neocolonial states).

TOWARD TRANSNATIONAL COSMOPOLITANISM

Based on these resources, I propose a transnational cosmopolitanism with three dimensions: (a) transnational cosmopolitanism is possible in theory because injustice within a polity cannot be neatly tied to exclusively domestic processes and because these broader processes also oppress groups whose ills cannot be neatly defined as citizens' grievances against their government or states' grievances against other states, i.e., the ontological point; (b) transnational cosmopolitanism may emerge from communication and interaction across borders whenever political resources at the disposal of actors facing a hostile, domestic or international sphere exist in realms that do not neatly coincide with the original framing of the problem and is likely to lead to an enriched understanding of the nature of injustice, i.e., the political point; and (c) when these connections take place and joint action ensues, significant transformations in the consciousness of the individuals involved in such struggles follows, i.e., the ethical point. In other words, creative problem solving and the opening of opportunities for exchange across borders lead to the discovery of affinities and the formation of alliances that will benefit from the leveraging of different realms of politics (i.e., domestic, international, and transnational cosmopolitan) against each other. These processes, in turn, lead to the reconsideration of the nature of injustice and the transformation of the consciousness of participants in the struggle.

Thus, the transnational cosmopolitanism I build finds synergy between loyalty to and work toward domestic justice and coalition making with those affected by similar threads of injustice abroad. This synergy does *not* follow from a virtuous republic that conducts itself benevolently toward others abroad – as neo-Kantians imagine – but from marginalized members of a polity, who must resort to alliances beyond borders to struggle against the lack of progress within the polity *because* of the transnational roots of domestic arrangements. Transnational cosmopolitanism tracks those spaces of politics that are neither domestic nor international, and those forms of coalition that disrupt the taken-for-granted governance practices at the domestic and international level.

The notion of transnational cosmopolitanism proposed can be contrasted with a prominent view of cosmopolitan patriotism that echoes neo-Kantians' focus on Western democracies as the initiators of cosmopolitan change. This is the view that certain forms of patriotism or national identification can train citizens to eventually develop ties of solidarity toward other countries. This form of gradual enlargement of circles of concern characterizes the work of Martha Nussbaum on cosmopolitan patriotism but is also present in Elizabeth Anderson's work on integration (Anderson 2010, 2; Nussbaum 2008). Nussbaum's account of cosmopolitan patriotism (which reconsiders the one she articulated in the 1990s) puts forward the following grounds for the embrace of patriotism:

National states of the sort described need the moral sentiments even more if they are going to undertake projects that require considerable sacrifice of self-interest, such as substantial internal redistribution or copious foreign aid, the overcoming of discrimination against traditionally marginalized groups, or the protection of allies against unjust domination. Such projects are good projects for nations to undertake. Therefore, we have even stronger reasons for the cultivation of nation-directed moral sentiments.

(Nussbaum 2008, 81–2)

Nussbaum's assumption is that a gradual development of moral sentiment will gradually enlarge citizens' ability to care for larger groups, including fellow citizens (that would benefit from redistribution) and non-nationals (like citizens of developing countries who would benefit from foreign aid). But this unidirectionality seems to exclude forms of critical loyalty of the kind Du Bois enacts. This loyalty involves discovering the connections between one's group's cause and that of others' abroad, based on a stark critique of the domestic polity and its exclusionary character. The persistent theorization of the domestic and the cosmopolitan as sequential obscures the productive virtuous connections, the multiple forms of loyalty, and that political action must sometimes skip the national to be most effective in addressing genuinely transnational injustice, including racism, labor exploitation, and other forms of economic injustice. Transnational cosmopolitanism endeavors a critical political practice and concomitant transformation of political subjectivity that can best challenge those divisions and *also* endeavor to create an alternative, global, political imagination.

CONCLUSION

The previous analysis shows that while Kant and Du Bois could initially be seen as a study in contrasts, juxtaposing them shows the radical possibilities of redeploying Kantian concepts from below. The notion of transnational cosmopolitanism allows us to see that the full productivity of complementarity and hospitality is reached when these concepts are transfigured. Transfiguration follows from transnational alliances among marginalized groups in the West and the Global South that expose Western-led global, institutional formations as cooperation for exploitation. To capture these moments, it is necessary to attune theorizing to silenced currents of thought and action that connect power structures to particular localized instances of injustice, including both the postcolonial condition and racial injustice within Western states. This conceptualization follows from an aesthetic understanding of politics that focuses on the appearance and speech of marginal subjects considered inferior and non–self-governing – in Du Bois's time – or poorly governing – as today's chosen narratives of corruption and failed states go. Attending to similarly excluded subjects and instances of politics today still holds the potential to spur deliberate reflection and upset everyday practices of hierarchical multilateralism (Hopf forthcoming, 13; Pouliot 2016; Rancière 1999). The aesthetic is also relevant vis-à-vis contemporary scholarship on cosmopolitanism because it can normatively enrich accounts of hospitality and interconnection beyond the limits set by the problem space that motivated Kant's intervention. The framework of transnational cosmopolitanism shows the myriad unexplored dimensions of complementarity and hospitality, once we attune ourselves to the overlooked radical thinking and action taking place within and outside the West.

Only with a transfigured hospitality do accounts of complementarity become genuinely cosmopolitan, by which I mean equally concerned with the experiences of injustice and the notions of emancipation of a broader array of subjects, particularly those currently denied a voice. This account of complementarity helps us see that domestic and cosmopolitan loyalties can interact differently than the way they have been made to in the neo-Kantian literature, which expects a gradual sequence in which virtuous (Western) republics will develop a cosmopolitan consciousness and lead the way toward global justice.

In sum, transnational cosmopolitanism seeks to realize equal concern by taking seriously the political craft underlying the struggle against colonialism and post-slavery racial injustice and the insights that this injustice follows from common transnational origins (the ontological point) and needs to be addressed jointly and politically (the political point). In the process, transnational cosmopolitanism relocates the cosmopolitan subject away from the charitable Westerner and takes seriously the question of the political subjectivity of localized, marginalized subjects located in the West or outside of it (the ethical point). Chapters 4 and 5 expand on the three dimensions of transnational cosmopolitanism. Chapter 4 argues that transnational practices of coalition have the potential to deeply transform the consciousness of subjects, who find new purpose and solidarity for their struggle beyond the nation-state. The new "place in the world" attained by the oppressed groups that come together is at the core of the proposed notion of transnational cosmopolitanism. This place and the emancipatory subjectivity it carries with it solidify the domestic struggle against injustice through the access to new resources and spaces to stage claims. Chapter 5 traces the way in which the formation of transnational solidarity proceeds alongside the creation of an anti-colonial counter-public contesting imperial hegemony. Through reciprocal exchanges, domestic struggles can empower each other and also collaborate in creating a cosmopolitan sphere that can develop a genuinely public will unintelligible in sanctioned realms.

4

Race, Identity, and the Question of Transnational Solidarity in Cosmopolitanism

To the extent that the literature on cosmopolitanism has engaged with questions of identity and solidarity, it has devoted most of its energies to deflating identity's normative credentials, which stand in the way of cosmopolitan projects. This likely follows from the fact that prominent literature in political theory defines national identity in contrast to, or against, an Other, an opposition that is sometimes claimed to be self-evident. Scholars who support particularist claims do so either by positing the necessity of this form of identification in agonistic understandings of politics or its intrinsic value as a form of identification that facilitates valuable societal goals, like distributive justice among liberal nationalists (Abizadeh 2005, 45). Because the particularistic and/or oppositional notions of identity assumed in these literatures put in question the desirability and feasibility of a cosmopolitan normative orientation, cosmopolitans see the rejection of identitarian claims as connected to the defense of projects of global solidarity. As a consequence, positive engagement with the potential affinities between identity and cosmopolitan projects is still sparse.

Yet, this exclusively negative engagement with identity has prevented cosmopolitan scholars from theorizing the importance of race-based forms of domination prevalent domestically and internationally, which are tightly connected with race-based forms of mutual identification, both of the controlling, essentializing kind, and of the solidaristic, contestatory kind. This is a loss because identity – alongside other factors – plays an important role in establishing mutual links of solidarity and leads to emancipatory forms of political subjectivity among racialized subjects

(Alcoff 2006; Barvosa 2011). This solidarity, moreover, need not be limited to tightly knit groups or to national collectives. Instead, as I show in this chapter, political solidarity can be transnational, and, when it is, it becomes an effective political craft that can underlie projects of cosmopolitanism. These configurations offer productive models for considering how identity, political subjectivity, and solidarity figure in questions of motivation and political feasibility that underlie cosmopolitanism. In other words, this exploration is central to understanding the range of ways in which cosmopolitan projects take shape, and the kinds of subjectivities and political linkages that make them possible.

An examination of scholarship on questions of identity shows that identity can shape subjects in ways that are controlling and essentializing (Brown 1995; Markell 2003) or that it can underlie freeing forms of political subjectivity (Bickford 1997; Hooker 2009; Shelby 2005). Solidarity is similarly Janus-faced. While ties of solidarity may serve to sustain schemes of cooperation that uphold deeply unjust and undemocratic arrangements (Hooker 2009, 40–54; Stanley 2017, Chapter 6), identity-based forms of solidarity can also bring together people who have experienced common forms of injustice and serve to organize collective action to contest it (Hooker 2009; Shelby 2005).

But when cosmopolitanism either shies away from questions of identity and solidarity, or considers only national forms of identity that must be overcome there is a twofold risk. First, there is a risk that cosmopolitans discard all forms of identity and solidarity and miss those that can fuel projects of cosmopolitanism. Second, there is a risk that cosmopolitans inadvertently retain forms of "Western solidarity" as supposedly non-identitarian forms of cooperation that nonetheless warrant scrutiny because they may carry uncosmopolitan implications, as explicated in Chapter 2 and discussed further in this chapter. One of the few examples of scholarship that highlights the communitarian aspects of cosmopolitan processes is Alexander Wendt's theorization of world-state formation (2003). He notes that processes of integration are fueled by struggles for recognition operating at different levels, leading eventually to a world state. His focus, however, is on struggles for recognition between states. Even if Wendt acknowledges that "domestic struggles for recognition" will affect this process, these struggles appear to be contained – and ultimately resolved – within the domestic sphere (2003, 516). My approach explicitly does not see domestic group forms of identification as contained but rather operating in solidarity with other groups located beyond the national community. This solidarity emerges from racial and political commonalities that tie together disparate subjects throughout the West and the non-West. These commonalities, in turn, follow from the imperial and postimperial structures of oppression that operated world-wide through the institutions of the slave trade, colonialism, slavery, and the diverse forms of oppression, segregation, and apartheid that characterized Western and non-Western societies. Given the foundational role of empire in the international system, the interstate struggles for recognition that are the focus of Wendt's work are likely to leave out the important currents of identity formation and counter-publics that traverse state borders that I outline in this and the next chapter.

W. E. B. Du Bois's thought on transnational consciousness, political subjectivity, and solidarity is an inescapable resource to explore normatively the role that identity-based solidarity can play in contemporary projects of cosmopolitanism. Du Bois is well-known for his theorization of a double form of consciousness that characterizes the experience of blacks in the US polity (*SBF*). However, the development of his notion of black consciousness after *Souls* shows that he grappled with how identity, solidarity, and political subjectivity operated beyond the nation-state. In particular, Du Bois underwent and advocated for a transformation of black consciousness toward the transnational in an effort to support more robust forms of political subjectivity, which came accompanied by the formation of anti-colonial networks of political solidarity. The emerging transnational consciousness did not replace black consciousness or make black solidarity obsolete, instead, it added to this form of identification by acting upon shared values and/or goals with subjects located throughout the world. The question of racial identity was both central and secondary to the experiment. It was central to the extent that it was exclusion of a *racial* kind – implemented via slavery, apartheid, colonialism, or disenfranchisement – which was at the root of the shared identity supporting networks of solidarity. Yet, it was secondary to the extent that it did not require racial *commonality* in order to be operative, but instead built upon and included the experience of racialization that differently affected Africans, African diasporas, Asians, and other dark peoples subject to colonial and neocolonial power. Moreover, this commonality built upon racialization and the mutual trust developed through exchange also allowed for a future-oriented politics, through which subjects could exit relationships of misrecognition and develop shared values and goals to orient emancipation struggles.

In the rest of this chapter I develop these claims. The next section builds upon Tommie Shelby and Juliet Hooker's writings on identity and solidarity to introduce twin concepts of transnational political subjectivity and solidarity. The section titled 'Black Transnational Subjects' further develops this concept through an examination of the evolution of black consciousness in Du Bois's writings. The section titled 'Transnationalism and Segregation: An Elective Affinity?' shows that group identity can be more conducive to transnational forms of solidarity and political subjectivity than forms of identification and narratives associated with the nation-state. The section titled 'Complicating Identity and Solidarity within Cosmopolitanism' contrasts the proposed account with the way in which identity figures in Habermas's account of cosmopolitanism.

My engagement with Du Bois's context of writing, political action, and political thought in this chapter theorizes two of the three dimensions of transnational cosmopolitanism that I have argued are required for a robust account of cosmopolitanism. By reconstructing the deep transnationalization of US space in the 1920s, I show that Du Bois was moved to further elaborate on the common transnational origins of injustice (i.e., the ontological point). By offering a nuanced account and praxis of black self-definition and transnational consciousness, Du Bois relocates the cosmopolitan subject away from the charitable Westerner and theorizes the possibility of solidarity, tying together marginalized subjects located inside and outside the West (i.e., the ethical point). In the next chapter, I further theorize the way in which the accounts of identity and solidarity that develop in the present chapter allow for the inauguration of political arenas beyond the domestic and international spheres, so that the transnational origins of injustice can be traced and accountability sought (i.e., the political point).

IDENTITY, SOLIDARITY, MULTIPLICITY, AND THE POLITICAL CRAFT

Tommie Shelby's classic definition of solidarity includes five dimensions: mutual identification, special concern or partiality, shared values or goals, loyalty, and mutual trust (2005, 67–70). By incorporating mutual identification as one dimension of solidarity, Shelby acknowledges that members of a solidarity group tend to "identify, both subjectively and publicly, with each other or with the group as a whole" and think of themselves as "sharing a special bond" based on a "shared ethnic or cultural heritage (whether real or imagined)" or a "similar plight"

(2005, 68). While Shelby is interested in theorizing solidarity among US blacks, nothing in his definition excludes the possibility that ties of solidarity may exist to bring together subjects that are distant from each other. This is particularly the case if we adopt two amendments of the framework that Juliet Hooker proposes. Hooker argues, first, that not all of the dimensions in Shelby's definition need to appear in all forms of solidarity (2009, 32). This becomes evident when we consider that communities will often have people who are, in significant ways, "not like us" (Allen 2004; Hooker 2009, 32–3), but with whom we can nonetheless share goals or develop mutual trust as a result of doing political work together. But this also means that, as Hooker notes in her second amendment to Shelby's account, "individuals experience multiple and overlapping solidarities, and . . . find themselves negotiating how to balance the competing obligations derived from these allegiances" (2009, 31).

These two amendments are important in theorizing the question of identity and solidarity in a cosmopolitan framework. If solidarity can be built upon a variety of grounds and individuals by definition establish different kinds of solidaristic relations with different groups, then we can argue further that cosmopolitan solidarities are possible and can coexist with other forms of allegiance. This is consistent with Catherine Lu's understanding of cosmopolitan unity as not entailing homogeneity, but instead encompassing diverse subjects, who can nonetheless have bonds of affinity, "grounded in multiple roots and bound by diverse compelling obligations" (2000, 257–8). This focus on multiplicity echoes conceptualizations of multiple identities in Latina/o political thought. Scholars in this tradition note that identity need not be conceptualized "as a coherent set of attributes shared by all members of the group and essentially closed or stable" (Alcoff 2006, 45). Edwina Barvosa, in particular, notes that the challenge for scholars of identity is to consider how they relate to "solidarity building in productive ways under various conditions" by examining concrete practices of solidarity work that also constitute the subject as a political agent (Barvosa 2011, 122, 130; Yarbro-Bejarano 2006, 87, cited in Barvosa 2011, 130). Du Bois's advocacy work in the 1920s and 1930s grappled with these questions, as is evident from his advocacy of both self-segregation *and* transnationalism – examined below.

Opening up the discussion to the question of cosmopolitan solidarities, however, requires normative judgments about the character of the identities that underlie solidarity as well as the goals and values that orient them. Not all forms of solidarity are devoted to advance goals that are inclusionary or democratic (Gutmann 2003), and the same can be said regarding how identities operate vis-à-vis cosmopolitan justice. In fact, Du Bois's early work reminds us that US national identity was tragically narrow and supportive of an unjust regime of racial domination. His later work, on the other hand, contains vocal complaints about the international system, which facilitated "Western solidarity" and allowed for peace among European states and the more effective pursuit of goals of territorial control and racial and imperial domination (WC, 431). In fact, the following sections make clear Du Bois's intellectual and political turn toward transnationalism responds partially to the persistent closure of emancipatory avenues in the domestic sphere. This closure was connected to forms of national identity tied to white supremacy, which supported sustained racial segregation and violence in the American polity adn imperialism abroad. Thus, valuable forms of identity and solidarity play central roles in advancing goals of cosmopolitan justice. If this is the case, it is necessary to expand the cosmopolitan tradition in order to explore and theorize the ways in which identity and solidarity could and do in fact underlie successful projects of justice beyond the nation.

In particular, I am interested in forms of solidarity that facilitate emancipatory forms of political subjectivity, hospitable political exchanges, and coalition making that contest exclusionary forms of transnational governance, which variously operate in localized political realms. These ties of solidarity may depend on forms of race-based identity, which may have emerged from an oppositional relation with imperial structures of domination but provided resources for self-definition that could support emancipatory projects. These forms of identity and solidarity can fuel a process of *political* subjectivation or subject formation. In other words, the forms of solidarity and identity in which I am interested are those conducive to forms of political subjectivity that allow individuals to critically navigate the trappings of misrecognition offered to oppressed subjects. This political subjectivity is "freeing" because it allows subjects to critically engage with the power structures and destructive discourses that confine them, and leads them to imagine alternative political arrangements (Valdez 2016). This freedom is not the one that exists when all structures of power have been dismantled. By contrast, it is the freedom that is required precisely because these structures are in place. The twin processes of identity-based solidarity and subjective emancipation are well captured in Ralph Ellison's assessment of the prospects for racial justice in the United States:

This society is not likely to become free of racism, thus it is necessary for Negroes to free themselves by becoming their idea of what a free people should be.
(Ellison n/d)

It is the oppressed group that can work together within an oppressive society in order to define itself as a group and imagine that it can be otherwise. This is what Satya Mohanty argues regarding claims and feelings about racial or cultural identity; that they embody "alternative and anti-hegemonic accounts of what is significant and in fact necessary for a more accurate understanding of the world we share" (1997, 236–8). Only armed with such anti-hegemonic accounts can the group act politically in ways that are truly emancipatory. In Du Bois's case, as I show later, his "idea of what a free people should be" involved a political subject who recognized the common origins of injustice affecting African-American, Afro-diasporic, and colonial subjects and their shared political fates.

Accordingly, the forms of identity, solidarity, and political subjectivity that can undergird cosmopolitanism are those that, in the process of self-definition, engage critically with the social, political, and economic character of their oppression, find these conditions to be genuinely transnational and move to act politically at such a level. This is the "political craft" that is central to the success of cosmopolitan projects that I am interested in pursuing through Du Bois's trajectory between the turn of the century and the 1930s. This is a normative and theoretical interest to the extent that it orients accounts of what cosmopolitanism is, where it is found, and what institutional structures can better channel variously located subjects into such a cosmopolitan project. In the following sections, I offer Du Bois's own transnational, political craft as a resource for this theorization. In particular, I trace how his notion of black consciousness and racial emancipation became transnationalized after World War I and the forms of solidarity and political subjectivity that he posits as necessary for a project of global justice. In so doing, I support three claims (a) that solidarity may emerge among extremely diverse and variously located groups; (b) that only certain forms of identity are normatively valuable and conducive to cosmopolitanism; and (c) that identities and their transformation are always the work of politics.

BLACK TRANSNATIONAL SUBJECTS

In this section I show how Du Bois's mature work provides the political and ethical scaffolding of the relation between United States and transnational forms of racial domination by revisiting his earlier notions of consciousness, political subjectivity, and solidarity. This is not to say that Du Bois's work was unconcerned with transnationalism at the time he wrote *Souls* or that this topic was absent in *Souls* itself.[1] Instead, it is to note that his theoretical work on solidarity, political subjectivity and the public – which interest me in this chapter and the next – were still primarily concerned with the domestic realm in Du Bois's early writings. His transnationalism, on the other hand, was part of Du Bois's philosophy of history and thus less engaged with questions of identity, subjectivity, and political agency.

After *Souls*

The literature on *Souls of Black Folk* is extensive and a mere survey of it would warrant a chapter of its own. However, my concern is not to contribute to, arbitrate between, or settle for one of the alternative interpretations of *Souls* (see Gooding-Williams 2011, Lewis 1993; Reed 1997; among others). Instead, I aim to single out the notions of consciousness and subjectivity that appear in this work *in order* to show, on the one hand, that they are predominantly grounded in a domestic – rather than transnational – understanding of injustice and politics. On the other hand, I show that some of Du Bois's worries around the "peculiar problems of inner life" (*SBF*, 155) remain central when he develops the notions of transnational consciousness, identity, and political subjectivity. Regarding the first point, it is worth noting that despite the varied interpretations of this work, all scholars agree in understanding Du Bois's claims in his book – including those about subjectivity – to be about the domestic sphere of politics. This is the case in interpretations that privilege an exegetical and/or historical reading of this work (Gooding-Williams 2011; Reed 1997), as well as those who are more interested in

---

[1] See, for example, brief references to world conflict in "Of Our Spiritual Strivings," to American colonial expeditions in "Of the Quest of the Golden Fleece," and to contact between Europe and "undeveloped peoples" in "Of the Sons of Master and Man" show (*SBF*, 43, 125, 33).

relying on *Souls* anachronistically as a normative resource to address pressing questions of today (Balfour 2011; Rogers 2012).

Du Bois's most well-known theorization of subjectivity is undoubtedly his notion of double consciousness. Despite the inordinate amount of attention this notion has received among political theorists, this concept seems to have disappeared from his later writings (Reed 1997, 124), and in any case may depict only the experience of educated African Americans who came into social contact with whites (Kent 1972, 50), rather than that reflecting a broader set of preoccupations in Du Bois's theorization of consciousness. These preoccupations included the particular forms of consciousness that freedmen and women and workers in the Black Belt developed in the post-slavery era.

Double consciousness is a burdensome yet insightful form of consciousness associated with the "inevitability of seeing oneself through the contemptuous eyes of others" (*SBF*, 38). Yet, the "two-ness" is not simply a burden. Instead, it provides a privileged insight into the divisions that plague America in ways that are beyond the reach of white citizens (*SBF*, 38). This second sight allows the black subject to glimpse "faint revelations of his power, his mission" and to hope that the "two world-races may give each to each those characteristics both so sadly lack" (*SBF*, 3, 41). Adolph Reed has interpreted this particular statement to fall squarely within the Lamarckian developmentalism, prominent at the time of Du Bois's writing (Reed 1997, 122–3). According to this interpretation, Du Bois aimed to present African Americans' "humility," "good humor," and the Sorrow Songs as an antidote to the "overcivilization" of America, a topic of extensive discussion at the turn of the century (Reed 1997, 122–3). Robert Gooding-Williams, on the other hand, sees this portion of *Souls* as depicting a search for true self-consciousness, which would allow for a mutual and educative dialogue between "Negro's ideals, judgments, and strivings" and American ideals, without subordinating one perspective to the other (Gooding-Williams 2011, 86–7). The focus on double consciousness has limited the attention given to *Souls'* concerns with forms of consciousness associated with different social and economic contexts enveloping African Americans. For example, African Americans in the Black Belt of Georgia were facing a new form of slavery made up of high rent, poor land, and inflexible landowners. *Souls* also denounces the cruelty and mistreatment that black convicts faced and the broader question of a police system originally "designed to keep track of all Negroes, not just criminals" and a criminal justice system devoted to produce government income through convict labor (*SBF*, 113–14, 142). The consciousness of these African-American subjects goes from "[c]areless ignorance and laziness here, fierce hate and vindictiveness there," and emerges from a world that gives black subjects no reason to strive (*SBF*, 113–14, 119–20, 129–30). Unlike the double consciousness of African Americans with access to white spaces and narratives, other black subjects are shaped by the failed transition from "feudal agrarianism to modern farming," which could have, but failed to, put an end to the gross inequality and dependence preventing the self-sustained citizenry and mutual cooperation necessary for democracy (Balfour 2011, 29–30).

In other words, the black farm laborers' self-consciousness was stunted by the "mockery" of freedom economic conditions allowed for, i.e., black laborers returning to new masters – doing "task-work" or "cropping" rather than "toil in gangs" – remaining "laborer[s] with indeterminate wages" (*SBF*, 123). Adding to this bleak situation was the problem of Southern disenfranchisement and the corrupt – if any – political engagement available for African Americans in the North. In *Souls*, Du Bois denounces plans to "eliminate the black man from politics," or reduce his political activity to the "bribery, force, and fraud" until black men become convinced that "politics is a disreputable and useless form of human activity" (*SBF*, 139–40).

In sum, *Souls* covers a few distinct forms of post-slavery subjectivity to be overcome (destructive double consciousness, a self-consciousness stunted by peonage, and a subject alienated from politics through bribery and violence). In connection with the critique of problematic forms of consciousness, *Souls* is concerned with self-definition, i.e., the process through which the various forms of misrecognition received from the oppressor could be overcome. This was necessary for the African-American subject to be "himself, and not another" and "attain their place in the world" (*SBF*, 41). The realization of an African-American self-consciousness was central in developing a critical political subjectivity that could lead to the political contestation of the continued denial of their due. In this sense, one reason Du Bois worried about misrecognition, i.e., the "contempt and pity" that characterized the reflection received from whites, is that it could imperil a democratic project of emancipation (*SBF*, 38).

This concern with self-definition and the way it was threatened in the emancipation era fueled Du Bois's effort to reconfigure African-American identity in ways that exceeded the partitioned subjectivity that characterizes double consciousness, the incomplete form of selfhood that emerges from centuries of slavery, and the new forms of victimization experienced by the disenfranchized black peasantry. His pessimism about the visions that animated white America (Douglas 2015) and his worry about the internalization of shame and lack of striving among African Americans oriented him toward redefining the character of his overall political project by transforming and deepening his early transnationalism.

Du Bois's writings in the decades that followed *Souls* grappled with the problem of self-definition and political subjectivity and put the question of consciousness at the center. Yet this time its multiplicity redirected the African-American political imagination away from the United States and toward the worlds of color, and reconceived African-American identity as a process of self-definition that is practiced alongside others subjected to imperial power. The new form of consciousness that Du Bois developed during this period relies on forms of kinship that are racial but in a deeply political sense. On the one hand, kinship emerges from being associated with undergoing domination on behalf of racial belonging:

But one thing is sure and that is the fact that since the fifteenth century these ancestors of mine and their other descendants . . . have suffered a common disaster and have a long memory. . . . But the physical bond is least and the badge of color relatively unimportant save as a badge; the real essence of this kinship is its social heritage of slavery; the discrimination and insult; and this heritage . . . extends through yellow Asia and into the South Seas. It is this unity that draws me to Africa.

(*DD*, 117)

The importance of the "common disaster," however, is not limited to the injury and a resentful request to partake of the goods of the privileged – as identity politics critics fear (Brown 1995). Instead, the common disaster is a starting point that enables new forms of mutual identification among those subjected to "the insult" in ways that may enable coalition making against racialized domination. Most of Du Bois's 1920s writings go beyond the "common disaster" to carve out a space for the African-American subject and his imagination in world history. These works provide a transnational account of racial oppression that includes – but is not exhausted by – the African-American experience and looks toward the future. In particular, *Darkwater* (1920) was Du Bois's first attempt to articulate a less civilizational anti-imperialism and reconstruct the particular constellation of transnational forces that enveloped the United States in the 1920s. This constellation reframes the problem of oppression as properly transnational and underpins the transnationalism and transnational subjectivity he developed during this period. Du Bois's utopian novel *Dark Princess* (1928) further conceptualized the particular reorientation of subjectivity toward the transnational that Du Bois put forward. *Dark Princess*, as well as "The Negro Mind Reaches Out" (1925), is more clearly concerned with the political possibilities that open when solidarity among differently located peoples of color is established and relied upon for political pursuits. The transnational consciousness developed in these writings is based on a survey of instances of racialized domination that connect back to imperial ideologies and practices within and outside the United States. This project, while it proposed a substantive transnational orientation that is novel, also significantly expanded the political dimensions of Du Bois's earlier conception of race:

> a vast family of human beings, *generally* of common blood and language, always of common history, traditions and impulses, who are both voluntarily and *involuntarily* striving together for the accomplishment of certain *more or less vividly* conceived ideals of life.
>
> (CR, 817, my emphasis)

This early notion of race already allowed for groupings that bring together subjects who do not have "common blood and language" and that are brought together by events beyond their will. This claim is consistent with Paul Taylor's reading of Du Bois's race concept as focusing "on parallel individual experiences of certain social conditions," which hold the promise of a political activation of those affinities.[2] Thus Du Bois's post–World War I transnationalism is less a reconsideration of his notion of race than a more nuanced consideration of the mechanics of subjectivity and solidarity that would politically "stretch" his account of race through the politics of transnational coalition making. This shift must be understood in the context of the dramatic transnationalization of US space and racial relations and the generative post–World War I moment of intellectual production and soul searching. I term this a "shift" because of the way in which it contrasts with the teleological understanding of world history that characterized his earlier transnational thought. The next two subsections turn to these questions.

---

[2] A full engagement with Du Bois's concept of race is beyond the reach of this project, to the extent that my interest is more particularly in the related but distinct question of a political understanding of race consciousness rather than the concept of race in and of itself. In this debate, however, I find Joel Olson's notion of the race concept as political the most productive.

The Transnationalization of US Space

In the 1920s, African Americans witnessed persistent racial violence in the United States (including violent riots against Southern black workers in the North and the nativist frenzy that culminated in the 1924 ban on Asian immigration to the United States). The world, in turn, witnessed emerging home rule movements in India and the rest of the colonial world. During this time, white intellectuals grappled with the civilizational implications of the Great War, the threat of Pan-African solidarity, anti-colonial movements, and rising non-Western powers (Elam 2014, 15; Moses 1978, 251–3).

The aftermath of World War I witnessed a significant spatial and demographic transformation, fueled by continued immigration into the country as well as internal wartime migration of African Americans to the North. The nativist reaction that characterized this era – paradigmatically represented in the works of eugenicists Lothrop Stoddard and Madison Grant – responded to these two trends and to the aforementioned Western anxiety.[3] The nativist panic of the time has been widely studied but scholars tend to analyze it primarily in the light of one dimension: anti-black racism (Hooker 2017), immigration (Higham 2004), or anxieties about Western superiority (Lake and Reynolds 2008).[4] Du Bois's analysis of this period sees it instead as a thorough reorganization of American racial formations, emerging at the intersection of nativist reaction and imperial capitalism:

> Slowly they saw the gates of Ellis Island closing, slowly the footsteps of the yearly million men became fainter and fainter, until the stream of immigrants overseas was stopped by the shadow of death at the very time new murder opened new markets over all the world to American industry; and the giants with the thunderbolts stamped and raged and peered out across the world and called for men and evermore, – men!"
>
> (*DW*, 50)

Du Bois's account of 1920s nativism was alert to the fact that the capitalist need for labor remained and that new – European as well as

---

[3] As it is well-known, nativism fueled a series of bills banning Asian migration. The Emergency Act of 1921 and the Johnson-Reed Act of 1924 also established quotas that aimed to restrict Southern and Eastern European migration (Higham 2004; Ngai 2004).

[4] See, however, Nikhil Singh, who sees anti-black racism and anti-radicalism as inextricably linked (Singh 2004, 31).

American – forms of imperialism emerged to fulfill that need. The same racial prejudice that disenfranchised blacks closed off borders to foreigners and supported the violent recruitment of labor abroad through imperial means.[5] Du Bois's transnationalism understood immigration and the nativism that met it on arrival as dimensions of the transnational imperial formation rather than domestic phenomena.[6] This is clear in his assessment of United States–Mexico relations:

> [W]e stole Mexico's land and made it into Texas, Arizona, New Mexico and California to make more territory for stealing and working Negro slaves. We stole her soil . . . We filched her oil and minerals at an enormous profit, and when the stricken peons struggled up from their mud and pain and said "This land is ours and for us!" we sent our troops and our liars to threaten and browbeat the new Mexico. When the bluff failed and Mexico started to reclaim her soil and her heritage from predatory English and Americans; started to educate their peons and give them land; started to compel capital to pay a living wage – then with unparalleled impudence, we demanded pay and immediate pay for "our losses." We ought to be made to disgorge some of the millions we hijacked from Mexico in the last hundred years.
>
> (Du Bois 1940)

In Du Bois's eyes, the conquest of Mexico was part of the imperialist grab for land and natural resources, entangled with the past exploitation of slave labor and with the present extraction of freedmen's labor that characterized the United States. This explains that the Mexican Revolution, an effort toward self-determination, was met with US imperialist aggression. Moreover, as the previous excerpt suggests, the particular forms of entanglement between the United States and Mexico created obligations for reparation that Du Bois associated with racial injustice more generally. This logic extends to Du Bois's interpretation of other US imperial relations, like those with Cuba and the Philippines. About these countries, he argued that the United States held the former "by the industrial throat" and had the latter "on its knees, albeit squirming," (1914a, 79), an account that led him to see the fate of these imperial subjects as connected to those of African Americans and their self-definition.[7]

---

[5] For a more recent reading of the twin US dependence on foreign migrants and colonial peoples see Matthew Jacobson's *Barbarian Virtues* (2000).

[6] Notably, Du Bois's 1915 essay "The African Roots of War," partially reproduced in *Darkwater* was singled out in Stoddard's *The Rising Tide of Color against White World Supremacy* (1920).

[7] As he noted at the turn of the century, US imperial policy "doubles the colored population of our land" (*PODR*, 102; Balfour 2011, 118–19).

In discussing the American invasion of Veracruz in 1914, Du Bois noted US ambivalence over the desire for "millions of brown peons" and tied it to the fact these peons – unlike other colonial subjects – have known "food and opportunity" and would not be as pliant to US power (Du Bois 1914a).

Anti-Asian racism in the United States was also connected with broader international anxieties about the rise of Asia, and converged and was partly powered by the broader context of anti-radicalism (Gallicchio 2000, 33–7). In particular, immigration enforcement proved a useful tool to target anti-colonial Asian groups operating in the United States, including organizations like the Ghadar movement and the India Home Rule League and other Indian anti-colonial activist groups with whom Du Bois was connected, many of whose members were deported in the 1910s (Sohi 2007, Chapters 2, 3, and 5).[8] Along with Indians, Afro-Caribbeans – also subjects of empire – immigrated to the United States in this period and "helped internationalize and radicalize urban Black communities, already swelled by new arrivals from the South" (Slate 2012a, 47).[9]

Du Bois's reading of this juncture in an imperialist key is clear in a 1922 essay where he argued that "Americanization" is "the

---

[8] The Ghadar movement was the most widespread anti-colonial organization in North America, founded around 1913 in California. While its membership was predominantly Sikh, its leadership was made up of educated Hindus and Muslims, reflecting sectarian lines that were eroded by exile in North America (Horne 2009, 47–50). The New York branch of the India Home Rule movement was led by Lajpat Rai, who lived in the United States between 1914 and 1919 and was a close friend of Du Bois (Ahmad 2002, 787).

[9] Prominent among these migrants was, of course, the Jamaican Marcus Garvey, whose Universal Negro Improvement Association (UNIA) operated in Africa, the Caribbean, Europe, and Australia, in addition to the United States, and who cultivated a relationship of affinity with Indian anti-colonial thinkers, including Gandhi (Slate 2012a, 47–51). Garvey lived in New York from 1916 until his deportation in 1927. He founded the UNIA in 1914 in Jamaica before relocating it to New York, where he published a weekly paper and advocated race pride (Du Bois 1920, 58; Rogers 1955, 158; Slate 2012a; Stein 1986). Du Bois and Garvey were both Pan-Africanism proponents and perhaps the two most visible black leaders in the postwar period. I see Garvey's brand of transnationalism as one of several "alternative transnationalisms" that thrived in the post–World War I era. My focus on Du Bois does not imply that Garvey's project is not a worthy area of inquiry in and of itself, but it is outside of the scope of this book, which, with its focus on advancing a conversation on the political theory of cosmopolitanism, necessarily limits the space that I can devote to the ongoing conversations between Du Bois and other non-Western proponents of postwar subaltern transnationalisms, including the Pan-African and hemispheric ones, which have been reconstructed by other scholars (Hooker 2017; Slate 2012a).

determination to make the English New England stock dominant in the United States."[10] This dominance, he continued, relies on the "disenfranchisement of Negro, Jew, Irishman, Italian, Hungarian, Asiatic and South Sea islander" (*AMER*, 384). In a stark departure from his turn-of-the-century admiration for English civilization, Du Bois claimed that British imperial power is "one of the greatest foes of human liberty" and that it is being felt "this side the water," i.e., a land that accepts newcomers "only as dumb laborers or silent witnesses or as those willing to surrender their will and deeds to the glory of the 'Anglo Saxon'" (*AMER*, 384).

Du Bois evaluated these transformations through the prism of imperial domination, as instances of its variegated reach. In particular, these developments would permanently alter the management of racialized labor in the United States, an equation concerned centrally with African Americans (*BRA*, 5–6; Hahamovitch 2011). Unsurprisingly, Du Bois linked immigration restrictionism to a new stage of anti-black racism, i.e., the violence against African-American workers migrating to the North from the American South in 1917 and 1919:

The Unwise Men laughed and squeezed reluctant dollars out of the fists of the mighty . . . save for one thing, and that was the sound of the moan of the Disinherited, who still lay without the walls. When they heard this moan and saw that it came not across the seas, they were at first amazed and said it was not true; and then they were mad and said it should not be. Quickly they turned and looked into the red blackness of the South and in their hearts were fear and hate!

(*DW*, 50–1)

Divided labor, racism, and old wounds set the stage for the racial violence of the South reenacted in the industrial North. In this new world, the fate of the black subject was entwined with the yellow and the brown subject at home as well as abroad, all targeted, albeit in diverse ways, by the imperial project. These vast demographic and spatial transformations fueled Du Bois's reframing of his anti-imperial thought and his more nunaced consideration of political subjectivity and solidarity. Du Bois expected "those who suffer under the arrogance and tyranny of the white world" to unite and struggle politically against empire, as his utopian novel *Dark Princess* promises (*DP*, 12).

Du Bois's discussion of immigration in *Darkwater*, "Americanization," and *Black Reconstruction in America* reveals a particular interest on the

---

[10] In support of Du Bois's assessment, Desmond King (2000) has analyzed the coercive assimilationist and eugenicist policies of assimilation that characterized this period.

way in which racial structures and labor coimplicate each other. In particular, he noted the tragedy of the alignment between white immigrant labor and Anglo-Saxon whites rather than with black and brown workers. This reveals that Du Bois's hospitality toward transnational subjects was not restricted to those on his side of the color line but instead sought to construct an alliance against imperial formations that coopted white labor and preempted labor solidarity. Thus, Du Bois privileges black workers in the United States because they "had neither wish nor power to escape from the labor status" and to exploit other workers (*BRA*, 15). This was unlike white workers who could "by alliance with capital share in [the] exploitation of [black workers]." Yet again, this situation connected black workers to the "vast sea of human labor in China and India, the South Seas and all Africa; in the West Indies and Central America and in the United States" (*BRA*, 15). This common destiny brought the darker peoples together, those "on whose bent and broken backs rest . . . the founding stones of modern industry" (*BRA*, 15). As a consequence:

The emancipation of man is the emancipation of labor and the emancipation of labor is the freeing of that basic majority of workers who are yellow, brown, and black.

(*BRA*, 16)

Thus, the joint fate for the worlds of color emerges from their subjection to similar forces of empire and capitalism in the nineteenth and twentieth century, which relied on race as a central organizing principle of labor exploitation. The racial basis of the common fate is not related to any sort of racial essentialism or prepolitical racial identity but an artifact of empire and white supremacy. It is upon this basis, but going beyond the misrecognition it implies, that Du Bois constructed a political project to transform the consciousness of African Americans through novel forms of identification with subjects abroad and political action to allow for the emancipation of "that basic majority of workers." This coalition excluded white workers only to the extent that they choose to ally with white elites to partake in exploitation rather than struggle for labor emancipation.[11] This alliance, for Du Bois, implied a perverse vision in which subjects seek to "become emancipated from the necessity of continuous toil . . . [to] . . . join the class of exploiters," making the elevation of all workers less desirable as well as less possible for the average worker (*BRA* 17–18).

---

[11] As David Levering Lewis notes, "hardly a year passed in which Du Bois had failed to press against the anti-black policies of Gompers and now William Green's AFL" (Lewis 2000, 250).

Given the domestic alignment of white labor with elites, Du Bois's saw transnationalism as an exit from the racial prejudice and violence that structured the American polity and as the opening up of possibilities of political solidarity and coalition making with other racialized subjects targeted by nativist and imperial anxieties in this period. Among these groups, we find, notably, Asian migrants and Asian anti-colonial activists in the United States, but also a network of African and diasporic subjects operating in transnational networks (see also Lowe 2015, 170).

Vis-à-vis prevalent notions of cosmopolitanism, Du Bois's trajectory makes clear that the transnational orientation emerged from the sheer fact of the transnational character of injustice, which appeared locally in ways that were particular but not reducible to the domestic. Moreover, this trajectory demonstrates that it was the lack of hospitality of the US polity to questions of racial and colonial justice that fueled the search for alternative alliances and political spheres. This trajectory contrasts with the implicit assumption in the cosmopolitan literature according to which Western polities, with supposedly stronger democratic credentials than the rest of the world, will lead the project of cosmopolitanism. This involves an ahistorical maneuver that declares those at the helm of the imperial project redeemed and able to lead a project of global justice in the postcolonial world, thus erasing the past of colonialism but, most importantly, the present of neocolonial economic and political governance. Given this context, attending to Du Bois allows us instead to center the question of political subjectivity and solidarity among subaltern subjects who built upon a common experience of racialization an emancipatory project. The contrast with his earlier writings on transnationalism is noteworthy, as the next section notes.

Changing Anti-Imperialism and a Radical Cosmopolitanism

Darkwater contains Du Bois's early postcivilizational assessment of imperialism, reproducing and augmenting several essays he wrote during World War I (*ARW*, Du Bois 1914b). Yet, the critique of imperialism contained in these writings is still limited, because it is more concerned with appealing to the West's "better instincts" and warning them of the potential of rebellion than with delineating a project of emancipation for the non-West:

What, then, is this dark world thinking? It is thinking that as wild and awful as this shameful war was, *it is nothing to compare with that fight for freedom which black and brown and yellow men must and will make unless their oppression and humiliation and insult at the hands of the White World cease. The Dark World is going to submit to this present treatment just as long as it must and not one moment longer.*

(*DW*, 28)

He continues:

Today Japan is hammering on the door of justice. China is raising her half-manacled hands to knock next. India is writhing for the freedom to knock, Egypt is sullenly muttering, the Negros of South and West Africa, of the West Indies, and of the United States are just awakening to their shameful slavery. Is, then, this war the end of wars? . . . so long as sits enthroned, even in the souls of those who cry peace, the despising and robbing of darker peoples? If Europe hugs this delusion, then it is not the end of the war, – it is but the beginning!

(*DW*, 28)

The salient threat of violence by the darker world appears also in "The Hands of Ethiopia:"

if you were a man of some education and knowledge, but born a Japanese, or a Chinaman, an East Indian or a Negro, what would you do and think? . . . If the attitude of the European and American worlds is in the future going to be based essentially upon the same policies as in the past, then there is but one thing for the trained man of darker blood to do and that is definitely and as openly as possible to organize his world for war against Europe.

(*DW*, 34)

This narrative contains an anti-colonial impulse, but also problematic dimensions. In fact, it aligns with what Michel-Rolph Trouillot identifies as critiques of empire as "cautionary tale," in which "the voice of the enlightened West admonish[es] its colonialist counterpart," warning Europeans of the fatalities that await them if they do not change their ways (1995, 84–5). Du Bois's indictment of Western imperialism is strong and there is a definite effort to relocate Africa and its diaspora from the margins of world history to the center. At the same time, the cautionary tale narrative is not conducive to an engagement with the politics of emancipation – i.e., the kinds of subjectivity and links of solidarity that can give rise to emancipation transnationally.

A more political conceptualization of transnationalism took shape in Du Bois's 1925 essay "The Negro Mind Reaches Out," published as part of Alain Locke's landmark collection *The New Negro: Voices of the Harlem Renaissance*. Du Bois's essay is the sole text in the last section of the volume, *Worlds of Color*, and it prompts two turns: one toward the outside of the United States and the second toward the future. The former turn is prompted by his interest in the alternative colonial conditions and the promise of heterogeneous black subjectivities found outside of the United States. Du Bois's intention was to reassess the postwar situation and, in light of the meager recognition of African Americans' participation in the war effort, redirect the imagination of African Americans toward the transnational. This redirection first reconnects their lineage to Africa and then links their condition of oppression to a larger imperial structure.

Du Bois's survey of the different colonial conditions (which he calls "phases of European imperialism in Africa") is remarkable for its range and detail. He contrasts French and British colonial forms of exploitation, and the more marked importance of "caste lines" in the latter; he surveys "colored members of European parliaments," the obstacles that French assimilation of educated blacks in France pose to anti-colonial struggle, and the agitation for representative government in the British colonies in the Caribbean. He declares the task of "likening and contrasting each land and its far-off shadow" to be his field of inquiry. This inquiry includes exploring the heterogeneous black subjectivities and the varied coalitions that result from particular "color-line fights." About these, he offers the example of the boycott of Sao Thomé cocoa, which followed from complaints about working conditions at the British production sites:

> In this development note if you please the characteristic of all color-line fights – the tearing apart of all rational division of opinion: here is Liberalism, anti-slavery and cocoa capitalism fighting Toryism, free Negro proprietors and economic independence.
>
> (*NMRO*, 388)

In examining the variety of black subjects and colonial projects as well as the heterogeneous and unexpected character of coalitions that allow for resistance, he remaps the context of the American struggle against racial injustice as an instance of a vaster movement of emancipation. Moreover, he recognizes that racial oppression – while being a global phenomenon – is differently organized across locales, due to its intersection with local conditions and other overlapping forms of domination (see also Collins 2000, 231). Moreover, reconstructing the instances of defiance by oppressed groups works both to strengthen the denunciation of the violence of colonialism and speak against its totality:

Insurgent Morocco, independent Abyssinia and Liberia are, as it were, shadows of Europe on Africa unattached, and as such they curiously *threaten the whole imperial program*. On the one hand, they arouse *democratic sympathy in home-land*, which makes it difficult to submerge them; and again, they are *temptations to agitation for freedom* and autonomy on the part of other black and subject populations.

(NMRO, 389, my emphasis)

The text highlights the possibility of European sympathy for the colonies' democratic aspirations[12] and an interest in singling out emancipatory subjectivities – including those of African Americans – that can become blueprints for other subject populations:

Led by American Negroes, the Negroes of the world are reaching out hands toward each other to know, to sympathize, to inquire. There are few countries without their few Negroes, few great cities without its groups, and thus with this great human force, spread out as it is in all lands and languages, the world must one day reckon.

(NMRO, 412–13)

By providing a survey of localized instances of emancipation and tracing the connections between Africans of the diaspora Du Bois identifies what Frederick Cooper sees as – "the limits as well as the power of European domination, the unevenness and conflict within Europe itself," a task that postcolonial literature does not always embrace (2005, 416). Du Bois's focus on sympathy, inquiry, and the spatial reach of the African diaspora also aesthetically positions a universal – yet grounded – African subject at the center of world history. This appeal is not only to the world, but also to African Americans, the likely audience of the volume. In this context, it can be considered a call for the expansion of the imagination and a reconfiguration of the consciousness of African Americans, based on the entwined character of their fate and that of Africans and the African diaspora.

"The Negro Mind Reaches Out" lays down the foundations of Du Bois's cosmopolitan project and opens an arena for new ties of solidarity to emerge among the worlds of color and for their political imagination to craft an alternative worldview. African Americans had been uprooted from the African continent and deprived of a history; yet, the later Du Bois saw the twentieth century bringing Africans back together in the

---

[12] Although, as Robbie Shilliam (2016) convincingly argues, European solidarities with the colonies are not devoid of civilizational concerns.

form of a spread-out force with which the world must reckon, and one whose connections were rekindled and expanded to include other oppressed peoples. Kwame Anthony Appiah recognizes this shift, arguing that Du Bois globalized "his earlier bitter formula about the Negro being the person who rode Jim Crow in Georgia," making him "imbricated in larger, global systems of injustice; he could be defined by his victimization at the hands of "industrial imperialism" (Appiah 2014, 140). But this group did not come into existence only through victimization. As Vilashini Cooppan notes, the color line is "both that which has historically divided darker from lighter, and that which will eventually link darker peoples together in a global alliance that 'belts the world'" (2007, 36). The emergence of those linkages depends on politics, on particular forms of mutual identification, the formation of ties of solidarities, and the impulse to act together. This political craft is what takes the group "from striving to struggle" (Appiah 2014, 146–7, 159). *Dark Princess*, examined in the next section, moves forward this project, giving us a melancholic black character who emerges out of the corruption of American democracy to fuse his fate with an anti-colonial Indian princess.

Identity, Subjectivity, and the Transnational

Dark Princess narrates the story of Matthew Towns, an aspiring medical student from the South, who sees his plans frustrated by the reality of segregation. Having abandoned his studies, Matthew travels to Germany, where he encounters Princess Kautilya, a member of an anti-colonial coalition of Chinese, Egyptian, Indian, and Japanese leaders. Upon his return to the United States, and following Princess Kautilya's wishes, Matthew becomes engaged with a West-Indian leader and activist who plans a violent retaliation against lynch mobs and Ku Klux Klan members. After reneging from the group's violent goals, Matthew spends time in jail (a result of his attempt to protect the princess) and resurfaces as a politician in Chicago machine politics, under the protection of an astute political strategist, Sara Andrews. Matthew becomes increasingly involved in machine politics, while yearning silently for the experience of "world work" that he had briefly known. The novel closes with the reencounter between Kautilya and Matthew, who rejects a career in Congress in order to pursue a global struggle against colonial domination. The ending pages show us Matthew and Kautilya's meeting in the US South, welcoming their son: the "messenger and Messiah to all the Dark Worlds."

Dark Princess's story arc is a clear departure from the domestic focus of the postwar political imagination of African Americans and brings in instead the world as the proper realm to struggle politically for racial justice. In this sense, partly because of the failure of post–World War I politics to result in substantial progress toward racial equality, Du Bois himself departed from the wartime patriotism that he had espoused – however strategically (Du Bois 1918; Ellis 1992; Mennell 1999) – and turned instead toward internationalism. In the face of continued racial oppression in the United States, black loyalty to the American polity was misplaced and emancipation would require a turn outwards. *Dark Princess* is also an intervention against "the propaganda of poet and novelist" (*NMRO*) that maintained white supremacy. This propaganda is likely the fictional and nonfictional preoccupation with democracy, empire, and war that dated to the nineteenth century. According to Duncan Bell, the dream of perpetual peace in the early-twentieth century was embedded in a tradition of "white supremacist arguments about peace and global order" that embraced a "global racial peace," which promised the abolition of war following the imperial unification of white nations (Bell 2014, 649). Du Bois's novel explicitly addresses this tradition by opposing a multiracial, transnational utopia to the white and imperial notions of world peace that were then prevalent.

An engagement with a work of fiction such as *Dark Princess*, which belongs to the romantic and utopian genre, is particularly well-suited for parsing out questions of identity and subjectivity. The novel's attention to questions of emotional attachment and desire, on the one hand, and its opposites, aversion and alienation, on the other, allows us to reconstruct Du Bois's vision of shifting identities, and the emergence of transnationally oriented political subjectivities that underlie relations of solidarity beyond the group and the nation-state. The fantastic genre of the novel, moreover, puts Du Bois's aesthetic project to work for his politics, in which "the new stirrings" of black folk, new desires to create, as though they had just "awakened from some sleep that at once dimly mourns the past and dreams a splendid future" (*CNA*, 326).

Processes of subjectivation enhance freedom when they allow subjects to exit experiences of dehumanization and engage in solidaristic projects oriented toward the future. This is because, first, these projects radically expand the realm of the political imagination by making visible multiple points of resistance through coalition making. Second, these projects give

US blacks a "place in the world," making their unique location at the center of Western power a source of insight to anti-colonial transnational movements, which becomes a fulcrum for the anti-colonial cause (*DP*, 205; see also Weinbaum 2001).[13]

We see the transformation of black subjectivity involved in the turn toward transnational solidarity in the trajectory of the main character Matthew Towns, who must choose between committing to (corrupt and lifeless) American politics or rejoining the anti-imperialist work that the fictional Council of the Dark Peoples is pursuing. Du Bois's depiction of American politics is particularly bleak, even dystopian (Hooker 2017, 121). Town's political experience encompasses a stint as a Pullman porter and another one as the protégée of an African-American politician, deeply entangled in Chicago machine politics. While he depicts the latter as vastly corrupt and disconnected from the poor and marginalized blacks that he encounters in Chicago, the choice of the Pullman porters is also telling. The Pullman company was one of the largest employers of African Americans and its owner, George Mortimer Pullman, was known for having originally staffed his sleeping cars with freedmen, who, he thought, were "biologically adapted to a life of subservience" (Bates 2001, 17). The company, moreover, preferred paternalistic relations of patronage with its employees, predominantly located in the South Side of Chicago, rather than dealing politically with the porters, whose efforts to unionize – led by A. Philip Randolph – where violently opposed (Bates 2001, Chapter 3). In contrast to the corrupt or demeaning forms of incorporation offered by the US polity and paternalistic employers, the novel depicts the encounter with the transnational in a language that conveys possibility:

Now, as [Matthew] felt restless and dissatisfied, he laid it to nerves, lack of physical exercise, some hidden illness. But gradually he began to tell himself the truth. The dream, the woman, was back in his soul. The vision of *world work* was

---

[13] While outside of the scope of this project, the question of desire figures prominently in Du Bois's novel and could be productively extended to think about how the notions of freedom and political subjectivity that Du Bois envisions are centrally about the "education of desire," to use Ann Laura Stoler's term (Stoler 1995). Juliet Hooker's reading of *Dark Princess* in the context of Du Bois's writings on miscegenation is particularly illustrative of this question. In particular, Hooker's examination of Du Bois's "mulatto fictions" highlights the radical nature of the novel's story of interracial mixing in the context of the intimate and political connotations of the US prohibition of intermarriage (Hooker 2017, Chapter 3).

surging and he must kill it, stifle it now, and sternly, lest it wreck his life again. Still he was restless, *he was awakening. He could feel the prickling of life in his thought, his conscience, his body.*

(*DP*, 100, my emphasis)

World work opens the possibility of an enlarged imagination, an awakened and enlivened consciousness for black subjects. This is evident when Matthew refuses the nomination to become a Congressional candidate, after encountering Princess Kautilya,[14] acknowledging that the "Soul and Body [of the Princess qua transnationalism] spell Freedom to my tortured groping life!" (*DP*, 152).

Freedom results from the awakening of a transnational consciousness, the ability to escape for a moment destructive forms of identification offered by the American polity and to reenvision the political struggle against racial justice from a transnational perspective. Du Bois's increasing distrust of the ability of the American polity to nurture these forms of consciousness is behind his writings and political action on behalf of transnationalism, and his concern with forms of consciousness that will be able to foster freer political subjectivity. Yet, to fully understand the specificity of Du Bois's transnational turn and its relation to political subjectivity and cosmopolitanism, it is necessary to read it in the context of Du Bois's 1930s advocacy for segregation.

TRANSNATIONALISM AND SEGREGATION: AN ELECTIVE AFFINITY?

Du Bois's seldom examined writings on segregation are useful to further develop his concern with group identity and examine its compatibility and even symbiosis with forms of transnational identification. This examination serves to theoretically parse out the way in which multiple forms of mutual identification can coexist and potentiate each other. My analysis also shows how identity-based processes of self-definition can enable strong ties of solidarity between differently located groups, which can

---

[14] The symbolism of the princess's name is in line with Du Bois's broader project of resistance to Western domination. Kautilya was the name of a Brahmin who served as Chief Minister to the founder of the Mauryan Empire, Chandragupta (321–296 BC) – who successfully campaigned against the provinces Alexander the Great established west of the Indus river and who came to dominate a large part of the Indian subcontinent – and the alleged author of a famous treaty on government and foreign policy, the *Arthasastra* (Modelski 1964, 549).

lead to robust political subjectivities capable of underlying political action on behalf of cosmopolitanism.

In the 1930s, Du Bois published several articles defending segregation (*BAO; NNWN; NSS*), despite the fact that the struggle against segregation was one of the landmark causes of the NAACP. The Great Depression had shattered the country socially and economically, but the visible radical and democratic reformist movements had barely been interested in incorporating African Americans as their constituency, let alone contesting the racial prejudice that still dominated the American polity (*NNWN*, 265). Du Bois responded by suggesting that only segregated spaces are appropriate for achieving the kind of "race-consciousness" that should underlie emancipatory political actions. His focus on black churches, schools, and colleges is consistent with his earlier defense of "race organizations" in "The Conservation of Races" (*CR*) and is required because of the continuity of "color or race hatred" and the slim chance that African Americans will garner enough power to force compliance with egalitarian ideals in mainstream institutions such as "Church, State, industry or art" (*BAO*, 75; see also *NNWN*, 266; *NSS*, 328).

Absent the existence of dynamic segregated spaces, blacks' exposure to mainstream spaces makes them "ashamed of [them]selves" and unable to raise objections "when white folks are ashamed to call us human" (*BAO*, 73). This is akin to the integration of a new group into an old nation, which still "despises their color," providing for forms of identification and subjectivity that are not conducive to struggling for equality. To avoid this stunted integration, Du Bois's "far-sighted" plan advocated for increased segregation to potentiate the advances that had already occurred in "Negro churches, Negro schools, Negro colleges, Negro business and Negro art and literature" (*BAO*, 74–5). This return to the group facilitates self-definition, as opposed to the recognition offered by "integrated" institutions, which is nonrecognition, domestication, or, at worse, "racist recognition" (Coulthard 2014, 41). This is politically troubling for two reasons. First, the individuals educated will be schooled in race prejudice and taught to be ashamed of themselves. In Du Bois's words:

[R]ace prejudice in the United States today is such that most Negroes today cannot receive proper education in white institutions. If the public schools of Atlanta, Nashville, New Orleans and Jacksonville were thrown open to all races tomorrow, the education that colored children would get in them would be worse than pitiable. It would not be education.

(*NSS*, 328–9)

Du Bois goes as far as to equate education in these conditions to social death:

There are many public school systems in the North where Negroes are admitted and tolerated, but they are not educated; they are crucified.

(*NSS*, 329)

A second politically troubling feature of this juncture was the divisiveness that dynamics of assimilation brought to the struggle for racial equality more broadly. Du Bois feared that the few African Americans who had been able to progress were "desperately afraid of being represented before American whites by this lower group, or being mistaken for them" making them keen to "avoid contact with the poorest classes of Negroes" (*BAO*, 73).

One may worry that the defense of segregated spaces championed by Du Bois implies a retreat from his 1920s transnationalism, and, further, that such a move is essentializing and inherently connected to solidifying an identity to face a domestic political struggle. Against this interpretation, I argue that these fora – in contrast to the American public as a whole – allowed the aforementioned transnational affinities to become visible and active. The sense of opening that may come from such a retreat is well captured by Saidiya Hartman. For her, imagined places outside the state allow the African diaspora – otherwise "bound a hostile land by shackles, owners, and the threat of death" – to find "an imagined place" that might bring forward a vision of freedom, an alternative to defeat, and save your life (Hartman 2007, 97; see also Collins 2000, 233). The priority given to discourses of American democracy and exceptionalism in mainstream spaces means that we cannot think of forms of identification as concentric circles going from group to nation to cosmopolitanism. Instead, the nation-state denies the transnational linkages that are readily recognized by the group, making group identification more conducive to a cosmopolitan orientation. Segregated spaces as well as African-American media were the fora where the continuities between movements of colonial emancipation and the predicament of African Americans could be explored. These fora were most conducive to an understanding of race consciousness as rightfully including a Pan-African, diasporic, and ultimately global vision (Seigel 2005, 74; Singh 2004). In fact, in his 1930s writings on segregation, Du Bois explicitly connects segregation to a racial consciousness that extends beyond African Americans:

The next step, then, is certainly one on the part of the Negro and it involves group action. It involves the organization of intelligent and earnest people of Negro descent for their preservation and advancement in America, in the West Indies, and in Africa; and no sentimental distaste for racial or national unity can be allowed to hold them back from a step which sheer necessity demands.

(*BAO*, 75–6)

This turn toward self-definition is a move to cement African-American political subjectivity by reasserting the value of their heritage, but only in order to establish kinship with other groups affected by empire and devising – in coalition with these groups – a political imagination alternative to the one dominating the American polity:

And this race, with its vantage grounds in modern days, can go forward of its own will, of its own power, and its own initiative . . . It is their opportunity and their day to stand up and make themselves heard in the modern world.

(*CD*, 1258–9)[15]

Du Bois was searching for a more robust form of political agency among African Americans, required for free and freeing political action that could fuel projects of emancipation exceeding the democratic realm and addressing the imperial character of the US polity. Self-segregation and self-definition are thus a way of continuing the fight in order to develop a united opposition to racial injustice (*CD*, 1254; 1934, 1248). The establishment of links of solidarity with other colonized subjects complements this project of self-definition, whose primary goal is to shed the "almost morbid sense of personality" imposed by white Americans (*SBF*, 155), i.e., identities bestowed in a process of misrecognition (Coulthard 2014, 38–9; Fanon 2007, 9, 2008, 220–2).[16] Only after this step can racially oppressed subjects go beyond the notions of "white liberty" and "white justice" (Fanon 2008, 221; cited in Coulthard 2007, 450),which, even under the best of circumstances, cannot contest a worldwide imperial project to which the United States is no stranger.

The resulting collective identity provides promising roadmaps for supporting counter-hegemonic projects. A new transnational consciousness and the identification with subjects of empire makes African-American

---

[15] In this sense, Du Bois's project of segregation departed from Marcus Garvey's defense of race separation. The latter's belief that "all races should develop along their own lines" in order to be able to promote "their own ideas and civilization" and his argument for close cooperation between New World blacks and Africans (M'bayo 2004, 23; Rogers 1955, 160) did not contain a script for political reform and democratization of the broader polity or international sphere.

[16] See also Avram Alpert, who reads Du Bois's thought as a "practices of the global self" devoted to overcome an identity imposed "through stigma and violence" (Alpert 2019).

subjects no longer an anomaly,[17] and opens the door to a subjectivity that can foster freeing projects of political emancipation. In his writings on art, Du Bois refers specifically to the freeing aspects of the process of construction of an African-American political imagination to replace the flamboyant ideals of strength and accomplishment that otherwise fueled existing conceptions of American greatness (*CNA*, 325). Alongside his critique of the "competitive society" (Douglas 2015),[18] Du Bois attempted to map out alternatives and conduct the ethical work of self-definition to support them. Du Bois's frequent turn to the autobiographical and the literary in his writings, his interest in pedagogy and the student–teacher rapports established in segregated and integrated schools (*NSS*, 328) also highlights the importance of ethical work of subject formation in his account of emancipation.

The work of self-definition is thus conducive to a process of self-making (Butler 1997; Foucault 1997a; Valdez 2016) that is far from essentializing. Transnational consciousness and the forms of identification that facilitated it allowed for the emergence of an emancipatory subject that is a plural subject embedded in relations of solidarity. The exchanges facilitated by the moments of disclosure in hospitable collective spaces allow for changes in private meaning that could not have occurred in isolation (Beltrán 2010, 147; Warner 2005, 63). While this subject is undoubtedly embedded in power relations and social constraints, the forms of mutual identification allow them to be self-reflective and act politically against these structures (Foucault 1997b; Gutmann 2003, 192–3; Valdez 2016, 21).

In a transnational cosmopolitan framework, freedom and self-assertion flourish in sub-national realms (what Du Bois called the "nation within the nation") and transnational communities of racialized subjects. The cosmopolitan orientation that oppressed minorities can develop by exiting the confined terms of engagement of their domestic polities is based on the solidaristic recognition of common grievances. Against the Kantian conventional wisdom, a shift downward toward group identification and upwards toward transnational solidarity facilitate exploratory

---

[17] On this, see also Collins's discussion of black feminism in a transnational context (Collins 2000, chapter 10, especially 232–3).

[18] Douglas argues – following Michael Dawson – that Du Bois becomes a "disillusioned liberal;" a critic who had lost hope in the American creed. Such disillusionment with liberalism is not exclusive to Du Bois in his era, or later, as Eric MacGilvray traces in his account of market and republican freedom (2011), but it appears in Du Bois with a particular racial and transnational orientation.

practices tracing the evolving genealogy of transnational economic injustice, which the nation state merely mediates.

This account contrasts with that of Wendy Brown, who takes identity politics, broadly construed, to rely too heavily on the state to address social injuries, potentially requiring the very structure of oppression that freedom emerges to oppose (Brown 1995, 4, 18).[19] But scholars have noted that this cannot mean that all forms of identity are damaging (Alcoff 2006; Bickford 1997). Instead, as Patchen Markell notes, it is only those that reduce others' identities to a characterization necessary "for the sake of someone else's achievement of a sense of sovereignty or invulnerability" (Markell 2003, 7). Notably, the transnational forms of identity and solidarity outlined in this chapter contest sovereign and invulnerable formations that obscure the shape of injustice. They do so, however, without renouncing the theorization of the proper conditions for the development of agency are (McNay 2014), in contrast to approaches that emphasize "contingency, indeterminacy, and ongoing debate" as its condition of possibility (Zerilli 2005, 13, 166).

In other words, practices of self-definition and political exchange that eschew expected channels of claim making can make conceptions of identity contingent and open to a life shared with others. Acknowledging the role of the past in structuring identity does not make that past constraining or authoritative, nor does it claim sovereignty over the future, which is of concern to Markell (2003, 23–4). Instead, it provides an opening for the establishment of novel forms of solidarity in the present, which radically alter the identity with which one started the journey, and it fosters a transnational political imagination oriented toward the future. Despite this openness, however, the free political subjectivity is grounded and made possible by a racial and political identity that is historically grounded in a situation of domination to be overcome.

In addition to being grounded in a carefully reconstructed temporality, transnational identities are highly spatialized. It is through travel, migration, and localized encounters with others that the shared heritage of a past and ongoing insult can be found. These commonalities serve a diagnostic function, upon which a politics of emancipation can be developed. The localized transnationalization of the United States that Du Bois witnessed

---

[19] Similar objections have been raised against Pan-Africanism, namely, its indebtedness to Eurocentric essentialism and its problematic overshadowing of Afrocentric and/or African nationalist thought (Lemelle 1993; Nantambu 1998; Ndlovu-Gatsheni 2013).

informed his novel form of consciousness and enabled a transnational political subjectivity. As noted earlier, it is through internal migration that African Americans encountered new forms of racism at the hands of a native and immigrant white working class and discovered affinities with other racialized migrants. These encounters revealed the insufficiency of both the black–white racial binary and the national frame.

Such a form of identity, however, may elicit different concerns. In particular, identity constructions that straddle borders and claim to both recognize and synthetize group diversity may obscure the existence of contradictions within the process of identity construction, or the internal hierarchies that persist despite the commonalities. Du Bois's novel flags this problem when it portrays the reluctance to accept Africans and African Americans in the "Great Council of the Dark Peoples" and describes the suspicion of some of its members toward "mixed blood" (Hooker 2017, 140). Moreover, Du Bois himself argued – in *Dark Princess* and other work – that African Americans should stand *for* Africans, rather than alongside them, in the struggle against colonialism, something that he later amended (Du Bois 2005 [1955], 198). Paternalism also characterized Du Bois's relation to black women activists, whose agency he had trouble recognizing, and uneasiness with women's bodies and their presence in civic spaces (James 1996; cited in Alpert 2019; Threadcraft 2016, 92). Du Bois's friendship with Lajpat Rai offers another example of unresolved hierarchies within relations of solidarity. Whereas Rai – an India Home Rule activist who lived in New York between 1917 and 1920 – considered the case of African Americans akin to that of the untouchables in India, Du Bois sought broader affinities between African Americans and colonized India (Horne 2009; Sohi 2007, 71).

Thus, conceptions of identity are not free of the tendency to engage others "for the sake of someone else's . . . sense of sovereignty," as Markell fears (2003, 7). These moments of hierarchy within coalition making are to be expected, given the malleability of race as a historical and political category that can reconstitute itself in unexpected ways. Far from abandoning the task of theorizing identity and political subjectivity – which scholars who value indeterminacy are bound to do – it should direct us toward the critical examination of the work that those terms do in democratic forms of transnational coalition making while contesting the sovereign moments that preclude those forms. With this goal, the next section examines the role that identity has played so far vis-à-vis cosmopolitan frameworks and draws some productive contrasts with the proposed notion of transnational political subjectivity.

COMPLICATING IDENTITY AND SOLIDARITY
WITHIN COSMOPOLITANISM

Jürgen Habermas is perhaps the scholar who has best considered the question of identity in relation to the realization of republicanism and European integration (Habermas 2006, 131). He acknowledges that there is no reason identity should tie together national communities alone. Regarding Europe, he suggests that "decisive historical experiences . . . undeniably unite the European peoples" and could give rise to a "sense of belonging culturally and politically" (2000, 152). He goes on to note that the two catastrophes of the world wars should have provided enough warning about the mindsets that feed "nationalistic, exclusionary mechanisms" (2000, 152). These reflections suggest that Habermas considers European identity by definition superior to the forms of national identity that gave rise to the catastrophic conflict he mentions. This is consistent with the idea of "concentric circles" in which the expansion of the range of a collective identity gradually approximates cosmopolitanism. What the previous discussion suggests, however, is that identities and identity-based solidarities need to be scrutinized normatively before they can be endorsed as conducive to democratic justice and/or a cosmopolitan orientation. In fact, a central insight of the earlier discussion is that some group identities are more conducive to a cosmopolitan orientation than national identities. Similarly, there is no *a priori* reason to consider regional identities promising interludes to a cosmopolitan world. In particular, certain forms of European identity, rooted as they are in a common imperial past, can be as destructive and exclusionary as the national forms Habermas mentions. While Habermas is careful to note that European identity should be based upon a "non-pejorative differentiation from the citizens of other continents" (2006, 81), he is not particularly invested in theorizing how to turn European identity against the notions of racial and civilizational superiority and empire, which grounded its origins. This would be particularly important if – as noted in Chapter 2 – Habermas is interested in proposing the European trajectory of regional integration as an example to be followed. The transnational notion of identity and political subjectivity that I reconstruct in this chapter is – I believe – a crucial critical resource for the task of complementing, deconstructing and contesting the forms of Western solidarity and domination that supported the construction of empire and whose legacies structure the contemporary international, institutional architecture (Anghie 1999, 2006a, 2006b).

In particular, and in contrast to European identity formations that rely on notions of superiority that underpin both domination and cosmopolitan leadership ambitions, the aforementioned transnational identity formations rely on a shared experience of injustice and entwined histories connecting marginal subjects in the West with those in the colonies. The reliance upon a commonality of oppression is merely the starting point that allows for the development of cultural and political forms of identity based on joint political action and imagined freedom. So, the question we must ask of identity is what kind of narrative it is built upon and where does it position others, rather than necessarily aiming to move beyond it. Habermas's engagement with this register is also limited. For example, his account of postcolonial states remains in the "concentric circle" framework and emphasizes the opposition between identity and legality:

[t]he continuing tribal conflicts in formally independent postcolonial states serve as a reminder that nations only arise once they have traversed the difficult road from ethnically based commonalities among people who know one another to a legally mediated solidarity among citizens who are strangers to one another. In the West, this process of nation-state formation, which interconnects and mixes tribes and regions, took more than a century.

(Habermas 2000, 153)

Here, Habermas locates postcolonial states in the backward position of a linear trajectory, leading to European modernity. This is a maneuver of periodization that declares legal equality while introducing temporality as the medium of differentiation, suggesting certain groups represent the past of others and are in progressive motion toward the same destination (Gilroy 2004, 66). The extract also suggests an opposition between the identitarian and the legal, and these terms are again posited as two stages in a progressive temporality. The focus on certainly worrying forms of identification in the postcolonial world should not exclude the exploration of more promising alternative forms of transnational identities reconstructed in this chapter, or the projects of postcolonial state formation that posited alternative world economic orders but ran against the staunch resistance of the West (Bird 2016; Getachew 2019; van den Boogaard 2017).

The selective engagement with the postcolonial world marginalizes the experiences of subaltern groups who in fact developed valuable cosmopolitan scripts through transnational political craft. As noted in this book, these subjects were able to reach beyond the nation and develop grounds of commonality to fuel projects of emancipation to contest the racial basis of colonial and semi-colonial oppression as well as the political economy of neoimperialism. Habermas's consideration of the cosmopolitan sphere, in contrast, is depoliticized, i.e., it neglects the question of power, injustice, coalition making, and contestation to return to the moral. This is the case when he celebrates the gradual expansion of human rights principles within supranational institutions or when he focuses on the international criminal court:

> Shared moral outrage over gross transgressions of the prohibition of violence and egregious violations of human rights provides a sufficient basis for solidarity among world citizens . . . we can already observe the beginnings of the communicative structure which this requires . . . outlines of a cultural disposition required for a worldwide harmonization of moral reactions are already discernible . . . the functional requirement that the cosmopolitan society should be weakly integrated through negative emotional reactions to perceived acts of mass criminality (prosecuted by the International Criminal Court) should not represent an insuperable hurdle.
>
> (Habermas 2006, 80)

What is interesting here is the shift to the present. While his focus in Europe is on the lessons of the violent wars regarding the perils of nationalist identification, Habermas's focus in the cosmopolitan sphere is the acts of mass criminality prosecuted by the International Criminal Court, a body that to this day has only ever brought cases against Africans. This is not to say that acts of mass criminality are not horrific and worth opposing. Rather, it is to say that the form of cosmopolitan identification proposed by Habermas returns to the moral register by centering opposition to evil and rehearsing old tropes of the barbarism of non-Westerners. In so doing, Habermas depoliticizes the cosmopolitan sphere and makes it unable to host political critiques of structures of power that sustain Anglo-European dominance. Relatedly, Habermas's strategy prevents politically more productive forms of identification against the centuries of European imperialism, which would immediately focus our attention on how its legacies structure the world today. In other words, while arguably the most concerning democratic deficit at the world level is that between a Western-dominated international architecture and subaltern groups in the Global South, Habermas assumes that as long as the destructive forms of nationalism that fueled intra-European wars can be overcome and contemporary acts of mass criminality prosecuted, the prospects of a cosmopolitan union improve. In so doing, he returns to the assumption that virtuous republics will behave in cosmopolitan ways toward the rest of the world. Instead, the focus should be the past of imperialism, a question distinct from nationalism and intra-European rivalry, a cleavage that separates Anglo-European powers from the rest of the world. This is regardless of however internally cooperative (Mitzen 2013) or rivalrous they are. Thus, what Du Bois called the "solidarity of the West" (WC, 431) and the associated paradigm global whiteness are the constructs to be contested for cosmopolitanism to thrive.

In this vein, transnational cosmopolitanism enables a focus on the way in which transnational injustice affects particular groups within national spheres in ways that are common. Tracking instances of solidarity and collective action (i.e., the political craft) bringing together these groups provides clues to the shape of injustice a cosmopolitan project must address and alternative scripts for world solidarity and emancipation upon which a path to cosmopolitanism can be built. In so doing, transnational cosmopolitanism reverses the subject locations in some neo-Kantian approaches, including Habermas's. The latter posits advanced democracies and the European Union as cosmopolitan leaders and locates postcolonial states on their way to legality and insertion in an already formed society of states. In contrast, the former repositions advanced democracies and the European Union as important actors in sustaining unjust structures, and looks to grassroots and transnational instances of politics as the basis for a normative account of world injustice and the promise of cosmopolitan justice. By highlighting the affinities between heterogeneous processes of subject formation indebted to imperialism and neoimperialism, and thus upsetting the separation of spheres in which these grievances can be politicized, transnational cosmopolitanism remaps the sphere of political concern of the subjects involved and of the reach of obligation and responsibility, which needs to be adjudicated through political struggle away from the defaults of the nation-state and international arena.

CONCLUSION

In this chapter I constructed a notion of transnational consciousness and traced its emergence from group-based projects of self-definition that recognize the entwined character of their experience and that of other groups located throughout the world. I theorized the importance of these processes in supporting robust forms of transnational political subjectivity and solidarity. These practices were embedded in a process of self-definition, through which African Americans could critically engage narratives of racial exclusion and American exceptionalism and find a transnational political space where they could contest racial injustice and imagine alternative futures.

This account illustrates how creative and freeing forms of identity-based political subjectivity are conducive to emancipatory projects with transnational reach. Moreover, it shows that a transnational form of subjectivity does not require transcending or overcoming group identity, but may instead add layers of identification and networks of solidarity to already existing forms of identification. Transnational cosmopolitanism builds upon affinities that are both group-based and political, because they emerge from but also exceed the recognition of similar experiences of oppression throughout the world. In particular, group identification over-comes destructive domestic forms of identification and constitutes forms of subjectivity that are founded on solidarity with variously located groups. This is a deeply political process during which (a) the outlines of oppression are redefined as transnational; (b) the sites of contestation are reconsidered, and alternatives to the national and international level founded; and (c) alternative forms of political imagination are devised. This offers an "alternative path" to cosmopolitanism. Instead of thinking of the construction of cosmopolitanism via concentric circles going from group to nation to cosmopolitanism, this account recognizes that the nation-state operates to deny transnational linkages that are more easily recognized by the group, making group identification more conducive to a cosmopolitan orientation. The political subjectivity and solidarity that emerges from this process may be indebted to racial or other forms of group identity but it is also transnational and political. In the case analyzed, identity is racial because it relies on the commonality that emerges from the long memory of the "common disaster" and the kinship based on the "the discrimination and insult" associated with race as a regulatory category (*DD*, 117). It is transnational because it goes beyond each single one of those identities by pulling together causes and subjects that appear disparate when considered as the purview of the domestic and the international. It is political because, on the one hand, it addresses the question of power and oppression, and, on the other hand, it assesses the political possibilities of bringing different struggles together and inaugur-ating novel realms of politics (see also Olson 2005).

Finally, I have examined the way in which Habermas has conceptual-ized the question of identity in the cosmopolitan project and scrutinize the particular roles that he grants to Europe and postcolonial states. Trans-national cosmopolitanism contests Habermas's trust in Western democ-racies and Western-led regional formations to be at the forefront of cosmopolitanism. Instead, it suggests that our theorization of injustice and of the political craft required by cosmopolitanism can be better guided by groups involved in transnational coalition making than by a shift of register toward the moral. This is because such groups offer historically grounded accounts of injustice and novel scripts of justice upon which political theorists can build.

5

A Transnationally Cosmopolitan Counter-Public

This chapter builds upon the arguments of Chapters 3 and 4, which theorized transnational cosmopolitanism by developing the notions of transfigured hospitality and transnational solidarity, respectively. Chapter 3 offered a radical reading of hospitality that focused on horizontal exchanges among marginalized subjects. This move prompted a reconception of the world that makes visible transnational imperial structures and the localized ways in which they subjugate, marking the domestic and international realms as confining, and conceptualizing a third realm of transnational cosmopolitanism. Chapter 4 theorizes how identity-based ties of solidarity can be established among transnationally located marginalized groups, opening the way for transnational and cosmopolitan emancipatory political action. The present chapter theorizes a transnational counter-public, which constitutes the condition of possibility to challenging the injustice imposed by domestic and international polities. I historically reconstruct an account of the sphere of public opinion that enabled the transformation of commonality among colonial and neocolonial subjects from one built upon domination into one that can activate politically variously located subjects around the world and challenge sovereign delimitations of sanctioned realms. As such, it is a central building block in the framework of transnational cosmopolitanism. Moreover, the theorization of this sphere denaturalizes Western-centric accounts of cosmopolitan and domestic publics and complements accounts of imperial imaginaries by showing that these imaginaries were the object of contestation.

Engaging with Du Bois's writings and political action makes evident the waves of transnational solidarity and spheres of public opinion that swept under the radar of the interstate system in the early-to-mid–twentieth century. This was before political theorists declared the "crisis" of the Westphalian system brought about by neoliberal globalization and is part of the "urgent history" that recovers arguments delinking the state and sovereignty, thus empowering political theorists to reimagine global democracy (Morefield 2017, 15). These waves emerged from internal rifts of collective identities, colonial oppression, and/or lack of self-determination, and activated internal and transnational forms of political kinship, which in turn inaugurated spheres of exchange that fulfilled important roles in fueling an emancipatory political imagination.

In particular, Du Bois's transnational thinking and his utopian writing respond to imperial projects of integration based on racial utopian thinking contemporaneous to him. These argued that empires were central to the maintenance of world stability, and all agreed on the place of "backward" populations as dependent units in this scheme (Bell 2014, 654–5). As the century drew to a close, one vision that emerged from this debate contained an explicitly racial vision of peace, in which the unity of the Anglo-Saxon race, a "world historical force," was deemed capable of abolishing war (Bell 2014; Vucetic 2009, 2011). Alongside Du Bois, other subaltern subjects participated in a less visible but dynamic conversation about alternative transnationalisms, which instead saw Western crises as moments of opening for those under their yoke. Rather than attempt to reinforce structures of domination in the face of challenges or establish a sense of security at the expense of others, Du Bois's project appears as a counter-reactionary proposal to consider the question of solidarity, publics, and sovereignty *from below*.[1] Du Bois's writings and political action, and the spheres in which he operates, find meaning and overlap with a series of other discursive fora, such as the hemispheric conversation on race and racial mixing that Juliet Hooker has recently conceptualized (2017), or the currents of Ethiopianism and the black Pacific theorized by Robbie Shilliam (2015, 2016). In the face of the challenges, instabilities, and the aforementioned incipient delegitimization of colonial

---

[1] As Morefield's account shows, some projects were invested in critiques from below by highlighting transnational practices of democracy or challenging the democratic character of imperial powers (see, for instance, the writings of J. A. Hobson, Rosa Luxemburg, and Rudolf Hilferding, among others [Hobson 1975; Mommsen 1977). Yet, these projects were either invested in forms of transnationalism that did not directly problematize racial exclusion, like the workers' movement – a common target of Du Bois's critiques – or failed to consider the role of race in reinforcing the ability of organized industry to coopt the state and the democratic populace to legitimize colonial imperialism (*RA*, 725; *WC*, 444).

rule, Du Bois and his fellow travelers of color sought to capitalize on this moment to collectively think through an oppositional project to challenge imperial domination.

In the rest of this chapter, I first introduce the literature on imagined communities and counter-publics, upon which I build the notion of a transnational (anti-colonial) counter-public. The next section further reconstructs four functions of transnational counter-publics through an analysis of Du Bois's editorial work in the 1920s *The Crisis*. The fourth section argues that the anti-colonial counter-public theorized challenges neo-Kantian genealogies of cosmopolitan publics and provides a more rounded vision of "imperial politics" than critical accounts of developmentalism.

AN ANTI-COLONIAL TRANSNATIONAL COUNTER-PUBLIC

As early as 1909, Du Bois planned to write the Encyclopedia of the Negro, later reconceived as an "Encyclopedia Africana," a project ultimately supported by the Soviet Africa Institute and the Ghana Academy of Learning (Baldwin 2002, 199; Lewis 2000, 566–70).[2] This project echoes a preoccupation that Benedict Anderson's classic work attributes to nations: that of speaking on behalf of "large numbers of anonymous dead people," embedding them in secular, serial time and constructing a biography that both remembers and forgets exemplary events as their own (2006, 205–6). This is part of the process through which a sense of simultaneity emerges, which allows for a community to move through history (Anderson 2006, 24–6).

When assessed through this criterion, the panorama that we get from Du Bois's writings, his public interventions, and the intellectual and political networks that he addressed and to which he responded speaks of an active work of political imagination. This brought together diverse actors with a joint anti-imperial agenda and resulted in a sense of identity that was transnationally shared and willfully politically constructed, rather than natural or prepolitical. The experience both resembles the many dimensions of an imagined community as defined by Anderson and

[2] Interestingly, the Encyclopedia of the Negro failed to win the support of the Carnegie Corporation in the late 1930s because of doubts about the objectivity of the study, particularly in light of Du Bois's role as an editor and "propagandist" in the NAACP. The corporation would ultimately choose and fund Swedish economist Gunnar Myrdal to conduct a study (his first) on the topic (Lewis 2000, 444–51).

speaks against his privileging of the nation and sovereignty as limiting features of these dynamics (Appadurai 1996, 41).

The idea of a transnational imagined community often comes across as unattainable; critics argue that a "common spatio-temporal orientation for political judgment" is *absent* and, in any case, almost impossible to accomplish beyond Western domestic spheres of politics (Hutchins 2014, 106–8, 110–111). Yet, the anti-colonial sphere I describe in this chapter shows that differently located colonial subjects shared an understanding of what Kimberly Hutchins calls the "nature of their fate." Marginalized political actors in the West and the non-West possessed a clear sense of simultaneity and were constituted as subjects of this transnational sphere through the reflexive circulation of discourse. Moreover, organized counter-publics were built upon a common temporality, differing from that which grounded Western domestic and Western-centered international public spheres. This makes the anti-colonial counter-public, first, distinctive, rather than derivative. Second, the distinct temporality and sense of simultaneity also argues against the claims to universality of the international and domestic Western public spheres of the day and, with them, accounts that thought or think of inclusion simply in terms of expansion of such a sphere. Where the West saw territorial conquest and access to commodities and labor as associated with progress, the colonial world saw in these events oppression and dispossession, which gave rise to shared experiences with other colonial subjects and inaugurated a struggle for emancipation that could not possibly rely on Western-led understandings of progress. The character of this sphere, moreover, was not exhausted by its opposition to the dominant Western sphere, but was a forum where political imagination of alternative world arrangements could develop.

Therefore, this imagined community and the public sphere it constituted stood in a particular relation to the international sphere of states and the domestic realms of imperial polities. The dense networks of interaction among anti-colonial activists and intellectuals and the reach of these exchanges toward broader communities of racialized and/or marginalized Westerners and educated colonial populations amounts to what Michael Warner terms "counter-public." The transnational counter-public depicted here marks itself off from a dominant (white, imperial) public and contains discussions about race and colonialism that would have been regarded with hostility (Warner 2002, 86) in the dominant public domestically and internationally. Moreover, this counter-public is also "poetic," in the sense that it attempts to project a concrete and livable shape for a new world that emerges through the circulation of discourse itself (Warner 2002, 81). Yet, in addition to Warner's dimensions, i.e., marking itself off from a mainstream public and its poetic character, the anti-colonial counter-public also departs from the mainstream public morphologically. That is, this novel public straddled the sanctioned loci of politics by operating neither in the state-sanctioned sphere of domestic politics nor in international fora, inaugurating a space that was part of neither but could address both at once. This location followed from the irreducibly transnational origins of racial domination, and the need for political action that counters it to bring together the variously located subjects affected by it in order to target domestic and international spheres at once.

The transnational counter-public made up of anti-colonial activists and actors, however, is more "grounded" than the counter-public that Warner has in mind. This might sound counter-intuitive at first, to the extent that a transnational public by definition abandons the constrained and well-defined space of sovereign territorial authority. Yet, at the same time, the mere fact of distance highlights the way in which maps of allegiance and affiliation follow from historical labor flows, resulting in emergent racial solidarities and cartographies that are counter-national (Appadurai 1996, 51; Lowe 2015). Among these cartographies, the slave trade, even at the beginning of the twentieth century, still held a central place in the construction of identity and establishment of affinities between African Americans, Africa, and the African diasporas elsewhere in the world. Moreover, changing perceptions of time and space brought about by the late–nineteenth-century transformations in communications technologies also played a central role in making the transnational, anti-colonial networks possible. These transformations significantly impacted how the world could be imagined and shaped the perception of what political possibilities were available, giving rise to a series of transnational imaginaries in the West (Bell 2007a, 2013).

However, the experience of these transformations for the "worlds of color" departed from the Western experience. For subaltern subjects, the mass mobilizations of colonial and African-American troops in World War I, and the travel and communication allowed by this and other political developments, were perhaps more important than technological events in relaxing the strict regulation of mobility of bodies of color characteristic of empire and racialized polities, and resulted in sizeable African and Asian diasporas throughout the Western world. These trends also led to the transnationalization of domestic space, depicted at length in the previous chapter for the US case, which also contributed to the establishment of transnational publics of intellectual and political exchange. The term "public" here refers to a sphere of will formation and criticism of public authority, regardless of the fact that those doing the criticizing were not necessarily fellow citizens and the authorities being criticized were variously located at the domestic and international level. The mere possibility of exiting political realms that were encumbered by hierarchies of race, subjecthood, or unequal citizenship status and occupying realms that rested on a certain commonality opened the conversation to topics that were otherwise silenced. In other words, this counter-public was needed because public engagement on the topic of racial injustice within the American public was historically myopic and trafficked on understandings of American democracy that highlighted its exceptionalism, rather than one of critical debate, i.e., more akin to publicity than public opinion, in Habermas's terms (1991, 201). In this way, the inaugurated anti-colonial counter-public offered an alternative realm for affiliation, countering "approved sovereignties" and their attendant political subjectivities (Shapiro 1994, 482). In Du Bois's own words:

> If in decades or a century [my plans] resulted in such world organization of black men as would oppose a united front to European aggression, that certainly would not have been beyond my dream. But on the other hand, in practical reality, I knew the power and guns of Europe and America, and what I wanted to do was in the face of this power to sit down hand in hand with colored groups and across the council table to learn of each other, our condition, our aspirations, our chances for concerted thought and action.
>
> (*DD*, 274–5)

The process of learning about their conditions (past and present) and aspirations (future) is precisely the kind of exchange required for the poetic task of characterizing a community and – through this act – bringing it to life. In other words, the ability to consider these histories in a shared spatial or intellectual forum allows participants to make sense of them as threads of simultaneous – even if diverse – instances of imperial domination throughout the world. The mainstream public in opposition to which they stand is well defined: the domestic and international institutions defining peace narrowly as lack of conflict among Western powers and – through this concord – upholding Western aggression (*PE*). Thus, in the anti-colonial public sphere commonalities could be discussed and solidarity established, in ways that critically addressed mainstream channels of public discourse in fora such as the League of Nations.[3] This transnational public, in turn, depended on overlapping sets of discursive communities at the group level that would relay and amplify the terms of discussion in particular localities.[4]

The anti-colonial counter-public, moreover, also challenges conceptual accounts that tie the public sphere unproblematically to Westphalian states and national economic systems until the advent of globalization (Fraser 2014, 11–12). This is in keeping with the uncontained character of the political economy of empire. For example, the economics of colonial extraction in the Caribbean relied on importing slaves from West Africa, a trade that was significantly sustained by the newly independent United States (*SAST*; Balfour 2011, Chapter 6); industrial growth, in turn, required a new world system of food supply and social improvements for the masses in the West, partly enabled by colonial exploitation (*APMH*, 48; *ARW*, 708–9; *DW*, 27). There was also no obvious categorized group of members (i.e., citizens) or preexisting fora akin to the bourgeois public sphere of letters, but rather a simultaneous process of address and response that created a public whose members participated, in turn, in domestic counter-publics in the colonial and the Western world. The world-spanning organization of black men (i.e., a "united front") that Du Bois deemed unlikely, was only the institutionalization of a process of "reflexive circulation of discourse" that was well underway by the mid-twentieth century. The political work of setting up the sphere was a necessary, if perhaps not sufficient, condition to facilitate "concerted thought and action" in ways that could critically address the dispersed loci of authority that made up Western domination.

This is not to deny the distance between the aforementioned sphere and a publicly sanctioned public sphere that correlates with a sovereign power. As Nancy Fraser notes, the challenge for a transnational public sphere is twofold: to "create new, transnational public powers," on the one hand, and "to make them accountable to new, transnational public spheres," on the other (2014, 33). The political force of public opinion and the function of accountability are only ensured when both conditions are in place (Fraser 2014, 9). However, the necessary association between

---

[3] The Pan-African congresses, for example, explicitly directed their demands to specific imperial countries and/or to the League of Nations (see Chapter 3 and also Du Bois 1924a).

[4] In the case of Du Bois, addressing public spheres in segregated spaces of schools, churches, and other black public spaces was central for his transnational project. See Chapter 4 and also Michael Dawson's discussion of the black counter-public (1994, 199, 206).

public spheres and a sovereign authority can blind theorists to instances of transnational solidarity and association already in existence, which need to be made sense of theoretically. Moreover, as Janet Conway and Jakeet Singh note, an expectation that encounters must result in "collectively binding decisions" is not always normatively desirable, because it might hinder communication, solidarity, and cooperation (2009, 74). Thus, it is necessary to reconstruct transnational publics *not* tied to transnational public powers for at least two reasons. First, a historically grounded theorization of the process by which novel transnational publics are formed is central for one of the tasks suggested by Fraser: to link public powers to transnational public spheres. In other words, reconstructing historical instances of a transnational public speaks of the possibility of new publics emerging and supports a bottom–up approach to solving the challenge of transnationalism. In a bottom–up approach, public powers could be connected to an existing transnational public sphere, instead of an alternative in which new forms of public power are first constructed and then create – in a top–down manner – bureaucratized publics whose inclusionary character is limited. Scholars raising concerns about the feasibility of transnational publics note the unlikelihood of the emergence and/or existence of these publics. However, marginalized minorities in exclusionary communities gain by exiting their domestic public sphere; this allows them to do the work of self-definition away from painful currents of misrecognition and to reach out transnationally for constructive forms of mutual identification and solidarity. In this sense, the normative desirability of transnational forms of identification works not only at the level of tying global events to global publics, but also at the level of the subject, whose realization may depend on exiting oppressive national realms through the imagined communities that exceed these realms. Ultimately, if the goal of cosmopolitanism is to maximize the circulation of global emancipatory discourses and to mobilize dispersed actors with claims about injustice beyond the nation, a normative cosmopolitan project should strive to capture the dynamism of transnational counter-publics, while endeavoring to establish productive, if contested, conversations among these fora, and relying on these exchanges to guide processes of institutionalization when needed.

A second reason why it is theoretically relevant to reconstruct thinking and action constitutive of transnational public spheres is that these realms put forward an answer to the question of who is affected by particular structures of domination when the "who" is no longer unproblematically "citizens." In this case, the reconstruction I offer shows that it was precisely those for whom Westphalian institutions were ineffective, at best, and oppressive, at worst, who mobilized and reached beyond their confines, providing clues to the specific ways in which this system failed to legitimately include even marginalized groups within Western citizenry. The already diverse and transnational publics of the early-twentieth century, and the viable forms of interconnection that emerged as a consequence, speak of the way in which domestic polities under the Westphalian system of the first half of the twentieth century systematically fell short for their racialized citizens. In order to further substantiate the shape and character of a transnational counter-public and its connections to a radical cosmopolitanism, the next section proposes a fourfold conceptualization based on Du Bois's writings and editorial practices in the 1920s *The Crisis*.

THE STRUCTURAL TRANSFORMATION OF THE TRANSNATIONAL PUBLIC SPHERE

Four dimensions of the anti-colonial transnational counter-public are conducive to a bottom–up process of subjectivation and will formation. First, the *diagnostic function* of the transnational public contributes to disseminating information about variegated forms of (colonial) oppression. This information fuels a process of dialogue and exchange that contributes to tracing the particular character of transnational oppression, the common origins of forms of domination in different spheres and their linkages to domestic and supranational institutions. Second, the *connective function* of the transnational public sphere operates through the reflexive circulation of discourse that reaches and creates bonds among differently located marginalized groups (beyond bureaucratic/ academic elites) throughout the world. Third, the *political activation function* is operative when the public – not formally tied to an accountable public power – nonetheless identifies particular structures of formal authority and informal power, which it addresses directly with a claim about responsibility for particular grievances. And fourth, the *counter-sovereign function* of the transnational public destabilizes the legitimacy of sovereignty in two ways: (a) it exposes sovereignty as a force that conceals common/transnational/international sources of domination; and (b) it reveals the disenfranchisement of marginalized groups (the public's members) from access to political power as formally codified domestically and internationally.

Historians have, by now, provided excellent accounts of the transnational linkages between African Americans and African diasporas, and, in particular, of the connections between black nationalism and anti-colonial movements throughout the world. Du Bois holds pride of place in these accounts, as the cofounder of the Pan-African movement, as the editor of a central outlet in publicizing and cementing these connections (*The Crisis*), and as a visible political activist and intellectual in the interwar and post–World War II period. Du Bois lived, acted, and wrote constantly during this period of deepening interconnections and exchanges between anti-colonial groups and diasporas, which had been significantly emboldened by the two world wars. In the rest of this section I expand on the four dimensions of a transnational public sphere with a survey of Du Bois's 1920s writings and editorial work for *The Crisis*, a privileged outlet in which Du Bois takes up the task of political persuasion.

Diagnostic Function

A transnational counter-public provides a common space and temporality to diagnose the shared problems of domination structuring and orienting anti-colonial activists' critiques. In keeping with the analysis of Du Bois's transnationalism in this book, recent historical accounts have provided a wealth of evidence about the radical transnationalism of African, Afro-diasporic, and Asian anti-colonial movements and, in particular, the deep embeddedness of African-American radical movements in these networks.[5] In particular, historical reconstructions have shown that transnational networks among groups throughout the non-Western world built upon overlapping understandings of Western domination and the confluence of political projects of emancipation. These networks effectively resulted in what Kimberly Hutchins calls a "common spatio-temporal orientation for political judgment" spearheaded through travel, participation in international meetings, intellectual and journalistic production, as well as actual encounters. Notable among the latter were the

---

[5] This literature has engaged with the internationalism of nationalist and radical African-American movements in the United States (Blain 2015; Bloom and Martin 2014; Bush 2009; Frazier 2014; Gallicchio 2000; Makalani 2011; West et al. 2014); with the connections of these groups with India, Japan, China, and the Soviet Union (Burton 2006; Kelley and Esch 2008; Mullen 2004; Sohi 2007); and with the emerging cosmopolitan narratives and/or alternative philosophies of history that emerged out of these exchanges (Onishi 2013; Slate 2012a; Von Eschen 1997).

connections that resulted from the migration of radical Indian and Caribbean activists, who left British India or Caribbean possessions to settle in the United States, which enabled reciprocal learning between African Americans and other colonial subjects about their conditions and the familiarization of each of these groups and colonial activists back home with the other's radical writing (Horne 2009; Mullen and Watson 2005a; Slate 2012a; Sohi 2007).[6] These connections, importantly, extended beyond India and toward Japan and China because of the role that these countries played in the political imagination of anti-racist projects of both African-American and Asian intellectuals and the consideration of these causes as entwined and important for each other's success (Makalani 2011; Mullen 2004; Onishi 2013).

The regularity of these encounters and the mutual exchange of information about their experiences served the goal of both diagnosing the outlines of colonial domination throughout the world and of uncovering a common experience between African Americans and colonial subjects around the world. As the editor of *The Crisis* – appropriately subtitled "A Record of the Darker Races" – Du Bois contributed to the task of familiarizing his African-American readership with the conditions of injustice around the world. In the 1920s in particular, Du Bois's "Opinion" column regularly featured his own and/or reproduced texts covering Liberia, Haiti, the Pan-African movement, and colonial issues more broadly. The accounts of colonial oppression were often accompanied with an analysis of the chains of responsibility in the West, including the United States. For example, in an issue from 1922, Du Bois reproduced a speech made by Warren G. Harding (president at the time) during his campaign, condemning the Haitian intervention. By reproducing this excerpt, Du Bois pointed at the hypocrisy of the continuation of the invasion during Harding's presidency, arguing that:

Practically all we know now is that thousands of native Haitians have been killed by American marines, and that many of our gallant men have sacrificed their lives at the behest of the executive department . . . to continue at the point of domination which at this point requires the presence of no less than 3,000 of our armed men on that foreign soil.

(Du Bois 1922)

---

[6] Gerald Horne, in particular, underlies the grassroots reach of Indian anti-colonialism causes among African Americans and notes the little-known indebtedness of the Nation of Islam to the Ahmadiyya movement among Muslim Indian immigrants (Horne 2009, 39–43, 168)

Du Bois's denunciation of US colonial endeavors goes beyond his regular focus on Haiti (like his 1923 condemnation of the US invasion of the Virgin Islands [*LN*] and the critique of US interventions in Mexico, Cuba, and the Philippines discussed in Chapter 4). This attention to US imperialist enterprises accomplishes two goals. First, it counters accounts of US exceptionalism by realigning the United States with other imperial powers. Second, it illustrates the similarities between the conditions of US blacks and those of colonial and neocolonial subjects elsewhere. This is clear in Du Bois's engagements with questions of education, access to land, disenfranchisement, and labor exploitation in the colonies – something that is also highlighted in the 1923 Pan-African Conference declaration, reproduced in *The Crisis* in 1924 (Hunt et al. 1924, 121). In a similar move, in a later issue of 1924, Du Bois reports on the situation in Kenya, where Britain "segregate[s] black men into the worst and least habitable parts of their own land" and "established a government based on white suffrage" (Du Bois 1924b, 151). The phrasing chosen by Du Bois powerfully drives home the common currents between the US racial regime and the situation of colonialism.

Du Bois's transnational orientation exceeds Pan-Africanism not only in his focus on US imperialist endeavors in Central and South America, but also through his keen interest in the unity between Asia and Africa, an alliance he believed was necessary to ensure the world leadership of people of color (2005 [1933], 74). Thus, as examined at length in the previous chapter, Du Bois was deeply involved (through friendships, political connections, and study) with the Indian anti-colonial cause and the fate of China and Japan in the world sphere, and was invested in disseminating knowledge about Asian colonial and semi-colonial experiences among African Americans (2005 [1945]). The political importance of India in Du Bois's thought is further reflected in his extensive engagement with Gandhi, who qualifies as Du Bois's "most passionately admired statesman," and "a symbolic avatar of transnational cooperation, peace, harmony, and moral example" (Mullen and Watson 2005b, 114).

Thus, in this period, Du Bois's writings, reviews, and editorial work brought to the purview of his African-American readership varied and detailed accounts of the colonial condition that served to diagnose the particularities of injustice and draw lines of affinity among these conditions throughout the world, including with those of black Americans.

Connective Function

The reflexive circulation of discourse that is required to constitute a transnational counter-public sphere went well beyond the periodical meetings bringing African, Afro-diasporic, and African-American leaders together. While organizations such as the Pan-African Conference, the International African Service Bureau, the American Negro Academy, and the Council on African Affairs, among others, were central to this movement, the formation of a public opinion exceeded elites and took shape around "founding" moments of concerted transnational thought and action. These events included the Italian invasion of Ethiopia, the opposition to the lack of recognition of self-determination in the Atlantic Charter, the celebration of the recognition of black laborers by the World Federation of Trade Unions, and the support of striking workers in Africa by Africans and African diasporas throughout the world (Kelley 1999; Von Eschen 1997, 11, 26, 47–8, 55, 62).

The reflexive circulation of discourse required to connect sites of injustice around the world means transnational coalitional work and intellectual exchange among anti-colonial leaders must trickle down and become the subject of engagement of broader grassroots publics. A look at the material on Pan-Africanism in the W. E. B. Du Bois Papers[7] offers a glimpse of the multidimensional work required, on Du Bois's end, to make this diffusion possible. The archive tells the story of Du Bois's active participation in a series of transnational events associated with international solidarity and anti-colonialism, as well as his active contribution to the growth and diffusion of these activities among political actors and community groups in the United States and abroad. We find evidence of exchanges between Du Bois and American news outlets, peace organizations, African-American activist groups and black institutions of higher learning. Also evident are the international dimensions of these efforts, reflected in the coverage abroad of the activities of the Pan-African Congress and Du Bois's exchanges with white European peace activists and black intellectuals and activists from around the world. In addition to these exchanges, it is important to consider the wide circulation of the work of Du Bois and anti-colonial activists and intellectuals, including the reproduction of the latter's work in *The Crisis* and the extensive familiarity of anti-colonial intellectuals with Du Bois's work (Horne 2009;

---

[7] W. E. B. Du Bois Papers, University of Massachusetts at Amherst.

Sohi 2007; Vitalis 2015, 103). The connections with African and Afro-diasporic intellectuals was not peculiar to Du Bois, but characteristic of a broader set of African-American intellectuals who forged connections with "theoreticians of liberation and the future leaders of independent Africa and the island nations of the Caribbean," which Robert Vitalis groups under the term "Howard school of international relations" (2015, 12).

Within this group, however, Du Bois stood out for the prolific character of his writings, and their reach through a broad range of nonacademic outlets. In this sense, as a commentator who reached beyond academic circles, Du Bois not only contributed to the cause of familiarizing US black publics with current anti-colonial struggles, but also with the history and political economy of colonial areas. An overview of his book reviews (published in outlets such as *The New Republic, The Nation, The American Political Science Review*, and *The Crisis*) reveals that in the 1920s Du Bois covered a variety of questions related to the history of colonial locales and the question of imperialism, including the history and contemporary situation of Congo, East Africa, Haiti, India, Kenya, and South Africa. He similarly covered volumes on African poetry and mythology, education in Africa, and historical characters like Toussaint L'Ouverture, among other topics (Du Bois 1977, 65–7, 81–91, 101–3, 109–11, 115–121, 125, 129–131, 139).

The Crisis also featured pieces by Du Bois and other authors on history and current affairs pertaining to Africa, the African diaspora, and India. For example, the February issue of 1922 included a biographical piece on Gandhi and the non-cooperation movement, and the May 1929 issue included an essay solicited by Du Bois in which Gandhi sent a hopeful message to American blacks (The Crisis 1924; Young 2001, 17). The transnational orientation of *The Crisis* is a constant rather than an exception; the December issue of 1924 contained a critical commentary on the restriction of migration from the West Indies, called to the attention of the peace movement the millions of African and African-diasporic subjects living under oppressive conditions, and featured a piece by an Ethiopian author on the connected histories of Ethiopia and Egypt (Du Bois 1924c; Nerouy 1924). Lengthier features like the one on Ethiopia were a recurrent theme in *The Crisis*, spanning topics like the history of Brazilian slavery, nationalism in Egypt, Langston Hughes's account of his travels to West Africa, and a story on "Soviet Russia and the Negro" by Claude McKay (Fauset 1920; Hughes 1923; McKay 1923; Nash 1923).

The circulation of material acquainting differently located subjects with the cultural, historical, and political conditions of other colonial and neocolonial subjects was thus central in the editorial project of *The Crisis*, and supportive of the reflexive circulation of discourse required to connect marginalized groups. Du Bois acknowledged as much when he quoted approvingly from Leslie P. Hill's volume of poetry on Toussaint L'Ouverture, which he reviewed for *The Crisis*:

> The Negro youth of the world has been taught that the black race has no great traditions, no characters of world importance, no record of substantial contribution to civilization. The creative literature . . . must correct and counterbalance this falsehood of centuries. A worthy literature reared upon authentic records of achievement is the present spiritual need of the race.
>
> (Du Bois 1977 [1928])

Political Activation Function

A transnational counter-public is defined by its location outside of spheres of politics that are currently (and have been historically) formalized. Yet, even in the absence of a formally constituted transnational site of politics and authority, the emerging transnational counter-public reconstructed here addressed different loci of authority on behalf of their causes. This was accomplished through fora that, while not formally authorized, contributed to promoting causes of emancipation. For example, in 1919, the Pan-African Meeting denounced the exclusion of colonial peoples from postwar discussions of central concern to them, while in 1921 the Pan-African Conference provided a forum for the Haitian delegate to protest the American occupation (Los Angeles Times 1921; New York Times 1921).

The different ways in which African-American activists sought to influence the US government in favor of the fate of the colonies also falls under this category. For example, as already mentioned, in 1945, Du Bois was granted consultant status at the San Francisco conference as the NAACP representative and advocate for the colonies, an agenda that he also took to the US Senate (The Chicago Defender 1945a, 1945b). Soon after, African-American support was crucial for the progress and eventual passage of the Luce-Celler Act of 1946, which legislated an exception to the Asian ban by authorizing a quota of Indian and Filipino migrants to be admitted to the United States and to become naturalized (Horne 2009, 190).

These accounts illuminate the viability of political action in coalition with other subjects of empire, an issue Du Bois highlighted explicitly for his readers in a 1923 issue of *The Crisis*:

The Negro problem, the problem of the color line, is international and no matter how desperately and firmly we may be interested in the settlement of the race problem in Boston, in Kansas, and in the United States, it cannot ultimately be settled without consultation and coöperation with the whole civilized world.

(*PFR*, 9)

Lest we think Du Bois is referring to Western-led international organizations, he specifies a few lines below that "it is absolutely necessary that we seek to-day the harmony, self-knowledge and coöperation of the greater groups of people of Negro descent" (*PFR*, 9).[8]

Counter-Sovereign Function

Networks of exchange between differently located colonial and neocolonial subjects resulted in the constitution of a public that jointly reconstructed a composite picture of Western domination through the reflexive circulation of discourse connecting its members and allowing for cooperative political action. These actions challenged imperial sovereignty as a force concealing structures of domination and disenfranchised racialized groups from access to formal power.

Examples of counter-sovereign political actions abound in *The Crisis* of the 1920s. Du Bois reported often on his participation in transnational meetings. In 1924, for example, he covered the appearance of Haitian representative Mr. Hudicourt at the Pan-American conference, where he delivered remarks criticizing the "utterly indefensible action of the United States in these countries" (1924d, 153). In this intervention, Du Bois not only reproduced the specific complaint and the critical coverage of *The New York Times* on the issue, but chose to highlight a transnational sphere that amplified the voices of Caribbean peoples under American military occupation.

---

[8] The reference to "civilized people" was used by Du Bois and other Pan-African activists to refer to Africans, as in one of the articles of the resolutions of the Third Pan-African Congress that reads: "we ask for the civilized British subjects in WEST AFRICA and the WEST INDIES the institution of home rule and responsible government without discrimination as to race and color" (Hunt et al. 1924, 120).

Du Bois's interest in criticizing or highlighting moments of disruption in international fora is evident from his regular coverage of the League of Nations and other international organizations. In an issue of 1923 he asserts that "with all the sinister influence of Great Britain in its counsels, it has nonetheless recently shown its loyalty to humanity by admitting Ethiopia . . . to a seat in its council table" along with Liberia and "stolen Haiti" (*LN*). He contrasts the league with the Red Cross, for example, which he condemns for the "open prejudice that stains their actions."

In 1924, *The Crisis* reproduced the final declaration of the 1923 Pan-African Congress, coauthored by Du Bois, Rayford Logan, and Ida Gibbs Hunt. This document is particularly telling of the gradual emergence of a coherent public that problematized the conditions affecting differently located peoples as emerging from a common overarching structure of imperial and racial oppression. Demands included the extension of voting rights from Senegal and the West Indies to French West Africa, the restoration of the land rights of natives in Kenya, Rhodesia, and the Union of South Africa, and the end of lynching and mob law, along with the recognition of full citizenship regardless of caste in the United States, among other issues (Hunt et al. 1924). The resolution addressed a series of national governments (European colonial powers and the United States) as well as the League of Nations, which it enjoined to "investigate and report" on the conditions of the mandated territories (Hunt et al. 1924, 121–2). Addressing European-led fora like the League of Nations was a constant for Pan-Africanism, as well as Du Bois's commentary (*LN*, *PE*, *W*, 1921, 1923). The focus was usually on criticizing the exclusion of representatives of colonial peoples and the topics of racism and colonialism from their perspective. The goal of this criticism was not only to call attention to exclusions *per se*, but also to performatively highlight the existence of an opposing public – a "counter-public" in which the excluded subjects and people *could* and *did* pursue public and critical debate on those questions. Moreover, Du Bois was particularly aware of the consequences of silencing these topics in Western fora, which, by contributing to European peace, had the effect of facilitating violence toward the non-West. As Du Bois put it in his commentary on the Locarno peace pact between European powers:

Are we not facing a fairer future? We are not unless we are willing to face fairly certain hindering truths. England because of its dominant position in the League of Nations, where she controls the Secretariat . . . can yield to arbitration without fear. Through it she browbeats Turkey out of the Mosul oil fields and keeps her European enemies quiet while she enslaves India and Africa and China more securely. If France can be rid of the German menace she has a freer hand in Morocco and Syria. If Germany has no fear of England and France she can regain her industrial hegemony and therewith her lost colonies. If America can go into the World Court and the League of Nations with her hands red with the blood of Haiti and her pockets filled with the loot of Nicaragua, she will be free for further imperialism in Central and South America.

(PE)

Du Bois's caustic commentary on the celebratory tone of Western peace advocates brings home the lack of concern of this international public for the violence afflicting colonial peoples, African Americans in the United States, and the victims of US occupation in Central and South America. Du Bois notes as much when he notes "pacifists'" lack of action in response to growing tensions between the United States and Mexico and US meddling in Nicaragua in the late 1920s (W).

The fact that the political actions enacted in the anti-colonial counter-public meant a serious challenge to the status quo is clearest in the way in which attempts at transnational coalition were policed at every step by Western domestic and colonial authorities. The coordination between the British government, Canada, and the United States in order to surveil and restrict the movement of Indian anti-colonial activists (Sohi 2007, 106) is only one – if poignant – example of the way in which the narratives of imperialism that political theorists have masterfully reconstructed often required hard coercive power to do their work. Beyond the travel restrictions imposed on colonial and African-American subjects I have already mentioned, the high-profile accusation and trial against Du Bois during McCarthyism is also important evidence of this. Du Bois himself, in commenting on his trial and acquittal in 1951, argued in this direction:[9]

[O]f course this unjustified effort to make five persons register as the source of foreign propaganda for peace and particularly to scare fifteen million Negroes from complaint, was not the real object of this long and relentless persecution. The real object was *to prevent American citizens of any sort from daring to think or talk* against the determination of Big Business to reduce Asia to colonial subserviency to American industry; to reweld the chains on Africa; to consolidate United States control of the Caribbean and South America; and

---

[9] Du Bois was charged with being a foreign agent for his work for the Peace Information Center (*TA*, chapter 5; Von Eschen 1997, 137).

above all to crush Socialism in the Soviet Union and China. That was the object of this case.

(*TA*, 1104, my emphasis)

The role of policing and repression in bounding political imagination is clear in the previous extract. Thus, a theorization of a transnational public sphere should be able to develop critical tools to examine the extent to which policing powers are at the root of stunted publics that would otherwise challenge existing arrangements. In particular, it seems that Fraser's preoccupation with establishing "new, transnational public powers" cannot do without the equally important task of identifying, critiquing, and dismantling the national and international public powers systematically assailing them.

TRANSNATIONAL COUNTER-PUBLICS AND THE POLITICS OF EMPIRE

The previous section illustrates the four dimensions of a transnational counter-public via Du Bois's writing and editorial practices in *The Crisis* in the 1920s. These exchanges resulted in the gradual development of a sense of common space and temporality that could *diagnose* the character of domination. The increased connections facilitated by technological advances, as well as the growing readership among these groups, resulted in increased and fluid transnational *connections*. The anti-colonial counter-public successfully enabled and *activated political claims*, which it directed toward existing formal and informal spaces of authority. Finally, this sphere, while not officially tied to a sanctioned authority, appealed to and often destabilized Westphalian understandings of the domestic and the international as the exclusive realms of politics, thus serving a *counter-sovereign* function.

The reconstruction of this sphere and the recovery of these voices completes the dynamic literature of liberal imperialism by documenting "more varied sorts of political imagination," and new histories that are not national histories (Cooper 2005, 402; Dirks 1990, 26). It also contributes to politicizing critical intellectual histories of empire by highlighting the writings and actions of actors who confronted empire (Cooper 2005, 405, 412–13). In so doing, it goes beyond the reconstructions of imperial projects and developmental discourse by imperialist thinkers alone, or anti-imperialist Western thinkers (Bell 2007b, 2016; Mantena 2010; Mehta 1999; Pitts 2005, 2010), which could be enriched by accounts of the alternative discursive spaces proliferating alongside imperial projects.[10] Moreover, a reconstruction that stays close to the political context and the particular political practices that addressed Western authorities from below, as well as their responses, enriches our theorization of empire beyond the intellectual context. In particular, it shows the ideology of empire had to rely on different forms of repression and policing in order to maintain its rule.

Moreover, the proposed account of a transnational counter-public complements efforts to decolonize critical theory while conceiving of the sources for this critique in a more cosmopolitan and democratic manner, i.e., by relying on actual colonial or neocolonial subjects whose critiques were often more radical than those of Westerners. Among others (Livingston 2016; Muthu 2003), an example is Amy Allen's recent project to abandon vindicatory stories of historical progress in favor of a critical problematization of the present, based on a genealogical approach to progress that can retain the normativity of critique without romanticizing the past. Yet, Allen's approach continues to treat the Enlightenment as "self-correcting" and defers the "deep engagement, dialogue and learning across subaltern difference" she gestures toward (Singh 2016). Another example is the influential reconstruction of developmental thinking by Thomas McCarthy, which references Du Bois early on as representing an alternative tradition that considers racism to be foundational to modernity, as opposed to the narratives of progress McCarthy criticizes (2009, 24–5). Throughout the book, however, McCarthy does not engage with Du Bois's thinking but instead repeatedly notes the marginal character of his thought vis-à-vis mainstream historical and sociological accounts of progress (2009, 109n, 10, 41n, 83). Yet, it is clear that Du Bois was received and discussed in African-American and anti-colonial milieus at a level that – rather than marginal – was extensive and enthusiastic. For example, if we take one of the events considered in Chapter 3 (the participation of Du Bois as an NAACP consultant and advocate for the colonies at the San Francisco Conference) and examine its coverage by mainstream and African-American newspapers, the difference is remarkable. While *The New York Times* covered Du Bois's participation with one article, *The Chicago Defender* and *The Baltimore Afro-American* featured seventeen and eleven articles, respectively (not counting Du Bois's two columns in *The Chicago Defender* in March and May of 1945). These pieces

---

[10] As Jeanne Morefield notes, other works are currently challenging the focus on major figures of political thought in the literature on empire and political theory (Morefield 2016; Marwah 2017; Getachew 2019; Temin forthcoming).

inform the African-American reading public of the NAACP petition for the equality of races and its advocacy for colonial peoples, of Du Bois's critique of the lack of condemnation of colonialism by the United Nations (UN) (and the American alignment with it), and of the contested discussions around the system of trusteeship (Defender Staff Correspondent 1945; Durham 1945; Matthews 1945; The Chicago Defender 1945a). While this survey may suggest that Du Bois was indeed "marginal," it also brings to the surface a distinct realm of public discourse central to challenging the developmentalism McCarthy criticizes. Eliding the widespread coverage of Du Bois's political involvement in the black, Pan-African, and Asian anti-colonial counter-public and the way in which it contributed to cementing affinities between these groups is not just a simple omission, but a mischaracterization of the politics of empire and an act that reinforces the claim to totality of the developmental narratives under scrutiny.[11]

Such incomplete historical accounts of the politics of empire are often echoed by contemporary accounts of the origin of the cosmopolitan public sphere, as in Habermas's assessment that:

The first events that actually drew the attention of the world public sphere, and polarized its opinion on a global scale, were the wars in Vietnam and the Persian Gulf.

(Habermas 1997, 124)

Habermas goes on to argue that the series of conferences on "global issues", organized by the UN, were attempts to "bring some political pressure to bear on governments" by making them topics of discussion at the world level (Habermas 1997, 124–5). This assessment is telling of the lack of attention to the world-encompassing public opinion that formed around the question of colonialism and to the anti-colonial counter-public in particular. The UN global issues conferences, which Habermas acknowledges were still issue specific, are channeled through national public spheres rather than being genuinely cosmopolitan (1997, 125). The public sphere described in this chapter, by contrast, did rely on truly transnational spaces because it was forced out of national and international public spheres. Habermas comes closest to considering such a fora when he discusses organizations such as Greenpeace and Amnesty

---

[11] The same could be said of the frequency of treatment of African affairs in Du Bois's columns in African-American newspapers, his series of essays on African politics for *The People's Voice* in 1947–1948, and his extensive writing on African history (*APMH*; *APT*; Du Bois 1959, 2007 [1946]; *TN*).

International, which "creat[e] and mobiliz[e] transnational public spheres" and confront states from "within the network of international civil society" (1997, 125). While these organizations may be legitimately identified as members of a transnational public sphere, they are Western-led, nongovernmental organizations of the post–Cold War era, which deflected social and economic issues in favor of civil and political ones (Getachew 2019; Moyn 2010, 2018). This focus avoids the more contentious transnational public sphere considered in this chapter, and the more radical contestation of Western political hegemony built upon imperial capitalism that was staged.

CONCLUSION

The present chapter conceptualizes the transnational counter-public, made up of subjects and groups excluded from mainstream political spaces. I highlight four functions of these publics: diagnosis, connection, political activation, and counter-sovereignty. This conceptualization stays true to the focus on the political craft making up cosmopolitanism, i.e., theorization that is attentive to the particular way in which excluded groups setup relations of solidarity beyond the nation state and inaugurate public fora that serve to identify and challenge nodes of power responsible for injustice.

This is not to argue that these networks of solidarity exhaust the process of identification of chains of responsibility for domination or that their claims cover all potential political relations to be made accountable for injustice. After all, I have argued that particular forms of national identity facilitate, rather than prevent, injustice and can work to obscure affinities beyond the nation that are relevant to counter it.

Transnational counter-publics illuminate the deeply political character of the processes through which injustice is identified and problematized, and the need to theorize the conditions of political subjectivity and motivation that enable emancipatory politics beyond the state. The claims of identity reconstructed in the previous chapter support the establishment of this public and remain open to contestation and responsive to the forms of domination that motivate them as well as newly emerging forms. To the extent that global capitalism, in its imperial or postcolonial, neoliberal shape, radically affects the lives of a myriad of subjects throughout the world, the possibility of mutual identification and political solidarity based on experiences of oppression remains open. Du Bois's openings toward other oppressed subjects, including white workers, immigrants of all races, and Southern Europeans, testify to the potential of broader networks of solidarity (*AMER, DP,* 66, 255, *DW, WC*). The failure of these openings, on the other hand, underlines the tragic effectiveness of the color line at curtailing them and the need to continue unpacking its role in global injustice.

The historical account of the anti-colonial counter-public complements the literature on liberalism, empire, and developmentalism by providing a more nuanced picture of the politics of empire, including contemporaneous colonial and neocolonial subjects who challenged it. These challengers, acting in concert, inaugurated nonstate-centric networks of solidarity and public will formation that still nurture emancipatory politics today.

Theorizing transnational counter-publics based on the actual political practices of W. E. B. Du Bois and fellow black and anti-colonial activists speaks directly to the feasibility of these linkages, the potential pathways for their reproduction, and/or contemporary iterations of these efforts that can enrich theories of transnational and cosmopolitan justice. In so doing, this reconstruction joins efforts to bring political theory "down into the world of the *demos*" (Tully 2008b, 8–9), though it challenges the traditional sovereign demarcations of such a grouping. Reconstructing this sphere is ultimately a deeply theoretical endeavor, because by showing how political action exceeds what sovereign barriers and interstate fora demarcate, it questions the theoretical language that has been used to understand projects of justice beyond the nation. The proposed interpretive strategy goes beyond the call of intellectual historians to embed textual interpretation in the social and political worlds of the theorist (Moyn 2014, 2016). When a theorist – as in the case of Du Bois – is also an experienced political activist whose actions have been thoroughly investigated and accounted for by historians and biographers, we are able to move closer to what Brooke Ackerly identifies as "grounded theory," i.e., a theory that "wrestle[s] with the meaning within political contestation and resistance" and takes the "politics of practice" as the starting point (2018, 137). The theoretical insights emerging from an engagement with Du Bois are richer because of the grounded character of his theorizing and his well-known taste for autobiographical reflection. In other words, political theorizing of global injustice, and the conceptualization of the requirements of cosmopolitan justice, will be greatly enriched by our ability to incorporate thinkers and political actors who bring us closer to the "political craft" underlying the cosmopolitan project.

Conclusion

The Promise of a Transnational Cosmopolitanism

Immanuel Kant and W. E. B. Du Bois, brought into conversation in this book, lived in moments of historical rupture. As Kant conceptualized his cosmopolitanism, he witnessed the expansion of the European empire and expressed anxieties over the effects of colonial conflict on his project of European peace. Du Bois's 1920s recover the post-First World era, in which the West found itself – and its empire – in crisis. Partly motivating the West's anxieties was the consolidating awareness among the worlds of color of their status as a "world force" populating the globe, a force that could come together in the pursuit of emancipatory projects. This awareness came alongside the understanding of imperialism as a transnational form of power, which needed to be contested in the manifold instances and locations in which it took shape, without losing sight of its structural, world-encompassing character.

There are echoes between these historical moments and our present condition, which – at the time of writing – shows a divided West with recrudescent nativist domestic currents. Yet, it is the outline of transnational injustice and the sense of possibility that may follow from attending to transnational instances of politics that are missing from contemporary political theory's engagement with the global. Such an absence needs to be understood in the context of the heavy influence of Kant's framework, mistakenly taken to offer a global vision that is ultimately narrowed by disproportionate attention directed toward Europe as a cosmopolitan model. By contrast, I argue that cosmopolitanism is best theorized from the ground up by paying attention to the political craft of local groups who diagnose, alongside other differently located groups, the character of transnational injustice. Transnationalism removes the blinders of state and interstate thinking and allows us to theorize a cosmopolitanism that better illuminates the particular shape of injustice, the way in which injustice is connected across sites, and the networks of political action built upon solidarity and imagination that operate against these structures. For this task, I have argued, it is central to engage critically with the Kantian tradition through the neglected thought and political practices of W. E. B. Du Bois.

Based on this engagement, I conceptualize a notion of transnational cosmopolitanism. Transnational cosmopolitanism democratizes cosmopolitanism by relinking the theorization of justice and politics at the level of the cosmos to the interconnected struggles battling oppression in particular localities. I show Kantian cosmopolitanism to be too narrowly concerned with stability and peace in Europe to alone ground a framework of cosmopolitanism. I engage with the productive theorization of transnationalism by neo-Kantian scholars like Seyla Benhabib, James Bohman, Rainer Forst, and Lea Ypi, but note that the seemingly global Kantian framework is ultimately confining, and that without engaging with his principles "from below" we cannot fully account for the political practices and motivational structures that may advance a project of cosmopolitanism. For this I turn to the thought of W. E. B. Du Bois; this allows for a transfigured hospitality of horizontal exchanges that aim to disrupt and replace the exclusionary realms of domestic and international politics, rather than merely facilitate communication between them. The welcoming stance of marginalized subjects toward others around the world allows for the establishment of ties of solidarity, the reconstruction of the transnational character of injustice, and political action in concert. Coalition making is facilitated by forms of mutual identification allowing oppressed subjects to exit demeaning processes of misrecognition domestically and develop freer forms of political agency to support emancipatory projects. Such connections and joint action relies upon and further strengthens transnational counter-publics, which stand in opposition to sanctioned realms of politics and provide a common sense of temporality to struggling groups. This public serves to diagnose the common outlines of injustice, connect its members to each other, activate subjects politically, and put in question a system of sovereign states and interstate coordination that has historically organized world governance. In the rest of the conclusion, I reflect on the entwined question of hierarchy and hospitality, offer some reflections on the lessons of transnational cosmopolitanism for the global justice literature, and examine how the proposed framework illuminates the contemporary juncture.

THE GOOD, THE BAD, AND THE HOSPITABLE

The transnational cosmopolitanism proposed depends on a transfigured hospitality that is radical because it relies on forms of horizontal communication and exchange making visible the exclusions of existing realms of right. In Derridean terms, the problem of the host being at once that who welcomes and the master (*Wirt*) is lessened in two ways in these formations. First, it is the subaltern within the West who finds affinities with those subject to Western imperial power abroad and an escape from destructive forms of recognition at home. Second, the solidarity that results from this exchange is devoted to contesting the exclusionary character of existing institutions, rather than sustaining it. This represents a normatively important departure from the strategy of privileging the West as the model for normative projects of hospitable cosmopolitanism. These accounts tend to advocate for the extension of international regimes of cooperation toward non-Western countries, and encourage their democratization "Western style," rather than seeing radical reform as necessary.

However, this does not mean that the proposed transnational cosmopolitanism is a utopia devoid of hierarchies and conflict, far from it. Throughout the book I have brought up the particular blind spots evident in Du Bois's writings and political action, from his tendency to speak *for* Africans and his troubling discomfort with women's presence in civic spaces,[1] to his allegiances with regimes responsible for imperial and internal oppression, including Japan and the Soviet Union (on the latter, however, see Vaughn 2016). These attempts by Du Bois to establish mastery, however, need not undo the critical gains of relying on his thought for the construction of an alternative and transnational framework of cosmopolitanism. Rather, it is more productive to draw lessons from the hierarchies that emerge, even among subaltern actors struggling against imperial power. These lessons are about the always politically contested character of coalition making, in general, and the forms of solidarity that underpin cosmopolitanism, in particular. The contestation is characteristic of universality more generally, which I take to be the

---

[1] Recent scholarship has remarked upon the masculinist character of the project of black internationalism and recovered the neglected role of women activists in the Pan-African movement (Blain 2015, 2016; Blain et al. 2016; Makalani 2016; Stephens 2005). It should be noted that despite the noted gendered biases in Du Bois's activism, his scholarship has been productively utilized by feminist theorists (Balfour 2005; Hancock 2005).

continuous contestation of existing universals by the groups, in any given iteration, left out of it (Balfour 2011, 132–3; Butler 1996; Ingram 2013, 156–7). Grappling with this does not require us to retreat into indeterminacy or into abstract universals but, rather, should lead us to an agenda committed to tracing the outlines of power, the ways in which power constructs consciousness, and the forms of identification and subjectivity that can ground political struggle against it. In other words, the reproduction of difference and the permanence of hierarchy require us to more carefully engage with the circulatory character of power and its ability to reconstitute itself under different guises, even among subaltern groups.

This task can be better pursued when we depart from an abstract principle of equal concern and instead attend to the many particulars that make up the global (i.e., the transnational) in order to theorize what cosmopolitan equal concern requires. This involves becoming acquainted with the political dimensions of cosmopolitanism; i.e., the diverse interests that guide Western and subaltern cosmopolitan projects, the diverse ways in which overarching forms of oppression along lines of race, gender, class, and sexuality operate in different spaces, the subjects that are produced, and the ways in which those subjects contest those roles and inaugurate novel forms of subjectivity. It is only through a transnational lens that we can recognize and theoretically reconstruct the political practices through which differently located subjects coalesce and target sites of dominating power (i.e., the political craft). Attending to these instances of coalition making allows political theorists, in turn, to better understand the matrix of injustice that a cosmopolitan project must tackle, to better theorize its normative priorities, and to capture with more precision the motivational and political dimensions of such a project.

GLOBAL JUSTICE IN A TRANSNATIONAL LENS

The framework of transnational cosmopolitanism offers an important corrective to the ways in which identity is conceptualized in contemporary global justice debates. Liberal nationalists, on the one hand, assume that – rather than investigate whether – identity is unproblematically national; cosmopolitans, on the other hand, either deny the relevance of identity to their projects or subsume special relationships within universalist frameworks (Abizadeh and Gilabert 2008), rather than explore the specificity of identity and the political work it does, alongside solidarity, to further cosmopolitan projects. This missed opportunity emerges clearly in Richard Miller's comparative assessment of domestic and global injustice:

[I]n the United States, most reflective, generally humane people who take the alleviation of poverty to be an important task of government think they have a duty to support laws that are much more responsive to neediness in the South Bronx than to neediness in the slums of Dacca.

(Miller 1998, 202)

The assumption that Americans care more about African-American residents in the South Bronx than about vulnerable Bangladeshis who live in Dacca may be true in relative terms, but the actual level of concern for South Bronx residents would be put into question by Du Bois's critique of American democracy[2] and his account of transnational identity reconstructed in the previous sections. In particular, Du Bois's writings show that the degree of concern of privileged white American citizens for their African-American counterparts leaves something to be desired, but also that the plight of South Bronx populations and that of African and Asian subjects were – at least in his time – substantially connected and jointly explained by imperial domination, rather than two causes in tension that require adjudication.

Similarly, when a prominent liberal nationalist theorist like David Miller argues that "we owe special obligations to those we are bound to by ties of history, common culture, common language and so forth," he assumes unproblematically that there are no special obligations that tie subgroups in Western countries to non-national groups in ways that would give the latter's interests "special weight" (Miller 2008, 384). This is likely because, as Lu notes, national identity, in the effort to solidify one loyalty, often uproots entire groups and simplifies their otherwise multi-dimensional personalities into a more manageable "citizen" (Lu 2000, 257–8). Regrettably, discussions about national identity within the cosmopolitan literature – unlike discussions within democratic theory (Allen 2004; Gutmann 2003) – do little to examine the ways in which national culture has been invested in supporting projects of domination, and the ways in which marginalized groups have looked beyond the nation to counter them.[3] In the transnational cosmopolitanism proposed

---

[2] As well as by contemporary accounts of black and Latina/o political thought (Barvosa 2008; Dilts 2014; Shelby 2007; Taylor 2015; Threadcraft 2014, 2016).

[3] In his discussion of national responsibility, Miller acknowledges that societies may exclude and exploit one minority group and that there may be conflicting national cultures in any given society, in which case his claims would not apply (Miller 2007, 132–3). However, he

in this book, it is clear that domination, rather than cooperation can be and has been the goal of national identity (Mills 1997). Moreover, in the case of the United States, the narrative of American exceptionalism had the effect of obscuring the participation of the United States in the imperial trajectory established by European powers (Rana 2010). As shown in the second half of this book, a turn toward group self-definition among African Americans that led them to reconsider both the origins of US racial injustice and the site of emancipatory politics (both toward the transnational) was necessary to contest the confining tenets that organized the US polity. Compare this turn with the use of national identity to posit an idealized orientation toward cooperation with the most vulnerable within Western democracies, which does not obtain in reality and distracts from the political tasks needed to realize domestic justice. Yet, the argument for domestic cooperation nonetheless serves theoretically to *prevent* the consideration of obligations toward the rest of the world and, most importantly, to decline to scrutinize the interconnections between the oppression of minorities at home and overarching global injustice.

But transnational cosmopolitanism does not simply correct the approaches of liberal nationalists or special relations. It also shows – vis-à-vis cosmopolitans within the global justice literature – the gains to be had in departing from a predominant focus on deriving global justice obligations for Western subjects and instead attending to the particular claims of justice politically articulated by those subjected to injustice. These explorations would clarify that there is no simple divide between a wealthy West and a destitute Global South when it comes to working toward global justice. Instead, just as, or even more than, in Du Bois's time, the task for cosmopolitanism is to parse out the particular way in which transnational forms of injustice operate and become grounded in multiple spaces throughout the world, both in the West and the non-West. This should be uncontroversial in a world characterized by deindustrialization, the move of production offshore, mass migration, and refugee flows. However, it still stands at odds with the conventional wisdom on both sides of the global justice literature. While social liberals contend that inequalities at home should be given priority over global inequality, cosmopolitans claim that the West has to attend to the poverty and injustice that characterizes the Global South. Both accounts seem to

---

does not pursue the possibility that these groups may develop special relations beyond the nation and ultimately concludes that "outright alienation from national culture will be rare" (Miller 2007, 133).

rely on an overly simplistic picture in which domestic inequality is unconnected to global economic and political trends and either best addressed through domestic institutions or considered less urgent than the more extreme levels of poverty encountered abroad (Valdez 2019). Thus, both accounts prevent us from considering and theorizing injustice as an always-transnational question and the political actions and institutional reforms required to confront it. The transnational cosmopolitanism framework proposed in this book provides explicit guidance in this respect. A focus on local conditions of injustice should not rush to conclude that the state is the actor best placed to address them, but instead should inquire into the shared origins of injustice causing this and other instances of oppression throughout the world. Moreover, attention to the political craft by those so affected – including the forms of mutual identification, the political connections to and joint action with differently located subjects similarly affected, and the alternative futures that they imagine – can further enrich theorization. This enrichment emerges from putting into question existing institutions that allocate resources – material and symbolic – and working alongside marginal subjects in constructing a different world.

WESTERN CRISIS IN A TRANSNATIONAL LENS

It is worth considering what resources the proposed transnational cosmopolitanism offers for examining the contemporary anti-globalist backlash that has fueled the electoral victories of xenophobic populist projects like Trump in the United States, Brexit in the United Kingdom, and the victorious government coalition in Italy, among others. The purchase of right-wing populist projects depends on a notion of the national as opposed to the global, where the global (encompassing international law, trade, migration, and refugee flows, among others factors) has become an abstract and overarching victimizer of overwhelmingly white domestic groups. This picture elides both the role of Western elites in sustaining the global regimes that brought instability to previously sheltered groups within the West and the deep interconnections between the new forms of victimization and long-standing ways in which global regimes create pockets of vulnerability throughout the world. Recent accounts have tied the populist revival to a neoliberal left that "mixed together truncated ideals of emancipation and lethal forms of financialization," as Nancy Fraser puts it (2018), in what amounts to a "failure of progressive politics," as Michael Sandel has it (2018, 354). As much as they both criticize the particular globalism that the new left has embraced, their instinct is to return to the domestic by affirming the "New Deal Coalition" and the more egalitarian emancipation of the 1960s and 1970s (Fraser 2018) or by urging polities to seriously consider questions about the significance of national borders and the obligations we have toward fellow citizens vis-à-vis citizens of other countries (Sandel 2018, 357).

The concern for the last three decades of left-embraced, neoliberal globalization, while necessary, filters out from view a long history of global economic and political dynamics victimizing groups within Western societies. These were groups that the New Deal also left behind (Lowndes 2008; Skotnes 2012), and that constructed more radical visions, including the anti-imperial critique associated with the 1960s and 1970s civil rights movements (Rana 2018; Slate 2012b). Moreover, these views filter out the central role of racism – or what political scientists today call "racial resentment" – in structuring contemporary politics and making populist coalitions possible, over and above economic factors. Hence, this strategy assesses the vulnerability to global forces visited upon the downwardly mobile white working class as novel and unique, rather than addressing them alongside the long history of exposure to these forces by vulnerable groups in developing countries and vulnerable groups within the West – like racialized citizens in former colonial and slave societies. By disconnecting the narrative and reality of victimization of the white working class from the question of race and from that of other groups domestically and around the world misrepresents the character of globalization. The financialization of the economy, the flexibilization of labor markets, and the retrenchment of the welfare state were projects pushed by Western-led international organizations throughout the world, and to a greater extent in developing countries with less political clout.[4] Arguing for domestically centered progressive coalitions misconstrues the problem and curtails the potential of transnational coalitions that can better track the structure of injustice.

In other words, searching for solutions in nostalgic accounts of 1930s progressive national coalitions or reacting to global shocks by suggesting

---

[4] As much as trade and the "movement of jobs" away from the West have been made central in the US brand of right-wing populism, the movement of production offshore is hardly a boon for vulnerable groups in developing countries, whose states provide infrastructure and vast tax exemptions in exchange for low-quality jobs with a high turnover. Moreover, while trade agreements may depress certain sectors in the West, they are also behind mass dislocations in developing countries' small landholding sectors and small-and-medium enterprises.

that obligations to conationals have been forgotten falls into two problems. First, it forgets that when obligations to white conationals were served they relied on the exploitation of others through imperialism or neocolonial extractive and exploitative behaviors. Second, they correctly diagnose the neoliberal globalism tried by the mainstream left as wrongheaded, but retreat to the national rather than exploring the reach of the injustice of neoliberal globalization and aiming to form emancipatory transnational coalitions that can better track this reach. But the thriving black radical tradition in the 1920s and the 1930s reconstructed in this book diagnosed racial injustice in the US polity as entwined with US imperial injustice and made the case to address both at once. The transnational cosmopolitan approach that I build upon this tradition offers theoretical tools to exit the binary between the global and the domestic and consider alternative models of transnational engagement that foster justice domestically and globally. This framework contributes to drawing chains of responsibility that are not limited by domestic or international chains of accountability and can focus on the actions of multinational corporations, the international financial architecture that grants them enforceable rights throughout the world, and the role of Western elites and international organizations in sanctioning those powers (Anghie 1999; Isiksel 2016). But this reconstruction can most accurately track injustice when it proceeds from the bottom–up by paying attention to how oppression is organized – through race, gender, class, and sexuality – in particular locales and by normatively engaging with the political craft of groups that organize against injustice and reach out for alliances among similarly located subjects elsewhere.

In sum, the answers provided by transnational cosmopolitanism are neither a blanket defense of the global – as the heirs or spouses of "Third Way" politicians would have it – nor a recovery of nostalgic progressive moments that did not tackle the transnational question of race and empire head on. Instead, transnational cosmopolitanism decisively directs our sights to the lines of continuity between dispossession at home and abroad, along with a denunciation of the institutions and actors enabling that dispossession, as well as those who rely on the strategy – old and tired, Du Bois would say – of co-opting poor whites to the cause of imperial capitalism.

References

Abizadeh, Arash. 2005. "Does Collective Identity Presuppose an Other? On the Alleged Incoherence of Global Solidarity." *American Political Science Review* 99 (1):45–60.

Abizadeh, Arash and Pablo Gilabert. 2008. "Is There a Genuine Tension between Cosmopolitan Egalitarianism and Special Responsibilities?" *Philosophical Studies* 138 (3):349–65.

Ackerly, Brooke A. 2018. *Just Responsibility: A Human Rights Theory of Global Justice*. New York: Oxford University Press.

Adorno, Theodor. 1978. *Minima Moralia: Reflections from Damaged Life*. New York: Verso.

Ahmad, Dohra. 2002. "More Than Romance: Genre and Geography in Dark Princess." *English Literary History* 69 (3):775–803.

Ajei, Martin and Katrin Flikschuh. 2014. "Colonial Mentality: Kant's Hospitality Then and Now." In *Kant and Colonialism*, ed. K. Flikschuh and L. Ypi. Oxford: Oxford University Press.

Alcoff, Linda M. 2006. *Visible Identities: Race, Gender, and the Self*. New York: Oxford University Press.

Allen, Amy. 2016. *The End of Progress: Decolonizing the Normative Foundations of Critical Theory*. New York: Columbia University Press.

Allen, Danielle S. 2004. *Talking to Strangers: Anxieties of Citizenship since Brown v. Board of Education*. Chicago: Chicago University Press.

Alpert, Avram. 2019. *The Global Origins of the Modern Self, from Montaigne to Suzuki*. New York: SUNY Press.

Anderson, Benedict. 2006. *Imagined Communities*. New York: Verso.

Anderson, Carol. 2003. *Eyes off the Prize: The United Nations and the African American Struggle for Human Rights (1944–1955)*. Cambridge: Cambridge University Press.

Anderson, Elizabeth. 2010. *The Imperative of Integration*. Princeton, NJ: Princeton University Press.

Anghie, Antony. 1999. "Time Present and Time Past: Globalization, International Financial Institutions, and the Third World." *New York University Journal of International Law & Politics* 32 (1):243–90.

  2006a. "Decolonizing the Concept of 'Good Governance'." In *Decolonizing International Relations*, ed. B. G. Jones. Lanham: Rowman & Littlefield.

  2006b. "The Evolution of International Law: Colonial and Postcolonial Realities." *Third World Quarterly* 27 (5):739–53.

Appadurai, Arjun. 1996. "Sovereignty without Territoriality." In *The Geography of Identity*, ed. P. Yaeger. Ann Arbor: The University of Michigan Press.

Appiah, Kwame Anthony. 2014. *Lines of Descent: W. E. B. Du Bois and the Emergence of Identity*. Cambridge, MA: Harvard University Press.

Aviator. 1908. "Asia Contra Mundum." *The Fortnightly Review* 494:185–200.

Baldwin, Kate. 2002. *Beyond the Color Line and the Iron Curtain*. Durham, NC: Duke University Press.

Balfour, Lawrie. 2010. "Darkwater's Democratic Vision." *Political Theory* 38 (4):537–63.

  2011. *Democracy's Reconstruction: Thinking Politically with W.E.B. DuBois*. New York: Oxford University Press.

  2005. "Representative Women: Slavery, Citizenship, and Feminist Theory in Du Bois's "Damnation of Women"." *Hypatia* 20 (3):127–48.

Barvosa, Edwina. 2008. *Wealth of Selves: Multiple Identities: Mestiza Consciousness and the Subject of Politics*. College Station: Texas A&M University Press.

  2011. "Mestiza Consciousness in Relation to Sustained Political Solidarity: A Chicana Feminist Interpretation of the Farmworker Movement." *Aztlán* 36 (2):121–54.

Bates, Beth Thompkins. 2001. *Pullman Porters and the Rise of Protest Politics in Black America*. Chapel Hill: The University of North Carolina Press.

Beck, Lewis W. 1971. "Kant and the Right to Revolution." *Journal of the History of Ideas* 32 (3):411–22.

Bell, Duncan. 2007a. *The Idea of Greater Britain: Empire and the Future of World Order, 1860–1900*. Princeton, NJ: Princeton University Press.

  ed. 2007b. *Victorian Visions of Global Order: Empire and International Relations in Nineteenth Century Political Thought*. Cambridge: Cambridge University Press.

  2013. "Making and Taking Worlds." In *Global Intellectual History*, ed. S. Moyn and A. Sartori. New York: Columbia University Press, 254–79.

  2014. "Before the Democratic Peace: Racial Utopianism, Empire, and the Abolition of War." *European Journal of International Relations* 20 (3):647–70.

  2016. *Reordering the World: Essays on Liberalism and Empire*. Princeton, NJ: Princeton University Press.

Beltrán, Cristina. 2010. *The Trouble with Unity*. Oxford: Oxford University Press.

Benhabib, Seyla. 1986. *Critique, Norm, and Utopia: A Study of the Foundations of Critical Theory*. New York: Columbia University Press.

2004. *The Rights of Others: Aliens, Residents, and Citizens*. Cambridge: Cambridge University Press.

2006. "Another Cosmopolitanism." In *Another Cosmopolitanism: The Berkeley Tanner Lectures*, ed. R. Post. Oxford: Oxford University Press.

2009. "Claiming Rights Across Borders: International Human Rights and Democratic Sovereignty." *American Political Science Review* 103 (4): 691–704.

Bernasconi, Robert. 2001. "Who Invented the Concept of Race? Kant's Role in the Enlightenment Construction of Race." In *Race*, ed. R. Bernasconi. Oxford: Blackwell Publishers.

2003. "Will the Real Kant Please Stand Up: The Challenge of Enlightenment Racism to the Study of the History of Philosophy." *Radical Philosophy* 117 (January/February):13–22.

2011. "Kant's Third Thoughts on Race." In *Reading Kant's Geography*, ed. S. Elden and E. Mendieta. New York: SUNY Press.

Bickford, Susan. 1997. "Anti-Anti-Identity Politics: Feminism, Democracy, and the Complexities of Citizenship." *Hypatia* 12 (4):111–31.

Bird, Gemma. 2016. "Beyond the Nation State: The Role of Local and Pan-National Identities in Defining Post-Colonial African Citizenship." *Citizenship Studies* 20 (2):260–75.

Blain, Keisha N. 2015. "'[F]or the Rights of Dark People in Every Part of the World:' Pearl Sherrod, Black Internationalist Feminism and Afro-Asian Politics during the 1930s." *Souls* 17 (1–2):90–112.

2016. "'Confraternity Among All Dark Races': Mittie Maude Lena Gordon and the Practice of Black (Inter)nationalism in Chicago, 1932–1942." *Palimpsest: A Journal on Women, Gender, and the Black International* 5 (2):151–81.

Blain, Keisha N., Asia Leeds, and Ula Y. Taylor. 2016. "Women, Gender Politics, and Pan-Africanism." *Women, Gender, and Families of Color* 4 (2):139–45.

Blanning, Timothy C. W. 1996. *The French Revolutionary Wars, 1787–1802*. London: Arnold.

Bloom, Joshua, and Waldo E. Martin. 2014. *Black against Empire: The History and Politics of the Black Panther Party*. Berkeley: University of California Press.

Bob, Clifford. 2001. "Marketing Rebellion: Insurgent Groups, International Media, and NGO Support." *International Politics* 38 (3):311–34.

Bohman, James. 2007. *Democracy across Borders: From Dêmos to Dêmoi*. Cambridge: MIT Press.

Bowen, Huw V. 2005. *The Business of Empire: the East India Company and Imperial Britain*. Cambridge: Cambridge University Press.

Briggs, Charles L. 2005. "Genealogies of Race and Culture and the Failure of Vernacular Cosmopolitanisms: Rereading Franz Boas and W. E. B. Du Bois." *Public Culture* 17 (1):75–100.

Brown, Gregory Stephen. 2003. *Cultures in Conflict: The French Revolution*. Westport: Greenwood Publishing.

Brown, Wendy. 1995. *States of Injury: Power and Freedom in Late Modernity.* Princeton, NJ: Princeton University Press.

Bryant, John. 2007. "Witness and Access: The Uses of the Fluid Text." *Textual Cultures: Texts, Contexts, Interpretation* 2 (1):16–42.

Burton, Antoinette. 2006. "Cold War Cosmopolitanism: The Education of Santha Rama Rau in the Age of Bandung, 1945–1954." *Radical History Review* (95):149–72.

Bush, Roderick. 2009. *The End of White World Supremacy: Black Internationalism and the Problem of the Color Line.* Philadelphia: Temple University Press.

Butler, Judith. 1996. "Universality in Culture." In *For Love of Country? Debating the Limits of Patriotism*, ed. J. Cohen. Boston: Beacon.

1997. *The Psychic Life of Power: Theories in Subjection.* Palo Alto: Stanford University Press.

Cabrera, Luis. 2018. "Ambedkar and Du Bois on Pursuing Rights Protections Globally." *Global-E* 11 (1), www.21global.ucsb.edu/global-e/january-2018/ambedkar-and-du-bois-pursuing-rights-protections-globally (accessed 12/18/2018).

Cadahia, Luciana, Valeria Coronel, and Franklin Ramírez. 2018. *A Contracorriente: materiales para una teoría renovada del populismo.* La Paz: Vicepresidencia del Estado Plurinacional de Bolivia.

Cavallar, Georg. 2014. "Kant and the Right of World Citizens: An Historical Interpretation." In *Critique of Cosmopolitan Reason: Timing and Spacing the Concept of World Citizenship*, ed. R. Letevall and K. Petrov. Oxford: Peter Lang.

Clewis, Robert R. 2015. "Kant's Natural Teleology? The Case of Physical Geography." In *Reading Kant's Lectures*, ed. R. R. Clewis. Berlin: Walter de Gruyter.

Clulow, Adam. 2014. *The Company and the Shogun: the Dutch Encounter with Tokugawa Japan.* New York: Columbia University Press.

Cohen, Jean L. 2004. "Whose Sovereignty? Empire versus International Law." *Ethics & International Affairs* 18 (3):1–24.

2006. "Sovereign Equality vs. Imperial Right: The Battle over the 'New World Order'." *Constellations* 13 (4):485–505.

2008. "Rethinking Human Rights, Democracy, and Sovereignty in the Age of Globalization." *Political Theory* 36 (4):578–606.

Collins, Patricia Hill. 2000. *Black Feminist Thought: Knowledge, Consciousness, and the Politics of Empowerment.* New York: Routledge.

Contee, Clarence G. 1972. "Du Bois, the NAACP, and the Pan-African Congress of 1919." *The Journal of Negro History* 57 (1):13–28.

Conway, Janet, and Jakeet Singh. 2009. "Is the World Social Forum a Transnational Public Sphere? Nancy Fraser, Critical Theory and the Containment of Radical Possibility." *Theory, Culture & Society* 26 (5):61–84.

Cooper, Frederick. 2005. "Postcolonial Studies and the Study of History." In *Postcolonial Studies and Beyond*, ed. A. Loomba, S. Kaul, M. Bunzl, A. Burton and J. Etsy. Durham, NC: Duke University Press, 401–22.

Cooppan, Vilashini. 2007. "Move on Down the Line: Domestic Science, Transnational Politics, and Gendered Allegory in Du Bois." In *Next to the Color Line*, ed. S. K. Gillman and A. E. Weinbaum. Minneapolis: Minnesota University Press, 35–68.

Coulthard, Glen Sean. 2007. "Subjects of Empire: Indigenous Peoples and the 'Politics of Recognition' in Canada." *Contemporary Political Theory* 6 (4): 437–60.

  2014. *Red Skin, White Masks: Rejecting the Colonial Politics of Recognition.* Minneapolis: University of Minnesota Press.

Dawson, Michael C. 1994. "A Black Counterpublic? Economic Earthquakes, Racial Agenda(s), and Black Politics." *Public Culture* 7 (1):195–223.

Defender Staff Correspondent. 1945. "Hit U.S. Stand on Colonies." *The Chicago Defender*, May 19, 4.

Derrida, Jacques. 2000. "Hostipitality." *Angelaki* 5 (3):3–18.

Dhawan, Nikita. 2016. "The Canary Who Sings in a Predictable Monotone: Kant and Colonialism." *Postcolonial Studies,* www.tandfonline.com/doi/abs/10.1080/13688790.2016.1262203?journalCode=cpcs20.

Dilts, Andrew. 2014. *Punishment and Inclusion: Race, Membership, and the Limits of American Liberalism.* New York: Fordham University Press.

Dirks, Nicholas. 1990. "History As a Sign of the Modern." *Public Culture* 2 (2):25–32.

Douglas, Andrew J. 2015. "W.E.B. Du Bois and the Critique of the Competitive Society." *Du Bois Review* 12 (1):25–40.

Du Bois, W. E. B. 1914a. "Mexico." *The Crisis* 8 (2):79.

  1914b. "World War and the Color Line." *The Crisis* 9 (1):29–31.

  1918. "Editorial: Close Ranks." *The Crisis* 16 (3):111.

  1919. "Returning Soldiers." *The Crisis* 18 (2):13–4.

  1920. "Marcus Garvey." *The Crisis* 21 (2):58–60.

  1921. "The African Mandates." *The Crisis* 22 (4):151.

  1922. "Haiti." *The Crisis* 24 (3):106.

  1923. "The Turk." *The Crisis* 26 (5):201.

  1924a. "Haiti." *The Crisis* 27 (4):152–3.

  1924b. "Kenya." *The Crisis* 27 (4):151–2.

  1924c. "Opinion." *The Crisis* 29 (2):55–8.

  1924d. "The Third Pan-African Congress." *The Crisis* 27 (3):120–2.

  1934. "Segregation in the North." *The Crisis* 43 (4):1241–8.

  1940. "Mexico and Us." *The Amsterdam News*, September 21.

  1959. "The Africans and the Colonialist Tactic." In *Writings by W.E.B. Du Bois in Periodicals Edited by Others, vol. 4, 1945–1961*, ed. H. Aptheker. New York: Kraus-Thomson Organization, 289–91

  1977. *Book Reviews by W. E. B. Du Bois*, ed. H. Aptheker. Milkwood: KTO Press.

  1978 [1945]-a. "Letter to Edward R. Stettinius (03/10/1945)." In *The Correspondence of W. E. B. Du Bois. Selections, 1944–1963, Volume III*, ed. H. Aptheker. Amherst: University of Massachussets Press.

  1978 [1945]-b. "Letter to the American Delegation at the San Francisco Conference (05/16/1945)." In *The Correspondence of W. E. B. Du Bois:*

Selections, 1944–1963, Volume III, ed. H. Aptheker. Amherst: University of Massachusetts Press.

2005 [1906]. "The Color Line Belts the World." In *W. E. B. Du Bois on Asia: Crossing the World Color Line*, ed. B. Mullen and C. Watson. Jackson: University Press of Mississippi.

2005 [1933]. "Listen Japan and China." In *W. E. B. Du Bois on Asia: Crossing the World Color Line*, ed. B. Mullen and C. Watson. Jackson: University Press of Mississippi.

2005 [1945]. "The Colonial Groups in the Postwar World." In *W. E. B. Du Bois on Asia: Crossing the World Color Line*, ed. B. Mullen and C. Watson. Jackson: University Press of Mississippi.

2005 [1955]. "China and Africa." In *W. E. B. Du Bois on Asia: Crossing the World Color Line*, ed. B. V. Mullen and C. Watson. Jackson: University of Press of Mississippi, 196–201.

2007 [1946]. "The World and Africa." In *The World and Africa and Color and Democracy*, ed. H. L. Gates. New York: Oxford University Press.

Dubois, Laurent, and John Garrigus. 2006. *Slave Revolution in the Caribbean 1789–1804: A Brief History with Documents*. Boston: Bedford/St. Martins.

Dudziak, Mary L. 2011. *Cold War Civil Rights: Race and the Image of American Democracy*. Princeton, NJ: Princeton University Press.

Durham, Richard. 1945. "Parley Ducks Colonial Issue." *The Chicago Defender*, May 5, 1.

Economic and Social Council. 1947. *Summary Record of Thirty-Fourth Meeting*. New York: UN Commission on Human Rights, December 12.

Edler, Friedrich. 1911. *The Dutch Republic and the American Revolution*. Baltimore: The Johns Hopkins Press.

Egnal, Marc, and Joseph A. Ernst. 1972. "An Economic Interpretation of the American Revolution." *The William and Mary Quarterly* 29 (1):3–32.

Elam, J. Daniel. 2014. "Echoes of Ghadr: Lala Har Dayal and the Time of Anticolonialism." *Comparative Studies of South Asia, Africa, and the Middle East* 34 (1):9–23.

Ellis, Mark. 1992. "'Closing Ranks' and 'Seeking Honors': W. E. B. Du Bois in World War I." *The Journal of American History* 79 (1):96–124.

Ellison, Ralph. 1999. "Working Notes for Juneteenth." In *Appendix of Juneteenth*, ed. John Callahan. New York: Vintage.

Fanon, Frantz. 2007. *The Wretched of the Earth*. Translated by R. Philcox. New York: Grove Press.

2008. *Black Skin, White Masks*. New York: Grove Press.

Fauset, Jessie. 1920. "Nationalism and Egypt." *The Crisis* 19 (6):310–6.

Fine, Robert, and Will Smith. 2003. "Jürgen Habermas's Theory of Cosmopolitanism." *Constellations* 10 (4):469–87.

Fischer, Sibylle. 2004. *Modernity Disavowed: Haiti and the Cultures of Slavery in the Age of Revolution*. Durham, NC: Duke University Press.

Flikschuh, Katrin. 2010. "Kant's Sovereignty Dilemma: A Contemporary Analysis." *Journal of Political Philosophy* 18 (4):469–93.

2017a. "Kant's Nomads: Encountering Strangers." *Con-Textos Kantianos* 5 (June):346–68.

2017b. *What is Orientation in Global Thinking? A Kantian Inquiry.* Cambridge: Cambridge University Press.

Forst, Rainer. 2001. "Toward a Critical Theory of Transnational Justice." *Metaphilosophy* 32 (1/2):160–79.

2012. *The Right to Justification: Elements of a Constructivist Theory of Justice.* New York: Columbia University Press.

2015. "Transnational Justice and Non-Domination: A Discourse-Theoretical Approach." In *Domination and Global Political Justice: Conceptual, Historical, and Institutional Perspectives*, ed. B. Buckinx, J. Trejo-Mathys and T. Waligore. New York: Routledge.

Foucault, Michel. 1997a. "The Hermeneutics of the Subject." In *Ethics, Subjectivity, and Truth*, ed. P. Rabinow. New York: The New Press, 93–106.

1997b. "On the Genealogy of Ethics: An Overview of Work in Progress." In *Ethics, Subjectivity, and Truth*, ed. P. Rabinow. New York: The New Press, 253–80.

Fraser, Nancy. 2009. *Scales of Justice: Reimagining Political Space in a Globalizing World.* New York: Columbia University Press.

2014. "Transnationalizing the Public Sphere: On the Legitimacy and Efficacy of Public Opinion in a Post-Westphalian World." In *Transnationalizing the Public Sphere*, ed. K. Nash. Cambridge: Polity, 8–42.

2018. "The End of Progressive Neoliberalism." *Dissent* (January 2).

Frazier, Robeson Taj. 2014. *The East is Black: Cold War China in the Black Radical Imagination.* Durham, NC: Duke University Press.

Fremont-Barnes, Gregory. 2001. *The French Revolutionary Wars.* Oxford: Osprey Publishing.

Furnivall, John S. 2010. *Netherlands India: A Study of Plural Economy* Cambridge: Cambridge University Press.

Gallicchio, Marc. 2000. *Black Internationalism in Asia, 1985–1945.* Chapel Hill: University of North Carolina Press.

Gauthier, Florence. 2014. *Triomphe et mort de la révolution des droits de l'homme et du citoyen (1789–1795-1802).* Paris: Éditions Syllepse.

Geggus, David Patrick. 1982. *Slavery, War, and Revolution: The British Occupation of Saint Domingue 1793–1798.* Oxford: Clarendon Press.

Getachew, Adom. 2016. "Universalism after the Post-colonial Turn: Interpreting the Haitian Revolution." *Political Theory* 44 (6):821–45.

2019. *Worldmaking after Empire: The Rise and Fall of Self-Determination.* Princeton, NJ: Princeton University Press.

Gillman, Susan, and Alys Eve Weinbaum. 2007. "Introduction: W. E. B. Du Bois and the Politics of Juxtaposition." In *Next to the Color Line: Gender, Sexuality, and W. E. B. Du Bois*, ed. S. Gillman and A. E. Weinbaum. Minneapolis: University of Minnesota Press, 1–34.

Gilroy, Paul. 2004. *Postcolonial Melancholia.* New York: Columbia University Press.

Godrej, Farah. 2011. *Cosmopolitan Political Thought: Method, Practice, Discipline*. New York: Oxford University Press.

Goodhart, Michael. 2005. *Democracy as Human Rights: Freedom and Equality in the Age of Globalization*. New York: Routledge.

2018. *Injustice: Political Theory for the Real World*. New York: Oxford University Press.

Gooding-Williams, Robert. 2011. *In the Shadow of Du Bois: Afro-Modern Political Thought in America*. Cambridge, MA: Harvard University Press.

Gordon, Jane Anna. 2014. *Creolizing Political Theory: Reading Rousseau through Fanon*. New York: Fordham University Press.

Grewal, Inderpal. 2013. "Outsourcing Patriarchy: Feminist Encounters, Transnational Mediations and the Crime of 'Honour Killings.'" *International Feminist Journal of Politics* 15 (1):1–19.

Gutmann, Amy. 2003. *Identity in Democracy*. Princeton, NJ: Princeton University Press.

Guyer, Paul. 2005. *Kant's System of Nature and Freedom: Selected Essays*. New York: Oxford University Press.

Habermas, Jürgen. 1991. *The Structural Transformation of the Public Sphere*. Cambridge: MIT Press.

1996. *Between Facts and Norms: Contributions to a Discourse Theory of Law and Democracy*. Translated by W. Rehg. Cambridge: MIT Press.

1997. "Kant's Idea of Perpetual Peace with the Benefit of Two Hundred Years' Hindsight." In *Perpetual Peace: Essays on Kant's Cosmopolitan Ideal*, ed. J. Bohman and M. Lutz-Bachmann. Cambridge: MIT Press, 113–54.

2000. *The Inclusion of the Other: Studies in Political Theory*. Cambridge: MIT Press.

2001. *The Postnational Constellation*. Cambridge: MIT Press.

2006. *The Divided West*. Cambridge: Polity Press.

2008. *Between Naturalism and Religion: Philosophical Essays*. Cambridge: Polity.

2009. *Europe: The Faltering Project*. Cambrige: Polity.

Hahamovitch, Cindy. 2011. *No Man's Land*. Princeton, NJ: Princeton University Press.

Hanchard, Michael. 1999. "Afro-modernity: Temporality, Politics, and the African Diaspora." *Public Culture* 11 (1):245–68.

Hancock, Ange-Marie. 2005. "W. E. B. Du Bois: Intellectual Forefather of Intersectionality?" *Souls* 7 (3):74–84.

Hartman, Saidiya. 2007. *Lose Your Mother: A Journey Along the Atlantic Slave Route*. New York: Farrar, Straus, and Giroux.

Hedrick, Todd. 2008. "Race, Difference, and Anthropology in Kant's Cosmopolitanism." *Journal of the History of Philosophy* 46 (2):245–68.

Higham, John. 2002. *Strangers in the Land: Patterns of American Nativism, 1860–1925*. New Brunswick: Rutgers University Press.

Hill Jr., Thomas E., and Bernard R. Boxill. 2001. "Kant and Race." In *Race and Racism*, ed. B. R. Boxill. New York: Oxford University Press.

Hobson, J. A. 1975. *Imperialism: A Study*. New York: Gordon Press.

Hooker, Juliet. 2009. *Race and the Politics of Solidarity*. Oxford: Oxford University Press.

2017. *Theorizing Race in the Americas: Douglass, Sarmiento, Du Bois, and Vasconcelos*. New York: Oxford University Press.

Hopewell, Kristen. 2015. "Different Paths to Power: The Rise of Brazil, India and China at the World Trade Organization." *Review of International Political Economy* 22 (2):311–38.

Hopf, Ted. forthcoming. "Change in International Practices." *European Journal of International Relations*, https://journals.sagepub.com/doi/abs/10.1177/1354066117718041

Horne, Gerald. 1986. *Black and Red: W. E. B. Du Bois and the Afro-American Response to the Cold War, 1944–1963*. New York: State University of New York Press.

2009. *The End of Empires: African Americans and India*. Philadelphia: Temple University Press.

Hughes, Langston. 1923. "Ships, Sea, and Africa." *The Crisis* 27 (2):69–71.

Hunt, Ida Gibbs, Rayford Logan, and W. E. B. Du Bois. 1924. "Resolutions of the Third Pan-African Congress." *The Crisis* 27 (3):120–2.

Hutchins, Kimberly. 2014. "Time, Politics, and Critique: Rethinking the 'When' Question, Kimberly Hutchings." In *Transnationalizing the Public Sphere*, ed. K. Nash. Cambridge: Polity Press, 98–111.

Ingram, James D. 2013. *Radical Cosmopolitics: the Ethics and Politics of Democratic Universalism*. New York: Columbia University Press.

Isiksel, Turkuler. 2016. "The Rights of Man and the Rights of the Man-Made: Corporations and Human Rights." *Human Rights Quarterly* 38 (2): 294–349.

Jacobson, Mattew Frye. 2000. *Barbarian Virtues: The United States Encounters Foreign Peoples at Home and Abroad, 1876–1917*. New York: Hill and Wang.

James, C. L. R. 1973. "Reflections on Pan-Africanism, Part I." *Transcript of Speech given on November 21 and 22*. Retrieved from www.marxists.org/archive/james-clr/works/1973/panafricanism.htm.

James, Joy. 1996. "The Profeminist Politics of WEB Du Bois with Respect to Anna Julia Cooper and Ida B. Wells Barnett." In *WEB Du Bois: On Race and Culture*, ed. B. W. Bell, E. R. Grosholz and J. B. Stewart. New York: Routledge, 141–61.

Keene, Jennifer D. 2001. "W. E. B. Du Bois and the Wounded World: Seeking Meaning in the First World War for African-Americans." *Peace & Change* 26 (2):135–52.

Kelley, Robin D. G. 1999. "'But a Local Phase of a World Problem:' Black History's Global Vision, 1883–1950." *Journal of American History* 86 (3):1045–77.

Kelley, Robin D. G., and Betsy Esch. 2008. "Black Like Mao: Red China and Black Revolution." In *Afro Asia: Revolutionary Political and Cultural Connections between African Americans and Asian Americans*, ed. F. Ho and B. Mullen. Durham, NC: Duke University Press.

Kent, George E. 1972. "Patterns of the Harlem Renaissance." In *Harlem Renaissance Remembered*, ed. A. Bontemps. New York: Dodd, Mead & Company.

Khagram, Sanjeev, and Peggy Levitt. 2008. "Constructing Transnational Studies." In *Rethinking Transnationalism: The Meso-Link of Organizations*, ed. L. Pries. New York: Routledge, 21–39.

King, Desmond. 2000. *Making Americans: Immigration, Race, and the Origins of the Diverse Democracy*. Cambridge, MA: Harvard University Press.

Kleingeld, Pauline. 1993. "The Problematic Status of Gender-Neutral Language in the History of Philosophy: The Case of Kant." *The Philosophical Forum* 25 (2):134–50.

1998. "Kant's Cosmopolitan Law: World Citizenship for a Global Order." *Kantian Review* 2:72–90.

2007. "Kant's Second Thoughts on Race." *The Philosophical Quarterly* 57 (229):573–92.

2012. *Kant and Cosmopolitanism: The Philosophical Ideal of World Citizenship*. Cambridge: Cambridge University Press.

2014a. "The Development of Kant's Cosmopolitanism." In *Politics and Teleology in Kant*, ed. P. Formosa, A. Goldman and T. Patrone. Cardiff: University of Wales Press.

2014b. "Kant's Second Thoughts on Colonialism." In *Kant and Colonialism*, ed. K. Flikschuh and L. Ypi. Oxford: Oxford University Press.

Kofman, Sarah. 1997. "The Economy of Respect: Kant and Respect for Women." In *Feminist Interpretations of Immanuel Kant*. University Park: The Pennsylvania State University Press.

Krimmer, Elisabeth. 2008. "A Portrait of War, a Grammar of Peace: Goethe, Laukhard, and the Campaign of 1792." *German Life and Letters* 61 (1): 46–60.

Krishna, Gopala. 1947. "India Hails NAACP Stand." *The Pittsburgh Courier*, 1, 4.

Lake, Marilyn, and Henry Reynolds. 2008. *Drawing the Global Colour Line: White Men's Countries and the International Challenge of Racial Equality*. New York: Cambridge University Press.

Larrimore, Mark. 1999. "Sublime Waste: Kant on the Destiny of the 'Races'." *Canadian Journal of Philosophy* 29 (Suppl. 1):99–125.

2008. "Antinomies of Race: Diversity and Destiny in Kant." *Patterns of Prejudice* 42 (4–5):341–63.

Laurence, Keith Ormiston. 1995. *Tobago in Wartime, 1793–1815*. Kingston: University of West Indies Press.

Lawrence, Adria K. 2013. *Imperial Rule and the Politics of Nationalism: Anti-Colonial Protest in the French Empire*. New York: Cambridge University Press.

Lemelle, Sidney J. 1993. "The Politics of Cultural Existence: Pan-Africanism, Historical Materialism, and Afrocentricity." *Race & Class* 35 (1):93–112.

Leslie, Margaret. 1970. "In Defense of Anachronism." *Political Studies* 18 (4): 433–47.

Lewis, David Levering. 1993. *W.E.B. Du Bois: Biography of a Race (1868–1919)*. New York: Henry Holt & Co.

2000. *W. E. B. Du Bois: The Fight for Equality and the American Century (1919–1963)*. New York: Henry Holt & Co.

Livingston, Alexander. 2016. *Damn Great Empires! William James and the Politics of Pragmatism*. New York: Oxford University Press.

Los Angeles Times. 1921. "Foreign Briefs." *Los Angeles Times*, Sep. 7, 117.

Louden, Robert B. 1999. *Kant's Impure Ethics: From Rational Beings to Human Beings*. New York: Oxford University Press.

Lowe, L. 2015. *The Intimacies of Four Continents*. Durham, NC: Duke University Press.

Lowndes, Joseph E. 2008. *From the New Deal to the New Right: Race and the Southern Origins of Modern Conservatism*. New Haven, CT: Yale University Press.

Lu, Catherine. 2000. "The One and Many Faces of Cosmopolitanism." *The Journal of Political Philosophy* 8 (2):244–67.

   2018a. "Cosmopolitan Justice, Democracy and the World State." In *Institutional Cosmopolitanism*, ed. L. Cabrera. Oxford: Oxford University Press.

   2018b. *Justice and Reconciliation in World Politics*. Cambridge: Cambridge University Press.

Lugones, María C., and Elizabeth V. Spelman. 1983. "Have We Got a Theory for You! Feminist Theory, Cultural Imperialism, and the Demand for 'the Woman's Voice'." *Women's Studies International Forum* 6 (6):573–81.

M'bayo, Tamba E. 2004. "W. E. B. Du Bois, Marcus Garvey, and Pan-Africanism in Liberia, 1919–1924." *The Historian* 66 (1):19–44.

MacGilvray, Eric. 2011. *The Invention of Market Freedom*. New York: Cambridge University Press.

Mackinnon, Emma. 2019. "Declaration as Disavowal: The Politics of Race and Empire in the Universal Declaration of Human Rights." *Political Theory* 47 (1): 57–81.

Makalani, Minkah. 2011. *In the Cause of Freedom: Radical Black Internationalism from Harlem to London, 1917–1939*. Chapel Hill: The University of North Carolina Press.

   2016. "An Apparatus for Negro Women: Black Women's Organizing, Communism, and the Institutional Spaces of Radical Pan-African Thought." *Women, Gender, and Families of Color* 4 (2):250–73.

Maliks, Reidar. 2014. *Kant's Politics in Context*. Oxford: Oxford University Press.

Malleson, George Bruce. 2010. *History of the French in India: From the Founding of Pondichery in 1674 to the Capture of that Place in 1761*. Cambridge: Cambridge University Press.

Mantena, Karuna. 2010. *Alibis of Empire: Henry Maine and the Ends of Liberal Imperialism*. Princeton, NJ: Princeton University Press.

Marable, Manning. 1986. *W. E. B. Du Bois: Black Radical Democrat*. Boulder, CO: Paradigm Publishers.

Markell, Patchen. 2003. *Bound by Recognition*. Princeton, NJ: Princeton University Press.

Marwah, Inder. 2012. "Bridging Nature and Freedom? Kant, Culture, and Cultivation." *Social Theory and Practice* 38 (3):385–406.

2015. "Two Concepts of Liberal Developmentalism." *European Journal of Political Theory* 15 (1):97–123.

2017. "Rethinking Resistance: Spencer, Krishnavarma and the Indian Sociologist." In *Colonial Exchanges: Political Theory and the Agency of the Colonized*, ed. B. A. Hendrix and D. Baumgold. Manchester: Manchester University Press.

Matthews, Ralph. 1945. "Small Nations Seek Equality." *The Baltimore Afro-American*, May 12, 9.

Mazzini, Giuseppe. 2009. "Principles of International Politics." In *A Cosmopolitanism of Nations: Giuseppe Mazzini's Writings on Democracy, Nation Building, and International Relations*, ed. S. Recchia and N. Urbinati. Princeton, NJ: Princeton University Press.

McCarthy, Thomas. 2009. *Race, Empire, and the Idea of Human Development*. Cambridge: Cambridge University Press.

McKay, Claude. 1923. "Soviet Russia and the Negro." *The Crisis* 27 (2):61–4.

McKean, Benjamin L. 2017. "Ideal Theory after Auschwitz? The Practical Uses and Ideological Abuses of Political Theory as Reconciliation." *The Journal of Politics* 79 (4):1177–90.

McNay, Lois. 2014. *The Misguided Search for the Political*. Cambridge: Polity Press.

Meckstroth, Christopher. forthcoming. "Hospitality, or Kant's Critique of Cosmopolitanism and Human Rights." *Political Theory*, https://journals .sagepub.com/doi/abs/10.1177/0090591717719546.

Mehta, Uday. 1999. *Liberalism and Empire: Nineteenth Century British Liberal Thought*. Chicago: University of Chicago Press.

Mennell, James. 1999. "African-Americans and the Selective Service Act of 1917." *The Journal of Negro History* 84 (3):275–87.

Mikkola, Mari. 2011. "Kant on Moral Agency and Women's Nature." *Kantian Review* 16 (1):89–111.

Miller, David. 2007. *National Responsibility and Global Justice*. Oxford: Oxford University Press.

Miller, 2008. "National Responsibility and Global Justice." *Critical Review of International Social and Political Philosophy* 11 (4):383–99.

Miller, Richard W. 1998. "Cosmopolitan Respect and Patriotic Concern." *Philosophy & Public Affairs* 27 (3):202–24.

Mills, Charles W. 1997. *The Racial Contract*. Ithaca, NY: Cornell University Press.

2005. "Kant's *Untermenschen*." In *Race and Racism in Modern Philosophy*, ed. A. Valls. Ithaca, NY: Cornell University Press.

2014. "Kant and Race, *Redux*." *Graduate Faculty Philosophy Journal* 35 (1–2):125–57.

Milstein, Brian. 2015. *Commercium: Critical Theory from a Cosmopolitan Point of View*. London: Rowman & Littlefield.

Mintz, Sidney Wilfred. 1985. *Sweetness and Power*. New York: Viking.

Mitzen, Jennifer. 2013. *Power in Concert: The Nineteenth-Century Origins of Global Governance*. Chicago: Chicago University Press.

Modelski, George. 1964. "Kautilya: Foreign Policy and International System in the Ancient Hindu World." *American Political Science Review* 58 (3): 549–60.

Mohanty, Chandra Talpade. 1997. *Literary Theory and the Claims of History: Postmodernism, Objectivity, Multicultural Politics*. Ithaca, NY: Cornell University Press.

2002. "Under Western Eyes' Revisited: Feminist Solidarity through Anticapitalist Struggles." *Signs* 28 (2):499–535.

Mommsen, Wolfgang, J. 1977. *Theories of Imperialism*. Translated by P. S. Falla. Chicago: The University of Chicago Press.

Morefield, Jeanne. 2014. *Empires without Imperialism: Anglo-American Decline and the Politics of Deflection*. New York: Oxford University Press.

2016. "Political Theory as Historical Counterpoint: The Case of Schmitt and Sovereignty." *Theory & Event* 19 (1).

2017. "Urgent History: The Sovereignty Debates and Political Theory's Lost Voices." *Political Theory* 45 (2):164–91.

Morgan, Kenneth. 2007. *Slavery and the British Empire: From Africa to America*. Oxford: Oxford University Press.

Moses, Wilson J. 1978. *The Golden Age of Black Nationalism, 1850–1925*. Hamden: Archon Books.

Moyn, Samuel. 2010. *The Last Utopia: Human Rights in History*. Cambridge, MA: Belknap Press of Harvard University Press.

2014. "Imaginary Intellectual History." In *Rethinking Modern Intellectual History*, ed. D. M. McMahon and S. Moyn. New York: Oxford University Press.

2016. "History and Political Theory: A Difficult Reunion." *Theory & Event* 19 (1).

2018. *Not Enough*. Cambridge, MA: Harvard University Press.

Mullen, Bill. 2003. "Du Bois, Dark Princess, and the Afro-Asian International." *Positions: East Asia Cultures Critiques* 11 (1):217–39.

2004. *Afro-Orientalism*. Minneapolis: University of Minnesota Press.

2015. *Un-American: W. E. B. Du Bois and the Century of World Revolution*. Philadelphia: Temple University Press.

Mullen, Bill, and Cathryn Watson. 2005a. "Part III: World War II and the Anticolonial Turn." In *W. E. B. Du Bois on Asia: Crossing the World Color Line*, ed. B. Mullen and C. Watson. Jackson: University Press of Mississippi.

eds. 2005b. *W. E. B. Du Bois on Asia: Crossing the World Color Line*. Jackson: University Press of Mississippi.

Muthu, Sankar. 2000. "Justice and Foreigners: Kant's Cosmopolitan Right." *Constellations* 7 (1):23–45.

2003. *Enlightenment against Empire*. Princeton, NJ: Princeton University Press.

2014. "Productive Resistance in Kant's Political Thought: Domination, Counter-Domination, and Global Unsocial Sociability." In *Kant and Colonialism: Historical and Critical Perspectives*, ed. K. Flikschuh and L. Ypi. Oxford: Oxford University Press.

Nantambu, Kwame. 1998. "Pan-Africanism versus Pan-African Nationalism: An Afrocentric Analysis." *Journal of Black Studies* 28 (5):561–74.

Nash, Roy. 1923. "The Origin of Negro Slavery in Brazil." *The Crisis* 26 (6):264–7.

Ndlovu-Gatsheni, Sabelo J. 2013. "The Entrapment of African within the Colonial Matrices of Power." *Journal of Developing Societies* 29 (4):331–53.

Neblo, Michael A. 2015. *Deliberative Democracy between Theory and Practice*. New York: Cambridge University Press.

Nerouy, Kantiba. 1924. "Tutankh-Amen and Ras Tafari." *The Crisis* 29 (2): 64–8.

New York Times. 1921. "Denounce Our Haiti Policy." *New York Times*, Sep. 6, 15.

Ngai, Mae M. 2004. *Impossible Subjects: Illegal Aliens and the Making of Modern America*. Princeton, NJ: Princeton University Press.

Nicholson, Peter P. 1992. "Kant, Revolutions, and History." In *Kant's Political Philosophy*, ed. H. Lloyd Williams. Chicago: The University of Chicago Press.

Niesen, Peter. 2007. "Colonialism and Hospitality." *Politics and Ethics Review* 3 (1):90–108.

2014. "Restorative Justice in International and Cosmopolitan Law." In *Kant and Colonialism. Historical and Critical Perspectives*, ed. K. Flikschuh and L. Ypi. Oxford: Oxford University Press.

Nussbaum, Martha. 2008. "Toward a Globally Sensitive Patriotism." *Daedalus* 137 (3):78–93.

O'Neill, Onora. 2000. *Bounds of Justice*. Cambridge: Cambridge University Press.

Olson, Joel. 2005. "W. E. B. Du Bois and the Race Concept." *Souls* 7 (3–4): 118–28.

Onishi, Yuichiro. 2013. *Afro-Asian Solidarity in 20th-Century Black America, Japan, and Okinawa*. New York: New York University Press.

Pagden, Anthony. 2014. "The Law of Continuity: Conquest and Settlement within the Limits of Kant's International Right." In *Kant and Colonialism: Historical and Critical Perspectives*, ed. K. Flikschuh and L. Ypi. Oxford: Oxford University Press.

Palmer, R. R. 1954. "Much in Little: The Dutch Revolution of 1795." *The Journal of Modern History* 26 (1):15–35.

Pateman, Carole. 1988. *The Sexual Contract*. Stanford, CA: Stanford University Press.

Pearson, Charles H. 1894. *National Life and Character*. London: Macmillan and Company.

Pitts, Jennifer. 2005. *A Turn to Empire: The Rise of Imperial Liberalism in Britain and France*. Princeton, NJ: Princeton University Press.

2010. "Political Theory of Empire and Imperialism." *Annual Review of Political Science* 13:211–35.

Pouliot, Vincent. 2016. *International Pecking Orders: The Politics and Practice of Multilateral Diplomacy*. New York: Cambridge University Press.

Pouliot, Vincent, and Jérémie Cornut. 2015. "Practice Theory and the Study of Diplomacy: A Research Agenda." *Cooperation and conflict* 50 (3):297–315.

Pradeep, Barua. 2011. "Maritime Trade, Seapower, and the Anglo-Mysore Wars, 1767–1799." *The Historian* 73 (1):22–40.

Rana, Aziz. 2010. *The Two Faces of American Freedom*. Cambridge, MA: Harvard University Press.

2018. "Against National Security Citizenship." *Boston Review* 43 (1):81–91.

Rancière, Jacques. 1999. *Dis-agreement: Politics and Democracy*. Minneapolis: Minnesota University Press.

2009. "The Aesthetic Dimension: Aesthetics, Politics, Knowledge." *Critical Inquiry* 36 (1):1–19.

Rawley, James A. and Stephen D. Behrendt. 2005. *The Transatlantic Slave Trade: A History*. Lincoln: University of Nebraska Press.

Rawls, John. 1999a. *The Law of Peoples with 'The Idea of Public Reason Revisited'*. Cambridge, MA: Harvard University Press.

1999b. *A Theory of Justice*. Cambridge, MA: Harvard University Press.

Reed, Adolph L. 1997. *W. E. B. Du Bois and American Political Thought: Fabianism and the Color Line*. New York: Oxford University Press.

Rees, Dafydd Huw. 2017. "Decolonizing Philosophy? Habermas and the Axial Age." *Constellations* 24 (2):219–31.

Ripstein, Arthur. 2014. "Kant's Juridical Theory of Colonialism." In *Kant and Colonialism*, ed. K. Flikschuh and L. Ypi. Oxford: Oxford University Press.

Roberts, Christopher N. J. 2014. *The Contentious History of the International Bill of Human Rights*. New York: Cambridge University Press.

Rogers, Ben F. 1955. "William EB DuBois, Marcus Garvey, and Pan-Africa." *The Journal of Negro History* 40 (2):154–65.

Rogers, Melvin L. 2012. "The People, Rhetoric, and Affect: On the Political Force of Du Bois's *The Souls of Black Folk*." *American Political Science Review* 106 (1):188–203.

Sandel, Michael. 2018. "Populism, Liberalism, and Democracy." *Philosophy and Social Criticism* 44 (4):353–9.

Sapiro, Virginia. 1998. "Feminist Studies and Political Science – and Vice Versa." In *Feminism and Politics*, ed. Anne Phillips. Oxford: Oxford University Press, 67–89.

Saward, Michael. 2011. "Slow Theory: Taking Time over Transnational Democratic Representation." *Ethics & Global Politics* 4 (1):1–18.

Scheffler, Samuel. 2002. *Boundaries and Allegiances: Problems of Justice and Responsibility in Liberal Thought*. New York: Oxford University Press.

Scott, David. 2004. *Conscripts of Modernity: The Tragedy of Colonial Enlightenment*. Durham, NC: Duke University Press.

Seigel, Micol. 2005. "Beyond Compare: Comparative Method after the Transnational Turn." *Radical History Review* (91):62–90.

Sending, Ole Jacob, Vincent Pouliot, and Iver B Neumann. 2015. *Diplomacy and the Making of World Politics*. Cambridge: Cambridge University Press.

Shapiro, Michael J. 1994. "Moral Geographies and the Ethics of Post-Sovereignty." *Public Culture* 6 (3):479–502.

Shapiro, Stephen. 2008. *The Culture and Commerce of the Early American Novel: Reading the Atlantic World-System.* University Park: Penn State Press.

Shelby, Tommie. 2005. *We Who Are Dark: The Philosophical Foundations of Black Solidarity.* Cambridge, MA: Harvard University Press.

    2007. "Justice, Deviance, and the Dark Ghetto." *Philosophy & Public Affairs* 35 (2):126–60.

Shilliam, Robbie. 2015. *The Black Pacific: Anti-Colonial Struggles and Oceanic Connections.* London: Bloomsbury Academic.

    2016. "Ethiopianism, Englishness, Britishness: Struggles over Imperial Belonging." *Citizenship Studies* 20 (2):243–59.

Singh, Jakeet. 2016. "Colonial Pasts, Decolonial Futures: Allen's The End of Progress." *Theory & Event* 19 (4).

Singh, Nikhil Pal. 2004. *Black is a Country: Race and the Unfinished Struggle for Democracy.* Cambridge, MA: Harvard University Press.

Skinner, Quentin. 2002. *Visions of Politics.* Vol. 1. Cambridge: Cambridge University Press.

Skotnes, Andor. 2012. *A New Deal for All? Race and Class Struggles in Depression-Era Baltimore.* Durham, NC: Duke University Press.

Slate, Nico. 2012a. *Black Power beyond Borders: The Global Dimensions of the Black Power Movement.* New York: Palgrave Macmillan.

    2012b. *Colored Cosmopolitanism: The Shared Struggle for Freedom in the United States and India.* Cambridge, MA: Harvard University Press.

Sohi, Seema. 2007. *Echoes of Mutiny: Race, Surveillance, and Indian Anticolonialism in North America.* New York: Oxford University Press.

Spivak, Gayatri Chakravorty. 2004. "Righting Wrongs." *South Atlantic Quarterly* 103 (2/3):523–81.

Stanley, Sharon A. 2017. *An Impossible Dream? Racial Integration in the United States.* New York: Oxford University Press.

Stein, Judith. 1986. *The World of Marcus Garvey.* Baton Rouge: Louisiana State University Press.

Stephens, Michelle Ann. 2005. *Black Empire: The Masculine Global Imaginary of Caribbean Intellectuals in the United States, 1914–1962.* Durham, NC: Duke University Press.

Stoddard, Lothrop. 1920. *The Rising Tide of Color against White World-Supremacy.* New York: Blue Ribbon Books.

Stoler, Ann Laura. 1995. *Race and the Education of Desire: Foucault's History of Sexuality and the Colonial Order of Things.* Durham, NC: Duke University Press.

Storey, Ian. 2015. "Empire and Natural Order in Kant's 'Second Thoughts' on Race." *History of Political Thought* 26 (4):670–99.

Tarling, Nicholas. 1958. "The Relationship between British Policies and the Extent of Dutch Power in the Malay Archipelago 1784–1871." *Australian Journal of Politics & History* 4 (2):179–92.

Taylor, Kirstine. 2015. "Untimely Subjects: White Trash and the Making of Racial Innocence in the Postwar South." *American Quarterly* 67 (1):55–79.

Temin, David M. forthcoming. "Custer's Sins: Vine Deloria Jr. and the Settler-Colonial Politics of Civic Inclusion." Political Theory, https://journals.sage pub.com/doi/abs/10.1177/0090591717712151.

The Chicago Defender. 1945a. "Du Bois Pleads in U.S. Senate for Colonials." *The Chicago Defender*, May 19, 1, 4.

1945b. "Du Bois Pleads in U.S. Senate for Colonials: Shows Need for Governing Body." *The Chicago Defender*, July 21, 1.

1945c. "U. S. Failure to Back Freedom of Colonies Blasted." *The Chicago Defender*, June 2, 1, 6.

The Crisis. 1924. "Gandhi and India." *The Crisis* 23 (5):203–7.

Threadcraft, Shatema. 2014. "Intimate Injustice, Political Obligation, and the Dark Ghetto." *Signs* 39 (3):735–60.

2016. *Intimate Justice: The Black Female Body and the Body Politic*. Oxford: Oxford University Press.

Trouillot, Michel-Rolph. 1995. *Silencing the Past: Power and the Production of History*. Boston: Beacon Press.

Tully, James. 2008a. *Public Philosophy in a New Key, Volume I: Democracy and Civic Freedom*. Cambridge: Cambridge University Press.

Tully, James2008b. *Public Philosophy in a New Key: Volume II: Imperialism and Civic Freedom*. Cambridge: Cambridge University Press.

Turner, L. C. F. 1966. "The Cape of Good Hope and Anglo-French rivalry 1778–1796." *Historical Studies: Australia and New Zealand* 12 (46):166.

Valdez, Inés. 2012. "Perpetual What? Injury, Sovereignty, and a Cosmopolitan View of Immigration." *Political Studies* 60 (1):95–114.

2016. "Non-Domination or Practices of Freedom? French Muslim Women, Foucault, and the Full Veil Ban." *American Political Science Review* 110 (1):18–30.

2017. "It's not about Race: Good Wars, Bad Wars, and the Origins of Kant's Anti-Colonialism." *American Political Science Review* 111 (4):819–34.

2019. "Association, Reciprocity, and Emancipation: A Transnational Account of the Politics of Global Justice." In *Empire, Race, and Global Justice*, ed. D. Bell. Cambridge: Cambridge University Press.

Valentini, Laura. 2015. "On the Distinctive Procedural Wrong of Colonialism." *Philosophy & Public Affairs* 43 (4):312–31.

van den Boogaard, Vanessa. 2017. "Modern Post-Colonial Approaches to Citizenship: Kwame Nkrumah's Political Thought on Pan-Africanism." *Citizenship Studies* 21 (1):44–67.

Varden, Helga. 2017. "Kant and Women." *Pacific Philosophical Quarterly* 98 (4):653–94.

Vaughn, Rasberry. 2016. *Race and the Totalitarian Century: Geopolitics in the Black Literary Imagination*. Cambridge, MA: Harvard University Press.

Vitalis, Robert. 2010. "The Noble American Science of Imperial Relations and Its Laws of Race Development." *Comparative Studies in Society and History* 52 (4):909–38.

2015. *White World Order, Black Power Politics: The Birth of American International Relations*. Ithaca, NY: Cornell University Press.

Von Eschen, Penny M. 1997. *Race against Empire: Black Americans and Anticolonialism, 1937–1957*. Ithaca, NY: Cornell University Press.

Vucetic, Srdjan. 2009. *The Anglosphere: A Genealogy of Identity in the International Sphere*. Columbus, Political Science, Ohio State University.

2011. *The Anglosphere: A Genealogy of Racialized Identity in International Relations*. Stanford: Stanford University Press.

Walker, R. B. J. 2010. "Democratic Theory and the Present/Absent International." *Ethics & Global Politics* 3 (1):21–36.

Warner, Michael. 2002. "Publics and Counterpublics." *Public Culture* 14 (1): 49–90.

2005. *Publics and Counterpublics*. New York: Zone Books.

Weinbaum, Alys Eve. 2001. "Reproducing Racial Globality: W. E. B. Du Bois and the Sexual Politics of Black Nationalism." *Social Text* 19 (2):15–41.

Wendt, Alexander. 2003. "Why a World State is Inevitable." *European Journal of International Relations* 9 (4):491–542.

West, Michael O., William G. Martin, and Fanon Che Wilkins, eds. 2014. *From Toussaint to Tupac: The Black International since the Age of Revolution*. Chapel Hill: University of North Carolina Press.

Whalan, Mark. 2011. "Not Only War: the First World War and African American Literature." In *Race, Empire, and First World War Writing*, ed. S. Das. New York: Cambridge University Press.

Whitaker, Arthur P. 1936. "Louisiana in the Treaty of Basel." *The Journal of Modern History* 8 (1):1–26.

Wilder, Gary. 2015. *Freedom Time: Negritude, Decolonization, and the Future of the World*. Durham, NC: Duke University Press.

William, Korey. 1998. *NGOs and the Universal Declaration of Human Rights: A Curious Grapevine*. New York: Macmillan Press.

Wood, Allen W. 1996. "General Introduction." In *Kant's Practical Philosophy*, ed. M. J. Gregor. Cambridge: Cambridge University Press, xiii–xxxiii.

1998. "Kant's Project for Perpetual Peace." In *Cosmopolitics: Thinking and Feeling beyond the Nation*, ed. P. Cheah and B. Robbins. Minneapolis: University of Minnesota Press.

1999. *Kant's Ethical Thought*. Cambridge: Cambridge University Press.

Young, Mary. 2001. "Asia." In *W. E. B. Du Bois: An Encyclopedia*, ed. G. Horne and M. Young. Westport, CT: Greenwood Press.

Ypi, Lea. 2012. *Global Justice and Avant-Garde Political Agency*. Oxford: Oxford University Press.

2013a. "The Owl of Minerva Only Flies at Dusk, but to Where? A Reply to Critics." *Ethics & Global Politics* 6 (2):117–34.

2013b. "What's Wrong with Colonialism." *Philosophy & Public Affairs* 41 (2):158–91.

2014a. "Commerce and Colonialism in Kant's Philosophy." In *Kant and Colonialism*, ed. K. Flikschuh and L. Ypi. Oxford: Oxford University Press.

2014b. "On Revolution in Kant and Marx." *Political Theory* 42 (3):262–87.

Ypi, Lea, Robert E. Goodin, and Christian Barry. 2009. "Associative Duties, Global Justice, and the Colonies." *Philosophy & Public Affairs* 37 (2): 103–35.

Yvi, James W. 1945. "Concerning Peace." *The Crisis* 52 (7):204–5.

Zerilli, Linda M. G. 2005. *Feminism and the Abyss of Freedom.* Chicago: Chicago University Press.

Index